D1219570

Ethnicity and power in the contemporary world

Edited by Kumar Rupesinghe and
Valery A. Tishkov

McK
GN
496
.E838
1996

**United Nations
University Press**

TOKYO · NEW YORK · PARIS

© The United Nations University, 1996

The views expressed in this publication are those of the authors and do not necessarily reflect the views of the United Nations University.

United Nations University Press
The United Nations University, 53-70, Jingumae 5-chome, Shibuya-ku, Tokyo 150, Japan
Tel: (03) 3499-2811   Fax: (03) 3406-7345
Telex: J25442   Cable: UNATUNIV TOKYO

UNU Office in North America
2 United Nations Plaza, Room DC2-1462-70, New York, NY 10017
Tel: (212) 963-6387 Fax: (212) 371-9454 Telex: 422311 UN UI

United Nations University Press is the publishing division of the United Nations University.

Typeset by Asco Trade Typesetting Limited, Hong Kong
Printed by Permanent Typesetting and Printing Co., Ltd., Hong Kong
Cover design by Jonathan Gullery/Abel Graphics, Thornwood, New York, USA

UNUP-908
ISBN 92-808-0908-3
03500 P

Contents

Contents

Acknowledgements

This volume is based on presentations made at the Conference on Conflict, Governance, and the Devolution of Power in Multi-ethnic States sponsored by the United Nations University, Tokyo, and the Institute of Ethnology and Anthropology of the Russian Academy of Sciences in Moscow in March 1992, under the UNU's Ethnic Conflict and Governance Programme. We are also extremely grateful to the Institute of Ethnology and Anthropology for hosting the conference and to the Institute's staff, in particular Senior Researcher Mara Ustinova and Marina Martinova, Scientific Secretary.

We would like to acknowledge the invaluable support of the UNU both in sponsoring the conference and through a lengthy editing process: particularly Dr Takeo Uchida, former Principal Academic Officer and in charge of the Ethnic Conflict and Governance Programme, for his guidance and great patience. To Rogie Kahlon and all the other staff at the UNU who helped with the production of the volume, we offer our sincere thanks. Stephanie Loomis ably assisted in the organization of the Moscow conference. We would also like to thank Susan Hoivik, David Israelson, Lucy Ackroyd, and David Lord for their work on the manuscript.

Introduction

Kumar Rupesinghe and Valery A. Tishkov

The continuing agonies of Rwanda, Somalia, Bosnia, Azerbaijan-Armenia, and Algeria, just to cite a few of the dozens of examples of the violent internal conflicts which are the predominant form of warfare in the world today, underscore the timeliness of this volume by pointing to the urgent necessity of improving the global community's understanding of the causes and consequences of violent conflict and options for their prevention, constructive resolution, or transformation.

While covering a wide geographic and experiential range, this volume has no pretensions to providing an exhaustive or definitive overview of the relationships between ethnicity, power, and conflict in the modern world. In fact, in the following pages readers will find opposing perspectives, definitions, arguments, and conclusions, all of which are part of a rich and dynamic process of analysis, debate, and discovery. The material contained in this volume, which explores conflicts and conflict resolution approaches in the Horn of Africa, some of the Soviet successor states, the former Yugoslavia, India, Northern Ireland, the Basque country, and the United States, leads to the conclusion that solutions to the dilemmas posed by the resur-

1

gence of ethnicity and shifting power relationships in the post-Cold-War world involve a plethora of factors which do not lend themselves to superficial analysis or pat solutions.

In reality, the nature of conflict is as complex as the global varieties of social life itself; a fact which should, but does not always, lead scholars to reject the temptation to make categorical classifications and avoid oversimplifications. Case-studies, whether drawn from the former Soviet Union, Africa, Asia, Western Europe, or the Americas, demonstrate varieties of entwined objective and subjective factors, as well as rational and irrational motives on the part of individuals and groups, that belie simple classification. The urgency of many current conflict situations also demands that scholars, policy makers, and ordinary people eschew blinkered methodological, political, or ethnic orientations when trying to understand conflict and build peace.

The importance of the issue of self-determination in any discussion of conflict and conflict resolution in the contemporary world is indisputable, an importance which is reflected in this volume in several of the case-studies, as well as in the more general discussions. But the viability of political arrangements between groups is only part of the intricate matrix of most conflicts, which can involve issues of governance and authority as well as issues of ideology, identity, economic disparity, competition for resources, and other factors, most often in complex combinations.

Co-editor Kumar Rupesinghe's contribution, entitled "Governance and Conflict Resolution in Multi-Ethnic Societies," describes some of the fundamental changes which will be needed in our perceptions of security and sovereignty if the global community is to manage peacefully the dynamics of ethnic conflict and the unresolved and largely unreflected issue of self-determination. The issues of governance, ethnicity, and conflict resolution are explored in the context of the evolving new world order, which is still encumbered with increasingly obsolete and ineffective international systems, mechanisms, and approaches. Rupesinghe argues that conflicts involving claims or resistance to claims of self-determination remain among the most intractable, partly due to the absence of mechanisms to address such claims.

In "Ethnic Conflict in the Horn of Africa: Myth and Reality," Hizkias Assefa offers a definition of ethnic groups as collectivities of people who share the same primordial characteristics, such as common ancestry, language, and culture. Ethnicity refers to the behaviour and feelings that emanate from membership of an ethnic group.

In looking at the resolution of conflict, Assefa contends that mechanisms must be sought to legitimize ethnic identity without making it incompatible with the formation of larger units of identity based on mutuality and beneficial collaboration, such as a loose federal system of governance.

Some of the theoretical underpinnings of current conflict resolution approaches, as well as their shortcomings, are reviewed by Valery A. Tishkov, this volume's other co-editor, in his chapter, entitled "Ethnic Conflicts in the Context of Social Science Theories." Looking at various conflicts in the former Soviet Union, Tishkov argues that it is not correct to label as "ethnic conflicts" these sometimes violent political struggles, because of the multi-ethnic composition of most of the areas involved. However, he notes that manipulative élites have not shied away from using "ethnic camouflage" to obscure other motives and inflame disputes. Tishkov states that although the choice for ethnic separation is usually driven by economic calculation, political factors are also important. That is why the "élite-based" theory of conflict, focusing on the mobilization of ethnic feelings by intellectuals and politicians, has been fruitfully applied in the analysis of a number of case studies in the Soviet successor states.

Emil Payin's chapter, "Settlement of Ethnic Conflicts in Post-Soviet Society," focuses on types of inter-ethnic conflict and their distribution. The Soviet Union's rapid and unprecedented disintegration is, in Payin's view, a contributing factor to mounting ethnic tensions brought to a head by plummeting living standards. The establishment of authoritarian-nationalist regimes has further inflamed nationalist passions and led to conflicts, which interact with each other and have a cumulative affect. Payin presents a scale of ethno-political stability based on three types of factor: potential conflicts based on the historical and cultural alienation of ethnic communities; conflict of ideas (ranging from nationalistic statements in the press to violent demonstrations); and conflict of action – sporadic clashes or prolonged armed conflict. Payin suggests that the prevention of ethnic conflicts ultimately requires radical socio-economic and political reforms, plus an ethnic conflict prevention system.

Airat R. Aklaev's chapter, "Dynamics of the Moldova–Trans-Dniester Ethnic Conflict (Late 1980s to Early 1990s)," argues that ethnic conflicts in the former Soviet Union are predominantly political and have been brought about by rapid socio-political change. The situation has been complicated, however, by artificial boundaries and complex territorial claims and demographic patterns within areas such as Moldova. Aklaev identifies five critical points in inter-ethnic political struggles in Moldova between late 1988 and mid-1992: the adoption of language legislation; local elections to Supreme Soviets; the reaction to the coup attempt in Moscow; referenda on independence in the Gagauzia and Trans-Dniester districts; and separatist authorities' attempts to subordinate local police offices. He singles out three major stages in the development of disruptive inter-ethnic confrontation between Moldova and Trans-Dniester: transition from non-violent to violent ethnic political action; transition to recurrent violent interaction in ethnically mixed urban and rural areas; and transition to warfare. Based on the Moldova case-study, Aklaev contends that the transition to violence often results from an ethno-political legitimacy crisis and that the dynamics of conflict are significantly influenced by fast-paced socio-political change.

In "Ethnic Conflict in the Osh Region in Summer 1990: Reasons and Lessons," Abilabek Asankanov analyses the causes of the inter-ethnic conflict in the Osh region of Kyrgyzstan and its common features with other conflicts in the Soviet successor states. Based on survey material and local reports, Asankanov contends that the primary cause of the conflict, which was characterized by its cruelty, was economic backwardness, which was tending toward even further decline. Unemployment, lack of housing, disputes over the allocation of land, and other problems created an environment for the emergence of a nationalist Kyrgyz group and an Uzbek separatist movement. But Asankanov notes that when survey respondents were asked what measures should be taken to prevent national conflicts, most focused on improvements in living conditions.

Klara Hallik introduces her chapter, "From Centre–Periphery Conflict to the Making of New Nationality Policy in an Independent State: Estonia," by describing how that country's cultural heritage and national identity were submerged under a wave of massive immigration during the Soviet era. Consequent demographic change has led to an ethnically divided society now shaping a new national identity. Estonia became the first former Soviet republic to enforce a language act giving its native tongue official status, which in turn led to conflict. Hallik favours the legal definition of citizenship as a response to problems involving national minorities, although she also states that resolution will be extremely complicated on a psychological level. According to the author, for Estonia to move from ethnic to civic nationalism it needs to rid itself of the ideology of a minority and create a pluralistic democratic society, free of polarization.

In "Conflict Management in the Former USSR and World Experience," Victor A. Kremenyuk describes conflict management as preventing the unpredictable development of conflict, providing a framework which can incorporate both "winning" and "compromise" approaches, and envisaging resolution or prevention as preferable outcomes. The author divides ethnic conflict into several different groupings, depending on whether ethnic minorities are seeking cultural autonomy, independence, or reunification, and suggests that the underlying rationale for the rise of ethnic conflicts is the fact that diversity is one of the world's most important and powerful locomotives of cultural development. In relation to the former Soviet Union, he contends that there is no model for managing ethnic conflicts that is fully suited to the new independent states, that the use of force is self-destructive, and that resolving ethnic conflicts must be seen as a long-term task.

Silvo Devetak's contribution, "The Dissolution of Multi-Ethnic States: The Case of Yugoslavia," raises a crucial question for those interested in conflicts and conflict prevention: whether the survival of the Yugoslav Federation could have avoided the carnage in former Yugoslavia. According to Devetak, the answer is no, because the dissolution of Yugoslavia had begun in the 1970s as a result of the abolition of market laws and legal obligations among economic entities, the ineffective decision-making process at the federal level, and the ineffectiveness of the political élite. Looking at the means of ensuring a future peace, the author suggests that what will be necessary will be economic revival and the resolution of socio-political problems, genuine democratization, improvements in inter-ethnic relations, and cooperation between states.

S.D. Muni contends in "Ethnic Conflict, Federalism, and Democracy In India" that diversity and heterogeneity do not necessarily produce conflicts, although the potential is often there. If India is to resolve its ethnic conflicts peacefully, he argues, political opportunism and expediency cannot be allowed to go uncurbed. The problem lies not with institutions and common people, but with leadership that surrenders values and larger gains for short-term and selfish advantages.

John Darby's chapter, "An Intractable Conflict? Northern Ireland: A Need For Pragmatism," examines how the violence which reached a peak in 1972 in Northern Ireland has declined with the implementation of social and military mechanisms to constrain it. Using the analogy of cancer, Darby likens conflict to a disease which was once seen as incurable but is now often successfully treated. Similarly, Northern Ireland's political problem is no longer viewed solely within a constitutional context but as a group of interrelated issues which include, as well as the constitutional issue, social and economic inequality, cultural identity, security, religion, and day-to-day relationships. Darby notes that progress in these areas provided the impetus for the political negotiations in late 1993 and early 1994 and has contributed greatly towards the peacemaking process.

"Political Autonomy and Conflict Resolution: The Basque Case," by Gurutz Jauregui and José Manuel Castells, weighs the practical results achieved in 12 years of autonomy for the Basque region of Spain against the practice of violence. Although autonomy has not resolved all the Basques' traditional demands, the authors suggest that its implementation has provided satisfactory results. Most importantly, it has been an effective instrument for recovering Basque identity, particularly in terms of language and culture.

In "Ethnic and Racial Groups in the USA: Conflict and Cooperation," Mary C. Waters argues that the historical experiences of ethnic groups in the United States significantly shape the various cultural lenses through which people understand inter-ethnic conflict. Based on four major bias incidents, Waters proposes that the treatment of people, along with the mode of their incorporation into social and cultural structures, influences meanings attached to racial and ethnic identities, the relationship of the group and its component individuals to the state, and the meanings attached to incidents of hate crimes, violence, and intergroup encounters.

Asbjørn Eide's contribution, entitled "Ethnic Conflicts and Minority Protection: Roles for the International Community," presents guidelines for peaceful and constructive ways to handle ethnic conflict through regulation of both processes and outcomes. The guidelines include non-discrimination and full participation; promoting the rights and development of minorities in ways which do not endanger regional peace; application of special measures and constructive development processes, such as preserving traditional languages, lifestyles, and cultures; and respecting the human rights of all majorities, minorities, and individuals. In Eide's view, conflicts cannot be resolved using ad hoc approaches; that is, without the application of basic standards which must be adopted at the early stages of conflict, when parties are still behaving rationally. Without rationality, there is a need for a much more complex step-by-step process, where peace enforcement could be required – a tremendously difficult undertaking for which tactics and strategy have yet to be learned.

In "The Right to Autonomy: Chimera or Solution?", Hurst Hannum analyses autonomy as a component of democratic governance and argues that autonomy arrangements respond to the three primary needs of self-expression, democracy, and the protection of human rights, although they do not guarantee them. The author suggests that the assumption that self-determination may lead to secession should not be accepted automatically, as it is a relative, not an absolute right, and different levels of self-determination may be appropriate for different groups. Hannum stresses that the right to effective participation in the economic and political life of a country is of crucial importance and would reduce demands for autonomy. While devolution of powers to sub-state components or even separation should remain options, they should only be exercised after a lengthy process in which the wishes of all parties can be accurately ascertained.

What is evident in the material contained in this volume is the specificity of particular conflicts, as well as the potential for sharing approaches and mechanisms for their peaceful prevention, resolution, or transformation. We believe that active cross-fertilization of ideas, methods, and mechanisms at the global level will increase the international community's capacity to transform the violent conflicts we currently face and to meet more effectively the challenges of the future. In that context, we believe it may be useful to put forward some general approaches for the reduction and management of conflicts rooted in issues of authority and governance. While these suggestions are derived to a large extent from experiences in the former Soviet Union, we also believe they could have validity in other societies.

The first approach involves the decentralization of state power through territorial federalism. Denunciations of ethno-populism or attempts at dismantling ethno-populist political practices are not enough. Lasting accommodation will only be likely if constructive alternatives are developed. In developing alternatives, the experiences of multi-ethnic countries, which consider themselves, and are considered, nation-states – such as India, Nigeria, Canada, and Switzerland – should be taken into account. At the same time, the components of federations should acquire a high level of real power, including rights to their own constitutions and legal systems, control of resources and environmental policy, and management of educational and cultural institutions. Federalism is a means to move the institutions and services of a state closer to the needs and interests of culturally diverse groups living within that state. It is a means to provide self-government for lower-level, less spatially extensive authorities, which, as a rule, are ethnically more homogenous. Federalism is *not* a means to implement the notion of "one ethnic group, one state."

A second mechanism concerns multi-ethnic participation at the federal level as a means of minimizing ethnic conflicts rooted in alienation or rejection of central authority by non-dominant ethnic segments of society. Effective and workable federative systems of governance can be realized not only through decentralization, but also by inclusion at high levels in central political and cultural structures of members of local and regional élites, which would provide them with additional competence, legitimacy, and a sense of being a part of a whole. Reservation of offices and informational channels on an ethnic basis can also foster intra-ethnic competition and thus reduce the potential for conflicts between groups.

The third mechanism involves special measures and inducements to stimulate inter-ethnic political cooperation. Where ethnicity has been central to the formation of political coalitions and for mobilizing those direly affected by crises and attracted to totalitarian solutions, developing substitutes for this powerful charismatic paradigm is not an easy task. As a first step, attempts should be made to entrench the practice of inter-ethnic electoral and political coalitions legally and constitutionally. Multi-ethnic countries should explore election procedures which guarantee that a candidate is nominated and elected by a multi-ethnic electorate. Within the Russian Federation, for instance, a politician could not be elected as president unless, besides getting a majority of votes, he or she received a mandate from at least a majority of the ethnically diverse constituent republics. This model, recently tested in Nigeria and elsewhere and proven to be a promising means of widening and strengthening multi-ethnic cooperation and coalitions, could also be implemented within the components of a federation and their administrative units. Another avenue is the stimulation of special interest groups and coalitions, including business interests, the professions, and territorial associations.

A fourth mechanism concerns probably the most deep-rooted issue of inter-ethnic relations – reducing inequality and ethno-social disparities. In complex societies there always exist along ethnic lines different forms of economic inequality, even when equal opportunities and justice are well established by legislation or by state and community politics. As Manning Nash states in *The Cauldron of Ethnicity in the Modern World* (Chicago: University of Chicago Press, 1989, p. 127), "Ethnicity is a reservoir for turbulence in a world where power, wealth, and dignity are unevenly and illegitimately distributed within and among nations." Along with a process of devolution and redistribution of political power, special measures should be undertaken in the economic field, including the widening of participation in highly-skilled jobs for representatives of underprivileged groups through skills training, equal access to land, and, in the case of Russia, provisions for balanced inter-ethnic participation in distributing shares in privatized enterprises.

The fifth mechanism concerns the strengthening of local self-government and community organizations involved in the management of issues of ethnicity at the grass-roots level. In the former Soviet Union, as elsewhere, when we look closely at how ethnic conflict emerges and escalates, it is evident that most of the disputed problems are local ones and could be resolved at the local level. Equally, when conflict escalates into open violence, it is more often than not local authorities, social institutions, and grass-roots organizations who are best able to play pacifying roles. However, it is essential that local governments and other actors have the authority and financial resources to implement constructive initiatives and policies affecting ethnic issues. An extremely important issue for local politics is a proper respect for the traditions and values through which small groups and individuals of different ethnic origin and religious beliefs realize and manifest their own identities.

Finally, it should be considered that the right of preserving and developing one's own culture is one of the most basic rights and one which helps to preserve the diversity of human societies and humankind as a whole. But there is no need of global "Balkanization" to achieve this goal. Self-determination can mean an individual or group determining its own identity and safeguarding its rights and interests based on this identity, irrespective of political-administrative borders. The practice of ex-territorial cultural autonomy for its multi-ethnic population, native languages, press, schools, associations, religious activities, and the like was widespread in the early years of the Soviet Union. In Russia at least, new mechanisms for governing conflicting ethnicity should include revitalizing old experiences and suppressed institutions. The US experience of affirmative action is another possible model, as is Canada's multicultural approach.

1

Governance and conflict resolution in multi-ethnic societies

Kumar Rupesinghe

The search for forms of governance in multi-ethnic societies is an important issue which needs to be addressed in the transition from one world order to another. It will require fundamental changes in our perceptions of global security, sovereignty, and multi-ethnic societies.

Global society is changing. We are moving towards a single world order, a single civilization. The collapse of the Berlin Wall was symbolic in that it drew attention to the fact that boundaries are tumbling and systems are becoming more open. The Wall's collapse also came at a time when apartheid, the most outstanding example of institutional racism, was being challenged and new forms of governance actively pursued in South Africa.

The end of the Cold War has led to new issues being placed on the political agenda, including the questions of self-determination and the pursuit of a truly multi-ethnic global order. At the highest level of abstraction, humanity is evolving towards a global system which is more complex and more varied, and where the concept of state sovereignty may assume new meanings. Global society is moving toward recognition of a multicultural, multi-ethnic, pluralistic global system.

But old ideas take a long time to disappear, particularly when these ideas have been trapped in institutions and attitudes.

In this paper I take as my starting point the idea that ethnicity is dynamic concept which has acquired a new and important historical significance. The revival of ethnicity and the search for identity is itself an aspect of modernity and leads to the democratization of structures. In this sense, the revival is positive and may not lead to violence and war if institutions are created for a multi-ethnic plural order.

My second point is that, unlike the old nations which had completed state formation projects, i.e. the so-called democratic zone, many states are still in the process of nation-building. The old historical process of achieving nation-building through a highly centralized state structure is not possible. State- and nation-building is therefore problematic. It requires policies which are not merely assimilationist and integrationist but which truly recognize a multi-ethnic plurality.

The third point is that the right to self-determination after decolonization has become an unresolved and largely unreflected domain of contention. These issues need to be addressed if the new world order is to have any universal significance. Should the right to self-determination be judged on a case-by-case basis, where the protagonists have to engage in a protracted civil war to obtain the status of a sovereign nation? Or should there be alternative arrangements, where people without states may enjoy a sense of nationhood and identity securely with a sense of participation? Given a new international climate favourable for democracy and human rights, should there be international bodies and mechanisms that could provide a framework wherein minorities' issues and cases of self-determination and independence are properly addressed?

My fourth contention is that the notion of governance requires a more expanded notion of conflict transformation. This is needed in order to take into account the various phases and evolutions of the conflict process and determine where timely interventions can be made to resolve and prevent the outbreak of violence and war. Changes in the global order need to be managed by transnational agencies, and a renewed United Nations must finally address the issue of self-determination and develop frameworks and mechanisms for the resolution of these problems.

A contingency approach to conflicts and their prevention is needed, which in turn suggests the need for an expanded role for regional and international bodies. Governance of multi-ethnic societies requires the active participation of civil society, and the development of a culture of negotiation and tolerance. Institutional mechanisms and frameworks must take into account the positive achievements of many societies which have lived and worked together for centuries.

1 Governance, ethnicity, and conflict resolution

Governance, at both the international and the national levels, refers to the objective of producing orderly, just, and peaceful relations to deal with the problems encountered in a complex and rapidly changing world. The essence of governance is that it is a process of continuing creativity in the search for adjustment and accommodation in the midst of uncertainty. Although we are moving towards a "new world order," the global order is still based on the old political order. The old political order was governed by the hegemonic domination of the two superpowers. Its thinking and practices on statehood, sovereignty, and security need to be examined.

There is a growing recognition that many global problems, such as ecological security, disarmament, and the escalation of internal wars and refugee flows, require global institutions to manage them. Some global institutions have already emerged, such as the United Nations, and global economic organizations such as the International Monetary Fund and the World Bank. These institutions sometimes impose on the sovereignty of states, through both rewards and sanctions. It is obvious, however, that no global institution has yet emerged to manage and prevent violent conflicts, protect minorities, or regulate and decide on the rights of peoples.

What is indeed paradoxical in the current global system is that while the United Nations has a clear mandate to deal with international conflicts, its mandate to deal with internal strife and the norms for intervention is still evolving. Today, inter-state conflicts are relatively rare, but the numbers of internal wars within a given state are increasing. Most of these wars are due to problems of state formation and ethnicity. According to the *SIPRI Yearbook 1992*, there were over 32 internal wars the previous year and the prospects for the increase in the numbers of these wars was highly likely. If we reduce the threshold of the definition of an armed conflict to less than 1,000 casualties, then the number of armed conflicts in the world would be over 150.

Internal war is no longer restricted to the South, however, as the war in former Yugoslavia demonstrates. Potential civil wars in the

Commonwealth of Independent States may make the figures even higher. More than 40 million refugees (including refugees outside the borders of a given country and internally displaced people) in the world today are victims of armed conflicts. It is likely that the figure will go up to 100 million by the year 2000.

1.1 Ethnicity and identity

"Ethnicity" is itself full of ambiguity in the Anglo-Saxon world, and perhaps it is this ambiguity which provides for its constant recurrence. But ask anybody to define ethnicity and the problem begins. We are left with a host of interpretations. The difficulty in defining ethnicity is that it is a dynamic concept encompassing both subjective and objective elements. It is the mixture of perception and external contextual reality which provides it with meaning. In political theory, "ethnicity" describes a group possessing some degree of coherence and solidarity, composed of people who are aware, perhaps only latently, of having common origins and interests. Thus, an ethnic group is not a mere aggregate of people but a self-conscious collection of people united, or closely related, by shared experiences and a common history. It is difficult to find a satisfactory definition of multi-ethnicity or multi-ethnic society. But the implication is that there is more than one group possessing some degree of coherence and solidarity, whose members have common origins and interests which they do not share with other groups. In this sense, few states are ethnically homogeneous and many are polyethnic in composition.

Much has been written about ethnic revival and there is no need to summarize the discussion. What is significant and important in the discussion is that there are particular factors that not only lead to the revival of identity but also to violence. Conditions of modernity give rise to ethnicity and make identity a powerful symbol of meaning and worth. Present-day ethnic conflicts have a scope and intensity that did not exist earlier. Anthony D. Smith even argues that "we are fully justified in isolating a broad historical trend in the modern era, and designating it as an 'ethnic revival'. [But] ... such a revival of ethnicity is also a transformation, and ... it possesses a unique character, shared by no previous ethnic revival" (Smith, 1983).

Those who perhaps are not patient with current terminology have decided that the concept of ethnicity should be replaced instead by the notion of identity. They define this as a continuous and dynamic development encompassing both existential and social components.

The search for identity is a powerful psychological driving force which has propelled human civilization. Identity is evocative: we are after all dealing with a myth or an imagined community which has all the power necessary for political mobilization. Identity has also been defined as an abiding sense of selfhood, the core of which makes life predictable to an individual (Northrup, 1989: 55). To have no ability to anticipate events is essentially to experience terror.

Identity can be conceived of as more than a psychological sense of self; it encompasses a sense that one is safe in the world physically, psychologically, socially, even spiritually. Events that threaten to invalidate the core sense of identity will elicit defensive responses aimed at avoiding psychic and/or physical annihilation.

The conditions for ethnicity have been the subject of great intellectual inquiry in recent times. What seems to be the unanimous view is that ethnicity and identity conflicts will be the dominant form of violence and war in the coming years. Ethnicity itself can be enhanced and reformulated under conditions of modernization. Myths of origin, enemy images, demonizing the other, are old and traditional myths of long historical duration. Most ethnic groups do have a myth of origin, a history of the group, chosen enemies, and stories of traumas. But what is it that gives these symbolic elements meaning and, in certain contexts, a possibility of actualization? When do self-fulfilling prophecies become actualized? It is at this point that the intersection between modernity and the revival of myth and ritual is of interest.

Most ethnic or minority conflicts today have a substantial international or transnational component, for various reasons. This may be because members of the minority community in one state form part of the majority community in a neighbouring state, such as the Tamils in Sri Lanka or Catholics in Northern Ireland, or because a minority or ethnic community cuts across borders and thus involves more than one state (e.g. Basques, Saamis, Kurds). At least 80 potential contemporary border and territorial disputes between states have been identified. Transborder conflicts may seem latent, but they have a tendency to flare up and escalate rapidly. Iraq's invasion of Kuwait and the Gulf conflict (1990–1991) illustrated the potential for such conflagrations.

The problem is that many states have denied the existence of ethnic conflicts. Barsh (1988) evaluates the extent to which international bodies responsible for the protection of human rights have recognized the significance of ethnic conflict as a destabilizing force in both developing and industrialized countries. The study concludes that a surprisingly large number of states refuses to acknowledge the possibility of ethnic divisions. Examples of such denial can be found in all regions, but most frequently in Asia and Africa, where evidence suggests that the contemporary threat from ethnic conflict is also the greatest.

1.2 Conditions for ethnic conflicts

The multiplicity of ethnic groups does not by itself lead to violence and conflict. The stages in the process between mobilization and civil war can be long and protracted and it is only under certain conditions that separatist or secessionist movements will emerge. There have been several suggestive attempts to delineate models of ethnic stratification. These can provide useful typologies which raise issues of relevance to conflict resolution. Joseph Rothschild suggests:

Societies may stratify their ethnic groups according to models of vertical hierarchy, of parallel segmentation or of cross-patterned reticulation. Only in the first of these, the vertical hierarchical model, is there a categorical correspondence among all dimensions – political, social, economic and cultural – of ethnic superordination and subordination. (Rothschild, 1981: 79–80)

To take one example, South Africa's apartheid system would easily fit this model.

In models of parallel ethnic segmentation, each ethnic community is internally stratified by socio-economic criteria and each has a political élite to represent its interest *vis-à-vis* the corresponding élites of the other ethnic segments. In the reticulate model, ethnic groups and social classes cross-populate each other but the system is not random, symmetrical, or egalitarian. Each ethnic group pursues a wide range of economic functions and occupations, and each economic class or sector organically incorporates members of several ethnic categories.

Rothschild suggests that the reticulate model provides the best conditions for the gradual and peaceful resolution of ethnic conflicts. Similarly, Donald L. Horowitz (1981) makes a distinction between ranked and unranked ethnic groups. He sees the distinction as resting upon the coincidence of social class with ethnic group. When the two coincide it is possible to speak of ranked ethnic groups. Where groups are cross-class, it is possible to speak of unranked ethnic groups.

Both Rothschild and Horowitz point to a major distinction in ethnic stratification. If ethnic groups are ordered in a hierarchy, with one group superordinate and another subordinate, ethnic conflict moves in one direction. But if groups are parallel, with neither subordinate to the other, conflict takes a different course. Stratification in ranked systems is synonymous with ethnic membership. Mobility opportunities are restricted by group identity.

In unranked systems, on the other hand, parallel ethnic groups coexist, each group internally stratified. Horowitz suggests that ethnic and class conflict coincide when ethnicity and class coincide in ranked systems. Ethnic conflict, however, impedes or obscures class conflict when ethnic groups are cross-class, as they are in unranked systems. It is obvious that this model describes two pure types which may not be so clear-cut in reality. It is crucial in the distinction to note that what we are mostly discussing with regard to modern ethnic conflicts are unranked systems, so characteristic of many multi-ethnic societies in the third world.

In distinguishing between types of ethnic conflict and stratification, important work has also been undertaken which could provide a fruitful basis for empirical research. The mobilization processes for political autonomy or secession would depend on certain conditions. Certain basic structures determine the course of the conflict and possibilities for resolving it. Rothschild suggests seven different outcomes of stratification from a conflict-resolution perspective:

1. Dominating majority;
2. Dominating minority;
3. Balanced relation with nation-building people and several ethnic groups or nationalities;
4. Division of power between territorially based and functional groups;
5. Oppressed but economically strong minority;
6. Many small groups in balance;
7. Multiplicity of ethnic groups of varying sizes and levels of politicization, manoeuvring within a relatively cohesive political system.

This can provide us with a useful typology for speculating on the types of conflicts each model can generate. With regard to secessionist movements, the worst possible situation is where both the majority and the minority have strong perceptions of being engulfed and dominated. In the dominant majority/minority model, the minority may have cross-border affiliations with a neighbouring country. The conflicts in Sri Lanka and Northern Ireland are examples.

The dominant minority model reflects the apartheid system in South Africa. Here the ethnic stratification system and class are coterminous, with a tendency to polarize the conflict. In both these cases there is a danger that complex issues and a range of conflicts may be reduced to a single win/lose conflict with strong potential for violence.

The third type represents typically large geographic units with multi-ethnic configurations, many nations, languages, and minorities. The Indian case, where the Hindu majority is surrounded by many nations and linguistic minorities, has given rise to a federal structure. In the former Soviet Union the nation-building people also expanded across their own border, and the entire commonwealth has today inherited a complex ethnic stratification system. In such instances conflicts are always multiple in character and the complexity cannot be reduced to a single conflict. The state has more room for manoeuvre and requires a strong management style.

Another interesting stratification system occurs when one group retains economic power and the other geographic control and political power. Examples include Malaysia, Fiji, and Guyana. In such instances there is a tendency towards intractability if political power is not shared by both communities.

The mobilization processes for political autonomy or secession depend on certain conditions. To understand the dynamics of mobilization aiming at political autonomy and secessionist solutions, we must analyse the ethnic balance of power. This reflects not only demographic conditions but also differences between the resource bases of the various ethnic groups, their economic power and organizational propensities. Certain basic structures may determine the course of the conflict and possibilities for resolving it.

Typologies can be created to specify the types of conflict that could be generated. These specifications help us to discuss more clearly the types of conflict reduction mechanism possible within each given structure. Some structures have a potential for direct violence, while others have a potential for mediation and reconciliation. This suggests that the propensity for violent conflict exists in some societies but not in all.

To develop models of ethnic stratification and types of conflict represents a welcome corrective to those who would suggest psychological approaches, which merely prescribe changes in attitudes. In many cases changes in structure and the unit of devolution are crucial variables in determining whether conflicts will be generated. A sig-

17

nificant variable is the politicization of ethnicity by political parties and political leaders of all shades. It is to be noted that so-called majoritarian democracies which require political power to be based on arithmetical majorities may be more prone to inter-ethnic mobilization. In such democracies political élites can appeal to ethnic loyalties as a base for political power.

2   The role of the state

The modernization project, as it were, has been accompanied by a highly centralized and standardized bureaucratic system. Its apotheosis has been the development and articulation of a centralized state, a concept which captured the imagination of many opinion leaders and decision makers throughout the world as the best vehicle for the evolution of human civilization. The evolution of the state has been the vehicle upon which violence has been mediated between itself and the people through the evolution of a technocratic bureaucratic structure that has taken upon itself the sole monopoly of violence.

The evolution of the state and the process of standardization meant that cultures and languages were either absorbed, eliminated, or incorporated into the modern project, and this continues. The state-building project is still not completed and there are many new nations which are demanding state sovereignty. The concept of "one nation, one state" continues to evoke passions and mobilize people.

What is new is that the process of centralization and state-building has been challenged by a variety of social and ethnic movements. The consolidation of state power in the future is problematic for a variety of reasons.

1. The concept of sovereignty is being gradually eroded;
2. The unitary state as a powerful centralizing agency is under challenge by sub-nationalist forces;
3. The monopoly of violence is no longer the sole monopoly of the state, and various transnational forces are able to arm, equip, and deliver lethal weapons of terror.

2.1   The concept of sovereignty

The modern state system has European origins. Beginning with a small number of states, it has today expanded to a proliferation of states, which itself constitutes a major global project of universal dimensions. The state-building project assumed new vigour after the Cold War, with a series of new states emerging. However, there has also been, under modern conditions, an erosion of the concepts of sovereignty and non-interference in internal affairs. The prerogative of the state has been challenged by many institutions, and the metaphor of the global village and modern communications have helped to serve this purpose. Further, international institutions which began as complementary to state-building projects have assumed their own autonomy, which enables them to impose their will on individual states. In the domain of human rights and humanitarian intervention, norms have been developed where states are scrutinized for their human rights performance.

2.2 The unitary state

The process of state-building was characterized by strong centralization and bureaucratic management. Often unitary state structures are controlled by hegemonic élites who marginalize the periphery and other identities. This process of the unitary state often means one language, one principal nation. State formations are in different phases of evolution. Some formations have achieved a high degree of integration, such as the European Union, where border controls for those within the community are all but abolished. But the majority of states are in different phases of evolution. There are variations of this pattern found in almost all decolonized societies, including the former Soviet Union and parts of Eastern Europe.

Often states are dominated not only by bureaucratic centralization, but by hegemonic élites with wide patron/client networks which exclude other nationalities. Some of these states may evolve into truly multi-ethnic societies. (The idea of the melting-pot as a paradigm for social integration may not be relevant to all segmented and deeply divided societies.) The uneven development of state formations means that there are highly developed states (often called the democratic zone), states in formation, and states yet to be born. Reform of the international system means recognizing this fact. While some developed states may transfer sovereignty to higher bodies, others may cling to a narrow definition of sovereignty.

Most emerging conflicts are about the nature of the state and its formation. Whether the conflicts are over the devolution of power, federalism, governance, or how resources are distributed, generally they concern the way the state manages its business. Several states are themselves products of violence and bloodshed. Some states are hegemonic states in that they are based on communal/ethnic or religious loyalties, where patterns of recruitment to the army or the bureaucracy are based on ethnic affiliations. Some states can be called defective states, in that they continue to foster their own retardation, but all states are confronted with similar challenges. The most significant challenge is the requirement for modernizing their economies within an accelerated, frenetic, shrinking world. Internal threats come from the military and from ethnic and religious fundamentalist forces, constituting twin challenges to democratic development. Unfortunately, the state, in dealing with these issues, has often become an agent of arbitrary violence, perpetuating force and militarism as a way of resolving conflicts. There is also another significant reason why conflicts are becoming increasingly difficult to manage. This is the proliferation of weapons and the diffusion of the technology of weapons. New armed actors tend to determine the direction of conflicts. There is a growing transnational network which trades in small weapons and this network is linked to the drugs trade.

3 The concept of self-determination

The right to self-determination remains one of the most intractable and difficult problems to be addressed by the international community. Many legal formulas have sought to define the existence of the right to self-determination, to define who constitutes a people and who has a right to a separate existence. The subject has been the basis for contention and war.

In a comprehensive analysis of the right to self-determination, Aureliu Cristescu wrote:

It is clear that the relevant provisions of the Charter have been interpreted in an increasingly progressive spirit over the years. Today, it is generally recognized that the concept of self-determination entails legal rights and obligations and that a right of self-determination definitely exists. (Special Rapporteur ..., 1981)

With two exceptions, South Africa and Palestine, colonial and alien domination was treated as a phenomenon that applied only where the dominator was European. There is nothing in the Charter or the Covenants, however, that restricts the definition to colonial and subject peoples. The Charter refers in general terms to the development of "friendly relations among nations based on respect for the principle of equal rights and self-determination of peoples." The Covenants assert that "all peoples have the right of self-determination. By virtue of that right they freely determine their political status and freely pursue their economic, social and cultural development."

Some of the problems associated with the current state of affairs have been identified as follows:

1. The United Nations has not established any formal procedures for adjudicating claims to self-determination. The Committee of 24, the Decolonisation Committee, entertains representations only on behalf of peoples whose territories they have listed, all of which are dependencies or former dependencies of European powers. But the Committee has no mechanism for examining claims from persons or organizations claiming to represent peoples aspiring to the right of self-determination, let alone of assessing them according to a set of agreed criteria.

2. A distinction is made in practice between so-called "salt-sea" imperialism, where the dominating and the dominated are separated by hundreds of miles, and "local" imperialism, where the two peoples are immediate neighbours. It has been assumed until very recently that peoples locked together within a state must remain so linked indefinitely. This means that many cases of "internal colonialism" do not come under the purview of any international body.

3. The right to self-determination is treated essentially as a political right, rather than one of international law.

The current discussion is taking place in the context of a new situation. The disintegration of the Soviet Union provides new impetus to the debate, in that within the Commonwealth of Independent States the right to self-determination has not only been exercised by republics but is also a point of contention within the republics themselves. It is highly probable that current experiences associated with the disintegration of the Soviet Union and Yugoslavia will have ramifications beyond their borders. There is no shortage of other empires or quasi-empires which have imposed internal colonialism and subjected peoples to national oppression.

In the debate on the right to self-determination, useful distinctions have been attempted between peoples who have the right to secession and minorities who have the right to protection within a given state. The protection of minorities has been a subject of great contention and debate, but attempts are being made to monitor states' performance. Standards are being established, such as the United Nations Declaration on the Rights of Persons Belonging to National or Ethnic, Religious and Linguistic Minorities, adopted on 18 December 1992. Regional organizations such as the Conference on Security and Cooperation in Europe (CSCE) have also developed their own standards and principles governing minority protection. However, there is still a long way to go between declaration and practice, and mechanisms need to be developed for monitoring and obtaining compliance by states.

The question which has not been answered is: how will it be determined exactly what constitutes a minority and what constitutes a people? Is this to be determined solely by the individual state and only internationalized after gross violations have been committed or when refugee flows become unacceptable to neigbouring countries? Or should there be bodies which can adjudicate and make decisions on this vexing question? Those who argue for an international body to adjudicate self-determination would say that there needs to be a framework for making such decisions. Subject peoples need not have to undergo violence and bloodshed before their case is heard.

Recently there has been a proposal for the appointment of a High Commissioner for Self-Determination, whose function would be to look at claims and report on them in the light of factors which might include the following:
– previous history of statehood or existence as a separate territorial entity;
– ethnicity, language, religion, culture;
– existence of special institutions;
– manifestations of the will to a separate identity.

The High Commissioner could refer cases to a Committee on Self-Determination. The Decolonisation Committee that was set up to adjudicate on former colonies could be given the mandate to address new claims. Such a body may be able to adjudicate and give fair and evenhanded judgments based on the establishment of clear principles and norms.

On the other hand, some argue for a case-by-case approach. They are apprehensive of creating an epidemic, where fresh claims are made for secession without considering alternative arrangements such as internal autonomy, federalism, confederation, and minority protection. It may well be that the complexity of the situation requires a case-by-case approach. The weakness of this argument, however, is that it does not offer an institutional arrangement by which this can be achieved. Whatever the merits of these approaches, it is clear that today the issue of who constitutes a people and who has the right to independence is one of the most important to be addressed by the world community.

3.1 Democratization and self-determination

The paradox is that democratization creates the space for ethnic revival and religious fundamentalism. Only under conditions of democracy do such movements become public issues. The resurgence of ethnic and nationality claims may expand the basis for democracy by providing for adequate representation and devolution, but it seems that centralized unitary states are not prepared to give an inch, except through confrontation and violence. In this sense the resurgence of ethnicity and religious extremism pose a major challenge to the global expansion of democracy. Both these visions still have the capability to challenge democracy from below, but they may be counterbalanced by other factors, such as a large middle class or a diffused professional cadre committed to stability and secularism.

4 Governance and conflict resolution in multi-ethnic societies

The application of theories on conflict and their relation to ethnic strife and future disputes remains one of the central challenges for scholars and practitioners. The subject matter of conflicts we are dealing with is largely based on visions of just societies and strong conceptions of identity.

4.1 Rationality and conflict resolution

A large and growing body of literature on conflicts and conflict resolution has consisted of theoretical reflection coming from the United States and Europe. This approach generally presupposes a domain of "rationality," where all the parties more or less share certain basic values based on rational argument. However, certain assumptions within this conventional theoretical conflict paradigm are largely unstated and need to be deconstructed. Failure to do this leaves unaddressed many crucial questions relating to the causes of endemic violence in third world societies, the undemocratic nature of many of these societies and their inability to resolve conflicts in a more humane and peaceful manner. Conflict resolution theory, fixed within

23

a rationalist framework, marginalises many of these dimensions, making the theory a limited tool in resolving violent disputes. It is therefore important to identify some of the stated assumptions behind the approach to conflict resolution mentioned above.

In Western approaches to conflict resolution it is assumed that the problem is getting the parties to the conference table through negotiations and that it is possible to get a win/win solution agreeable to both sides. The environment within which these conflicts occur is generally imbued with a strong ideological imperative of equality and recognition of the rule of law. The modern division of labour in Western societies assumes that their members are tied to multiple roles and are attached to a variety of interests which result in conflict. In recognition of this complexity, society develops institutions and mechanisms to resolve conflicts in a specified way. Gradually, a culture of negotiations emerges and a complex network of arbitration and dispute resolution becomes increasingly professionalized. Conflicts are amongst like-minded actors who speak a common language, denoting a shared universe of meaning. Normally, disputes are defined within a fairly developed regime of law, based on individual rights, which has had a specific historical evolution in the West. In this approach a high priority is given to getting all the parties to reach an understanding of their specific interest and how those interests can be satisfied using problem-solving approaches and negotiations.

4.2   Conflict theory as applied to protracted conflict

How relevant are these approaches to the protracted violent conflicts we are now experiencing? These conflicts are not based merely on interest but involve many social dimensions involving identity and security. Social conflicts involving groups within a society are taken as severe when they result in political violence (war, massacres, executions, disappearances, torture), or serious political repression (imprisonment, censorship, discrimination) on a large scale.

Conflicts which involve a core sense of identity between or among parties tend to be intractable: the intractability is generated by the dynamics of the conflict rather than by a rational reasoning process. Conflict resolution here means changing the conditions of this intractability. These conflicts are not single-issue disputes, but multiple conflicts being waged simultaneously.

In the most general terms, I would suggest that we see conflicts as collisions between projects. Projects are sequences of actions directed towards a goal. Conflicts occur when the projects of different actors start impinging on each other. Take missions, for example. Missions are projects of the largest historical scale: their space is the world, their time measured in millennia. Among the world's religions, two stand out as missionary creeds: Christianity and Islam. The collision of ideologies in this century – between concepts of capitalism, Marxism, nationalism, or the idea of progress – can also be seen as clashes between projects.

4.3   Governance and conflict transformation

In reviewing conflict resolution stratagems I think I have made it clear that those which have emanated from the discourse of rationality are only partially applicable to protracted social conflicts.

Research on past conflicts provides us with quite a few clues to address this issue. Conflicts have a beginning and an end. While some recent wars have lasted 30 years, inter-state wars are getting shorter and more random. On the other hand, internal wars are getting longer and more consistent. It is also apparent that the most difficult conflicts to resolve are ethnic conflicts, and they also seem to be the most violent, involving the highest number of civilian casualties. Third parties seldom intervene until the violence reaches a high level and casualties are very high. The United Nations is rarely involved in these conflicts and the cases are rarely brought to the Security Council. Intervention, third-party mediation, or negotiations usually come years too late, after the conflict has become intractable. It is therefore necessary to identify gaps in the conflict process and find ways of strengthening and building competence in these areas.

In recent years it has become abundantly clear that we must abandon linear approaches that seek single causes of conflicts and adopt multiple approaches to reduce the sources of intractability. Conflicts can only be resolved within a political process. Such an approach requires recognition that many actors and many institutions need to be involved, and that a division of labour needs to evolve which engages the United Nations, the international community, and the non-governmental world.

A conflict may be broken down into several phases: formation; escalation; endurance; improvement; and transformation. Each phase may require a different type of intervention:

1. formation   – early warning;
2. escalation   – crisis intervention;
3. endurance   – empowerment and mediation;
4. improvement   – negotiation/problem-solving;
5. transformation – new institutions and projects.

4.3.1   When conflicts begin: Conflict formation

The conflict formation phase is when there is a perceived disjuncture between actors in a given social system. Conflict prevention means controlling a situation where conflicting goals exist, in order to avoid the development of violence. Institution-building for conflict regulation is one form of conflict prevention.

The political institutions which will be discussed later fall into this category. There is very little recognition of early warning indicators that can lead to conflict management or resolution. Except for national intelligence services – notorious for their bias and lack of credibility – there is no agency to monitor potential conflicts. Similarly, there is no public agency which can work towards conflict prevention. Few societies have ombudsmen or other governmental bodies to facilitate preventive action.

Generally, the international system has been geared for the protection of victims and intervention only after a conflict has developed into pathological proportions. Only very recently have serious discussions started on the development of an early warning capability and the need for preventive diplomacy.

4.3.2   Conflict escalation and crisis intervention

Conflict escalation occurs when conflicting parties have gone into the phase of attrition, both verbal and military, and when a dispute enters into a spiral of violence and counter-violence. Very little is done to intervene when a conflict escalates into bloodshed. Far too often, states are clearly implicated in fomenting or tolerating riots and pogroms. The same is true when it comes to the investigation of crimes committed against civilians and when little is done to hold law enforcement agencies accountable.

Non-governmental and humanitarian organizations and citizen bodies may play a role in providing relief to the victims. This is when peace-keeping forces may be brought into play. The United Nations has developed competence in peace-keeping and this may be used increasingly in internal armed conflicts.

4.3.3   Conflict endurance: Empowerment and mediation

Conflict endurance refers to a phase in which the parties to a conflict have entered a state of war and the reproduction of violence becomes pathological. Civilian institutions are weakened and the civilian community is passive. Eventually, concessions for mediation may be made, due to war-weariness or when the conflict has reached sufficient maturity and one side has been able to press its claims through either violence or mass pressure. Generally, as far as the state is concerned, concessions are expressed through accords, round-table conferences, pacts, and agreements.

Recent accords, however, do not provide for any optimism. Rather than resolve conflicts, some accords merely serve to create new disputes. Instead of being an attempt to bring parties to a consensus, an accord may really represent the exercise of power and the imposition of the will of the state. This is the time when civilians need to assert themselves and create space for democratic action and the resolution of conflict.

4.3.4   Conflict improvement: Negotiation and problem solving

There are instances when negotiations begin in earnest between protagonists. But cease-fires and negotiations tend to break down for a variety of reasons: there may be too much secrecy involved, or a lack of professional negotiators, and cease-fires can be used for regrouping armed militia. Such setbacks occur despite the fact that there are now many examples of frameworks for negotiations at the UN, regional, and subregional levels.

4.3.5   Conflict transformation: New institutions and projects

This is a phase when popular forces are able to change the balance of power and there is a change of regime, through either an election or a coup. Such transformation can only be meaningful if it is not a mere transfer of power, if structural changes are achieved within the society and new institutions emerge to address themselves meaningfully to outstanding issues.

We can classify possible solutions to the kinds of conflict discussed above, as follows:

(i)   A high degree of regional autonomy for a minority which has already a strong territorial claim;

(ii) Fundamental social reforms such as land reform, labour rights, social redistribution of wealth, etc.;

(iii) Political democracy with a free press, multi-party system, civil and political rights;

(iv) Consociational democracy: more complex social contracts that combine universal political rights with special provisions for vulnerable groups;

 (v) Federal form of government which recognizes linguistic groups and nationalities as units of devolution.

A rationalist formula may be able to deal with some of the phases in the conflict process but not all. The timing of various interventions and the nature of the intervenor can be crucial to the way in which the conflict is transformed. The challenge falls on those who capture the democratic space available to determine whether conflicts can be transformed through collective non-violence or whether armed conflicts and criminality will dominate. In peace-building processes, I would suggest that each specific culture has the indigenous resources to resolve its own conflicts. It should be borne in mind that conflict transformation attempts to empower all the parties to a conflict. This approach recognizes that social conflicts need to be transformed in a less violent way. Admittedly, violence can achieve limited objectives, but contemporary violence and its manifestations maim and injure all sides, including large numbers of civilians.

5 International responses and mechanisms

Concern has been expressed at the lack of capacity of international institutions such as the United Nations and various regional organizations to manage ethnic and internal conflict.

5.1 The role of the United Nations

The UN has considerable potential for conflict prevention and conflict resolution, but it is obvious that it has a limited mandate when it comes to violent conflicts, often defined as internal disputes. Nevertheless, the organization has been involved in conflicts in countries such as the Congo, Cyprus, Lebanon, Somalia, and Guatemala, and has sent observer missions to Palestine, Kashmir, Cambodia, Afghanistan, and El Salvador. Over the years, the UN has developed considerable competence in peace-keeping, but not in peace-making or in peace-building. It is therefore necessary to continue exploring ways to advance the UN's role as peacemaker. Many suggestions have been made, from improving reporting systems to early warnings, strengthening the role of the Secretary-General, developing competence within the Secretary-General's office, and appointing special rapporteurs. The Security Council has not been able to ignore the growing political and public pressure to re-examine the scope of UN activities. Discussions within the Security Council have allowed world leaders to explore the weaknesses and strengths of the United Nations, discuss its role after the Cold War, and make recommendations for its evolution. Many of the leaders proposed that the United Nations should play a major role in peace-making. It was suggested that the UN should not only develop an early warning capability but address the issue of conflict prevention by early and timely intervention. The Secretary-General was requested to use his good offices in advancing the cause of peace-making and peace-building.

Research on the formation of conflicts and their maturation tells us of the many lacunae and gaps in the field. We know that early warning and early intervention are still the weak links in the chain. We also know that once a conflict matures there is a mismatch between the event and forms of intervention. Generally intervention through fact-finding or mediation comes too late. We need to mobilize and deploy much earlier the skills available to enforce and monitor cease-fires. Parties in conflict rarely find legitimate frameworks to discuss these issues.

Negotiation is not the business of amateurs but requires the use of organizations with an institutional memory. Different interventions are required at different stages, from early warning to conflict transformation. The problem is not only to reduce the duration of the conflict but also to reduce the mismatch between escalation and intervention.

The United Nations is rightly placed and has within its mandate the opportunity to address these issues. According to Brian Urquhart, the UN has exercised two options in the past: traditional peace-keeping or large-scale collective enforcement action, such as was seen in Korea and more recently in Kuwait. Urquhart suggests a third strategy of international military operation is needed, somewhere between peace-keeping and large-scale enforcement. It would aim

to put an end to random and uncontrolled violence and provide a reasonable degree of peace and order so that humanitarian relief work could go forward, and a conciliation and settlement process be undertaken.

Such armed police actions would use highly trained but relatively small numbers of troops and would not have military objectives as such. Unlike peacekeeping forces they would be required to take certain combat risks and if necessary to use a limited degree of force. (Urquhart, 1993: 93–4)

My proposal, however, is directed toward preventing large-scale conflicts and bloodshed. The dynamics of conflicts are such that we need to have an enlarged political package where many initiatives can have a consistent place. This is why a new framework needs to be provided by the international community. There must be early and timely intervention. A framework for discussion can provide a basis for negotiating territorial grievances within an international setting.

Furthermore, guarantees for minorities may also be secured by providing comparative knowledge, as well as constitutional provisions and other mechanisms tried out elsewhere. Given timely warning and early enough alert information, the United Nations and the Secretary-General should be able to make available their offices to provide such frameworks for dispute resolution.

There must be a quick and effective manner to bring impending violent situations to the attention of the Security Council. In this regard, fact-finding missions sent quickly can accomplish a lot. Providing forums for the parties to identify the issues can also help, as can the sending of skilled peace-makers to talk to the parties and the provision of competent negotiators as technical assistants. The point is that contingency plans should be comprehensive.

In the pursuit of peace-making initiatives the United Nations can also benefit by closer cooperation with non-governmental organizations in the field. A much better understanding is required of how these organizations assist by developing early warning information and research and collaborating with other groups in the field. This in turn would foster a better understanding of the comparative advantages of each type of organization and the coalitions needed to be built around particular issues. Just as the current discussion on the role of the United Nations is timely, addressing these relationships at the highest level could help the people of the twenty-first century live in a more peaceful world.

References

Barsh, Lawrence. 1988. "The Ethnic Factor in Security and Development: Perceptions of the United Nations Human Rights Bodies." *Acta Sociologica* 31, no. 4: 333–41.
Horowitz, Donald L. 1981. "Patterns of Ethnic Separatism." *Comparative Studies in Society and History* 23, no. 2.

Northrup, Terrell A. 1989. "The Dynamic of Identity in Personal and Social Conflict." In Louis Krieberg, Terrell A. Northrup, and Stuart J. Thorson (eds), *Intractable Conflicts and their Transformation*. Syracuse: Syracuse University Press.

Rothschild, Joseph. 1981. *Ethnopolitics: A Conceptual Framework*. New York: Columbia University Press.

SIPRI Yearbook 1992. 1992. Stockholm International Peace Research Institute. Oxford: Oxford University Press.

Smith, Anthony D. 1983. "Ethnic Identity and World Order." *Millennium* 12: 149–61.

Special Rapporteur for the UN Human Rights Sub-Commission on Prevention of Discrimination and Protection of Minorities. 1978. "Study of the historical and current development of the right to self determination on the basis of the Charter of the UN and other instruments adopted by UN organs with particular reference to the promotion and protection of human rights and fundamental freedoms." UN [E/CN.4/sub.2/404/Rev.1]

Urquhart, Brian. 1993. "Security After the Cold War." In Adam Roberts and Benedict Kingsbury (eds), *United Nations, Divided World: The UN's Roles in International Relations*. Oxford: Clarendon Press, pp. 81–103.

2

Ethnic conflict in the Horn of Africa: Myth and reality

Hizkias Assefa

Introduction

Most of the wars waged in the Horn of Africa during the past 30 years have been described in terms of ethnic conflict, both by the adversaries themselves and by external analysts. The first and second Sudan civil wars have been characterized as conflicts between the Arabized northerners and African southerners, with cleavages along religious, racial, cultural, and linguistic lines. The various civil wars in Ethiopia have been characterized as wars between the Amharas and the Tigreans, Oromos, Eritreans, and so on. The Somali conflicts have been described as conflicts between the Maraheens and the Isaaqs, or between the Darods and the Ogadenis, and so on; and the conflict in Djibouti as between the Afars and the Issas.

Although each of these wars has been termed "ethnic conflict", one encounters tremendous difficulty when trying to analyse what is meant by this term and what these conflicts have been about. In this chapter some of the problems associated with the concept of ethnicity and ethnic conflict as they apply to the Horn of Africa will be examined. A discussion will follow of various mechanisms that have been utilized or advocated in the region to remedy the problem of ethnic conflict. The chapter will conclude with remarks on some possible responses that might open ways for the transformation and hopefully the alleviation of the problem.

Conceptual problems

What are some of the difficulties with using the concept of ethnicity as a framework for understanding and addressing the conflicts in the Horn of Africa? First, it is not clear what is meant by the terms "ethnic group," "ethnicity," and "ethnic conflict." In the context of the Horn, many concepts, such as nationality, tribe, and now clan, have been used interchangeably with that of ethnic group, and it is very difficult to distinguish between them. A commonly used definition is that an ethnic group is a collectivity of people who share the same primordial characteristics such as common ancestry, language, and culture. (People have included religion in the category of shared culture.) Ethnicity then refers to the behaviour and feeling (about oneself and others) that supposedly emanates from membership of an ethnic group. Ethnic conflict has come to mean cleavages between groups based on differentiations in ethnic identities.

A major question that arises from the above definition of "ethnic group" is whether people must share commonalities in all the criteria mentioned to be members of the same ethnic group or to share the same ethnicity. There are instances in the Horn in which just belonging to the same religion seems to suffice to classify people as members of an ethnic group, although they might differ in other criteria. For example, in central and southern Ethiopia, if an Oromo is Orthodox Christian that individual may be classified as an Amhara regardless of his or her ethnic ancestry or lineage.[1] In other instances, as in the Oromo regions, language has been used as the criterion for determining membership, despite other differences. But there are also cases where commonality in language and religion has not signified membership of the same ethnic group. Especially where groups have interacted for a long time, there are situations where people might have overlaps in one of these ethnic criteria (religion, language, culture, or ancestry) but lack commonalities in the rest. How are people to be ethnically classified under those circumstances?

Some have argued that membership of an ethnic group is not determined by objective factors such as sharing common primordial characteristics. They point to subjective factors such as perception, belonging, self-identification, and the like (Hymes, 1968: 1220; Nadel, 1947: 13). They argue that a person, regardless of primordial commonalities, can become a member of an ethnic group if he or she feels and acts as a member and is accepted as such by the group. But this raises some problems. If the basis for the perceived commonality or belonging is not the primordial common factor, then what is it? Could the basis be commonalities in interests, aspirations, psychological orientations? If so, why should this kind of identity and bond be characterized as "ethnic"? Moreover, what happens in cases where some feel and act as if they are members but their membership is not accepted by the reference group?

In short, the definition of ethnic groups and the distinction between people based on ethnic criteria is difficult, inconsistent, and confusing. One could come up with different results depending on whether one uses objective or subjective criteria. This has led to great controversy concerning the identification and measurement of the phenomenon.[2] But the preoccupation with definition is not simply an academic exercise. It has very important practical implications. It should go without saying that we cannot develop effective mechanisms to deal with a problem if we do not fully understand it. Frustration with the inability fully to grasp and define the concept of ethnicity has led to a tendency which says: "Let us not waste a great deal of time trying to define the concept; instead let us recognize it as a major problem and put our energies into developing mechanisms to deal with it."

Some would take the approach used by a US Supreme Court justice to define pornography: you may not be able to define it, but you know it when you see it. The trouble with that attitude is that if we are not agreed on what the phenomenon is we might be wasting our energy by focusing on the wrong problems or by prescribing a remedy for a problem that has not been diagnosed correctly. As we will see in greater detail later, doing so could even run the risk of making the situation worse instead of remedying it.

Another difficulty with the concept of ethnicity and ethnic conflict is the common assumption that ethnic similarities and differences are the basis for social harmony or discord. Thus, it is expected that those who share a common ancestry, language, culture, and religion should have a relationship of solidarity and harmony with each other but one of cleavage and conflict with those who do not share their ethnic identity. This concept is also full of problems. There are societies in the Horn where ethnic similarity has not assured social harmony nor avoided the outbreak of large-scale conflict. Especially where there is no perception of external threat, there is a great deal of evidence that ethnic groups have divided into lower-level identities and fought each other with as much zeal as they might fight other ethnic groups. Alternatively, there are also societies in the region where ethnic diversity has not been a prescription for violent conflicts.

These problems can be illustrated by examples from various contexts in the Horn of Africa. As indicated earlier, in Ethiopia ethnicity has been identified by many as a major cause of conflict. That country's major civil wars were between the central government, which was seen to have been dominated by the Amhara people, and various insurgency groups bearing the names of ethnic groups such as the Oromo, Tigre, Afar, Ogaden, and Beni-Amer Liberation Fronts. The liberation fronts claimed they were fighting to break free of the political, economic, social, cultural, and religious domination of the Amhara people over their particular ethnic groups.

Problems of definition

Once one goes beyond the labels and begins to decipher the claims and counter-claims in the Ethiopian conflicts, all the problems associated with the concept of ethnicity discussed earlier begin to surface. To begin with, the definition of the "oppressors" and the "oppressed" in ethnic terms becomes an insurmountable task. Who are the dominating Amhara people? How is membership in this group defined? What is the Amhara culture? Is "Amhara domination" a code word that disguises other grievances or does it signify supremacy of one population over another, as the term implies?

It is true that most of the symbols of the Ethiopian state (official religion, official language, etc.) have taken the identity of what has been labelled "Amhara culture," and the persons who have occupied power and privilege have, by and large, borne Amhara names.[3] But this situation does not mean that the great majority of the Amhara people have been "dominators" or beneficiaries of the political, economic, or social system that bore their name.

First of all, not all people that speak Amharic as their mother tongue and are Orthodox Christians consider themselves as one ethnic group. The Gondare Amharas are distinct from the Shoan Amharas, as the Gojam Amharas are from the Wollo Amharas. There had been a history of rivalry and warfare between these subgroups. In the past several centuries, the subgroups had formed various alliances with other ethnic groups such as the Oromos, the

Gurages, and the Tigres to fight other Amharas. The same phenomenon of internal division and warfare has also prevailed among other
groups such as the Oromos, the Afares, and the Somalis.

Second, in the last century, the major beneficiaries of the "Amhara-
dominated" state were primarily the Shoans, who held most of the
government leadership positions, controlled much economic power,
governed most of the provinces, owned large estates in the southern
provinces, and managed to make Shoa's capital, Addis Ababa, the
centre of economic activity for the entire Ethiopian state. The other
Amharas (Wolloyes, Gojames, and Gondares) were excluded from
this system as much as those who belonged to other ethnic groups.

Third, even with "Shoan domination," the beneficiaries of such
privilege were the aristocracy and the educated élite, who constituted
a very tiny percentage of the Amhara population. The vast majority
of the Shoan Amharas have been as poor, powerless, and exploited
as any other Amhara or non-Amhara groups such as the Oromos,
Gurages, or Sidamas. In fact, the poverty of the Shoan Amhara peas-
ant was in some cases worse than that of the "subjugated peoples" of
southern Ethiopia such as the Kaffa and Adere people, who were
"outsiders" to the state system.

Fourth, even the ethnic identity of the Shoan rulers has been subject to controversy. As far back as the 1760s, Oromos have assumed
very significant leadership roles in the Abyssinian kingdoms or
empires based in Shoa and the other Amhara regions of Begemder,
Gojam, and Wollo. According to Clapham (1988/9: 217), the Shoan
leaders have been as much Oromo and Gurage as Amhara. He points
out that most of the Shoan emperors, and many of the generals and
governors who served these rulers in the expansion of Shoan control
to the south of the country, had Oromo or Gurage lineage. Emperor
Haile Sellassie, the latest and one of the strongest symbols of
"Amhara domination," was "in terms of his parentage more Oromo
than Amhara, and also had a Gurage grandmother. He married an
Oromo."[4]

Fifth, there is a big question as to whether the so-called Amhara
culture was merely the culture of one ethnic group which was
imposed on other ethnic groups. It has been pointed out that the
Amhara culture interacted with the cultures of other peoples in
Ethiopia not by assimilation but rather by acculturation.[5] Although
its name stayed "Amhara," the culture allowed others to influence
and change it. Asmeron Legesse (1973: 9) argues that "the process of

cultural exchange cannot be reduced to a simplistic picture in which Gallinna [Oromo] speakers [for example] become Amhara ... It is a rather complex situation in which many cultural vectors are interacting to produce a resultant [*sic*] that is fundamentally new." This aspect of the so-called Amhara culture has enabled Clapham (1988: 23–4) to call it a core element of a multi-ethnic culture which, despite its name, is not the exclusive property of any particular group of people.

In sum, Greenfield (1965: 58) scans the history of the Ethiopian peoples' interaction over the centuries and observes: "This latter word [Amhara] no longer has close definition and it is clear that the word 'tribalism' is not suited to Ethiopian studies."

Thus, we find the ethnic explanation of the conflict that has gripped Ethiopia for the past 30 years, such as the theory of "Amhara domination," very inadequate and misleading. This is partly because it is very difficult to define the actors in ethnic terms (for instance, who are the Amharas?). Secondly, even if it were possible to define the actors in ethnic terms (if one were to define easily who the Amharas were), the reality on the ground does not support a conclusion that what was witnessed in Ethiopia was ethnic conflict.

In fact, a good case can be made that ethnic conflict, in the sense of one ethnic group waging a war against another, or pogroms motivated by ethnic hatred, such as we have seen in some societies, has been a very rare event in the history of Ethiopia. The norm in the country, if not in the region, with the exception of recent developments in Somalia, has been ethnic coexistence rather than ethnic warfare.

Ethnicity and social harmony

Now let us look at the other problem with the ethnicity framework – the assumption that ethnic similarity or difference is the basis for social harmony or cleavage respectively. When we examine this assumption in the context of the Horn, we find that it is also full of difficulties.

Not long ago Somalia was the envy of many African states because it was one of the very few nation states that existed in the continent. It was a territory inhabited by people who shared the same ancestral origin, language, religion, and culture – all the elements of common ethnicity. But that ethnic or nationality bond was not strong enough to prevent disintegration. Currently an extremely bloody civil war is being waged between clans and sub-clans. In the capital, Mogadishu, alone, over 30,000 Somalis have been killed in the past two years from inter-clan clashes. Hundreds of thousands have been made re-fugees. Interestingly, some analysts have begun to describe the clan conflict as ethnic or tribal conflict. If the term "ethnic conflict" is being used synonymously with "clan conflict," could it also be used to mean conflict between sub-clans or between family groups? If so, how useful is a term that could mean so many different things in different contexts?

When we look at the Eritrean/Ethiopian conflict, however, we observe the opposite configuration. Some of the major justifications given for the independence of Eritrea from Ethiopia have been that the Eritrean people are different from Ethiopians; that Ethiopia itself is not a legitimate nation state since it is a conglomeration of very diverse peoples; and that, as a separate people, Eritreans have a right to exercise their right of self-determination. But when one examines Eritrea itself, one sees that it is also an entity composed of nine major ethnic groups, having nine different languages and cultures. The pop-ulation is divided into two major religions (Christianity and Islam) and two ecosystems (highland and lowland) which more or less correspond with the religious divisions. If we pursue the logic for Eritrean separa-tion, could we say that the lowland Beni-Amer and Beja Muslims in Eritrea, who are different peoples from the Christian highland Tigreans, and who constitute a large percentage of the Eritrean pop-ulation, have a right to self-determination and to a separate state? Where does the disintegration stop? Does it continue until we get to an area occupied by one pure ethnic group? Is that possible? Is it desir-able? As indicated earlier, there are always cultural, linguistic, ances-tral, and religious continuities between ethnic groups that have inter-acted with each other for long periods. How will it be possible to separate groups from each other without wrenching apart families and communities, and without provoking hostilities between the groups?

Alternatively, if such diverse ethnic groups could come together in Eritrea and form a nation, why shouldn't the same logic apply to the rest of Ethiopia? Do Eritreans believe that all these diverse people will make one nation, or is this just wishful thinking? Is it ethnic similarity in Eritrea that created a sense of common antipathy towards the Ethiopian state, or is it the oppression Eritreans com-monly experienced from the economic and political system imposed on them by the élites who controlled the Ethiopian state (which, by the way, also included Eritreans)? If so, is the remedy to the problem the removal of the oppressive system or is it separation and the creation of a new state?

Our analysis so far reveals some major problems with the concept of ethnicity as a framework for analysing the conflicts in the Horn of Africa. Is this framework helpful? Does focusing on the ethnic differences or similarities of people in the region give us a good understanding of the conflicts or of what needs to be done to contain them? Could there be other explanations that would capture these situations better?

Clapham (1990: 10) argues: "Viewed across the region as a whole, economic marginalisation provides a much clearer guide than either ethnicity or even political exclusion to the incidence of warfare in the Horn." On a more cautionary note, Bhardwaj argues:

The importance of the ethnic factor [in the Horn of Africa] is recognised by all. But it is our contention that, along with the role of the ethnic actors, the socio-economic basis of the ethnic hostility must also be given due weight. A clash of interest of the exploiters belonging to different ethnic groups and the masses in general precipitates the ethnic hostility. The struggle of the nomads of Ogaden and Tigre of lower Eritrea against the Amharas of the Ethiopian plateau – all bring ethnic differences to the fore and distort a basically socio-economic conflict into an ethnic one. (Bhardwaj, 1979: 169)

It can be argued that, to a large extent, what has been called ethnic conflict is élite-driven conflict. When one talks of ethnic conflict between the Amhara and the Tigre in Ethiopia, or the Arabs and the Africans in the Sudan, for example, it is more accurate to talk about conflict between élite groups who come from different ethnic backgrounds than about people-to-people violence among the masses arising from ethnic animosity, as the term "ethnic conflict" implies. However, such an élite-driven conflict has a powerful capability of turning into widespread conflict among the masses.

It is true that the region's ethnic groups have their own prejudices and stereotypes about each other. But these attitudes have not normally turned into conflict at the people-to-people level unless manipulated and organized by political leaders. Élites find ethnic prejudices and stereotypes fertile ground in which they can easily cultivate support for their political and economic aspirations. Expressing their objectives in ethnic or nationality terms (such as "advancing the interest of our own people" or "protecting ourselves from another ethnic group") ennobles the pursuits and gives them more legitimacy.

As we have seen in many instances in the continent, the major beneficiaries of such aspirations might be the élites, but the whole ethnic group becomes associated with these aims since they are pursued in the name of the entire group.

Once this cycle starts and conflict begins to be waged in the group's name, fear and further animosity pervade the whole group, since all members become perceived as the enemy by those against whom the conflict is being waged. Pre-existing ethnic prejudices further fuel the conflict because they simplify the complex motivations of the actors, making it easy to create an immediate "us" and "them" perception as well as to demonize the adversary. Thus, a conflict started by the élites ends up, in a self-fulfilling prophecy, engulfing the entire ethnic group. Interestingly, despite such efforts by élites, at least in the Horn of Africa, the incidence of people-to-people violence and pogroms has been quite rare.

Despite the confusion generated by the concept of ethnic conflict, many analysts have latched on to this simplistic concept, implying people-to-people antagonisms based on ethnic differences to describe the conflicts in the region. As Clapham and Bharwaj have indicated, analysis of "inequitable economic and class stratification" or "monopolisation of access to state and economic power by an ethnic based elite" (in the case of Ethiopia, a multi-ethnic élite under the name of Amhara oligarchy) might provide an equally sound if not better explanation of the conflicts in the region.

The role of ideology

In the case of Ethiopia, particularly in the past 20 years, ideology has also played a role in sustaining and exacerbating the notion that ethnic animosity and supremacy of one people over the other is at the root of the conflicts in the country. The radical student movement of the 1960s and the early '70s, which was the forerunner of the 1974 Ethiopian revolution, was strongly Marxist-Leninist in orientation. During the rise of this movement, Lenin's discourse on "the nationalities question" and his prescription of "self-determination up to secession" (along with other Marxist ideas of "dictatorship of the proletariat," "collectivization of agriculture," etc.) were lifted wholesale from the history of the Soviet Union and grafted onto Ethiopian realities, thereby forming a major tenet in the political discussions at that time. There was not much debate about these concepts' relevance to the Ethiopian situation or about the operational problems involved in implementing them. Although the term "nationalities issue" grated on many people's ears, they acquiesced to it, since it was the paradigm of the day.

After the 1974 revolution, the soldiers who took power from the monarchy did not have much knowledge or experience of how to restructure the society following the destruction of the old social order. The radical Marxist student leaders were brought into the government, where they became the revolution's advisers and ideological leaders. Those student leaders then had the opportunity to make the "nationalities question" a national agenda. According to Markakis:

As militant Marxists, the radicals [student leaders] were obliged to confront the national issue and, after some agonising, they opted for the Leninist principle of national self-determination and declared their support for the Eritrean rebels ... From then on, the national issue was forced on the agenda of every political movement in the country ... Since it [the government of Mengistu Haile Mariam] espoused Marxism as its ideology, the new regime could not formally reject the principle of national self-determination. (Markakis, 1989: 4–6)

Even after Mengistu's overthrow in 1991, the new government leaders were those who had been socialized in the radical Marxist-Leninist ideology of the 1960s and who still held entrenched views on the nationalities issue. As soon as they took power they declared that the most important issue facing the country was the "nationalities question," and proceeded to decree that all ethnic groups, nationalities, and peoples in the country could define their own territory, form their own governments, and exercise self-determination, including declaring independence.[6] Towards this objective, the map of the country was redrawn, eliminating the old multi-ethnic administrative provinces of the country and replacing them with ethnic zones. As demarcating boundaries based on ethnicity is never an easy task in Ethiopia, the new map has reportedly been redrawn at least twice already.

The fallout from this policy has already started. People have been forced out of land they have inhabited for generations and told to return to their ethnic homelands. Of course, there is no home awaiting them in their places of origin, for they migrated generations ago. In some areas violent conflict has broken out between members of different ethnic groups in attempts to draw their own ethnic boundaries or claim territories that were considered common in the past.

41

Ethnic claims over resources that were considered common, such as minerals, land, ports, etc., are likely to become very explosive issues.

In the 30 years prior to the demise of Mengistu's regime, the civil wars in the country were waged between the central government and insurgencies bearing ethnic names. But in the current situation people are being pitted against each other. Neighbours who have co-existed peacefully for decades, if not centuries, are being encouraged by official government policy to emphasize their ethnic differences so that ethnically homogeneous political structures can be created. Age-old relationships between peoples, intermarriages, cultural inter-actions and continuities, are in peril of being disrupted or wrenched apart. As the reality in the country has been a long history of co-existence and cooperation between ethnic groups at the grass roots, people are speaking out against the ethnic segregation that is being imposed on them from the top. However, unless the implications of this new ethnic policy are examined carefully and the policy itself revised, the government might end up creating more ethnic conflict than it deters.

Close observation of the Ethiopian situation makes one wonder whether the preoccupation with "the nationalities question" and its prescribed remedy of "national self-determination" are products of an ideological framework rather than an outgrowth of the country's realities. Instead of the reality on the ground determining the model of theoretical framework to be used in diagnosing, understanding, and dealing with it, an ideologically dictated theoretical framework seems to have been imposed on the reality, which is then forced to conform with the framework. As the saying goes, if the only tool you have is a hammer, then you think everything else is a nail.

Similarly, since the most dominant analytical framework in Ethiopian politics since the late 1960s was the ethnic framework, it seems that every problem in the country was viewed as emanating from this basic question. Class analysis, élite exploitation, or even regionalism would have gone a long way to explain the country's situation, rather than an exclusive focus on ethnicity and the nationalities issue. If those other frameworks had been used, the emergent remedies would have differed from the current proposed solutions, which could drag the country into another cycle of bitter civil war.

This is not to argue that political leaders invented the nationalities problem in Ethiopia. There is no question, however, that they dis-torted it, inflated it out of proportion, and exploited it.[7] Ethnicity all of a sudden became the predominant explanation of many of the things that went wrong in the society. Élites sold the idea to the people and now the people are carrying the banner. A myth is developing that the creation of new states will solve the problems people have experienced with the current state systems in the region.

Traditional remedies

Now, if we focus on the solutions that have been traditionally applied to the problem of ethnicity and the conflicts it generates, we notice that the remedies seem to present as many difficulties as the problem itself. The traditional responses have been either "nation-building," which has meant forging one nation out of diverse peoples, or, in rare cases, "self-determination," which in many people's minds has been associated with separation and the formation of another state.

Attempts at building new nation states out of a multitude of ethnic groups has generally taken two forms. One has been the creation of a multi-ethnic culture, which all groups identify with and voluntarily adopt as their own. The other is the assimilation of different cultures into a dominant one, usually by the direction of a highly centralized and coercive state. The first approach is complicated and normally takes a long time to develop. The second approach, seemingly expedient, has been adopted by many post-colonial African states in their eagerness to generate quick results. But this approach has often been associated with manipulation and at times outright repression by those in power. The 30 years of experience with this approach since independence has shown that not many new nation states have been forged in Africa. In fact, it might be said that the efforts made in this direction seem to have backfired. More recently, animosity and violence along ethnic lines has been on the increase in many African societies, especially as the highly centralized nature of these states is being challenged with the movement towards multi-party politics.

As another response to ethnic conflict, people have proposed "self-determination" as an alternative to "nation-building." But the concept of "self-determination" is so riddled with confusion that it does not provide a viable alternative. The term itself is composed of two concepts, "self" and "determination," whose definition and operation raise a multitude of problems. What constitutes the "self"? Is it a group that is connected by primordial ties like an ethnic group? Could any other group form the "self"? Can the "self" be engineered? And what is the meaning, implication, and scope of the term "determination"?

43

If the "self" were to refer to a group having primordial ties, we are again faced with all the problems discussed earlier regarding group definition, especially in cases of a long history of intergroup interaction. The distinction between objective and subjective criteria again becomes an issue. Mayall argues that it is not clear whether some of these aggregate identities like nations exist "as an objective reality, as claimed by nationalists, or should be understood as an imagined community or creative fictions as others have claimed" (Mayall, 1990: 2; see also Gellner, 1983).

If one uses the objective criterion of primordial ties for defining nations, then there are many who feel that their primordial roots do not solely dictate their interests, needs, aspirations, and ability to forge common purpose as well as affiliations with those who do not come from the same roots. If one uses the subjective criterion – and there is a lot of merit to that – a major problem becomes how to identify those who feel they belong to an ethnic group so that they are clustered in one territory? What if those who feel they belong are not accepted by others as belonging?

To the extent that self-determination has meant separation and creation of a state, how might it be possible to build a state around an ethnic group without provoking chauvinism, ethnic animosity, and the wrenching apart of communities, given the cultural, linguistic, ancestral, and religious continuities between ethnic groups that have interacted with each other for long periods? The search for the pure ethnic group as a foundation for building a state has led to fascism, Nazism, pogroms, massive dislocations, and genocides in many parts of the world, including the African continent itself.

If, on the other hand, the "self" refers to an "imagined community" or "creative fiction," as Mayall argues, could one then stretch one's imagination to include others in the community so that "the self" becomes a larger and more inclusive unit?

Aside from the definition of the "self," there is still a problem with the content of "self-determination." What is to be determined? What is the scope of the "determination"? Some have defined self-determination as the aspiration "to have control over one's affairs in order to ensure one's economic and social well-being" (An-Na'im, 1989: 21; see also Assefa, forthcoming (a)). But the ability to determine one's own affairs or economic and social well-being is increasingly being complicated by the realities of an interdependent world. One is constrained not only by one's own capabilities but the interests and capabilities of others. Except in a world of autarky or complete isolation, any actor must recognize how his or her needs and actions are compatible with those of others in the system. The more interdependent the world becomes, as the trend seems to indicate, the more one's orientation might need to be towards coalition-building, coordination, negotiation, and consensus rather than unilateral determination of one's own affairs. If so, how much autonomous control can one sensibly exercise in this modern and rapidly shrinking world? How meaningful is it to absolutize "self-determination" in such circumstances?

The major limitation in all of these approaches to defining the "self" for the purposes of "self-determination" is the failure to recognize that primordial elements constitute only one consideration in that definition. It cannot be denied that there are other considerations based on human choice rather than mere coincidence of birth. Common perceptions, needs, aspirations, and interests can also enable people to include others who share these sentiments in their definition of "themselves" even if they do not share primordial links with them. Therefore, to define the "self" exclusively in terms of primordial givens by creating ethnic states seems to ignore, artificially and detrimentally, the various dimensions that enter into people's definition of themselves. The challenge becomes how to recognize and legitimize the unavoidable and undeniable fact of primordial roots, but to temper its detrimental and exclusionary tendencies by encouraging broader definitions that can accommodate others. In other words, how might it be possible to encourage and emphasize the consociational aspect of "self"-definition as much as the primordial aspects?

An alternative approach

The two conflicting demands of "nation-building" and "self-determination" have embroiled the Horn, as well as much of the African continent, in decades of bloodshed and destruction. However, we have seen that both approaches suffer from severe limitations which prevent them from providing avenues for the effective creation of harmonious societies.

Given these limitations, a more promising direction, especially in the case of Ethiopia, might be to re-examine the notion that ethnic animosity and the domination of one ethnic group by another are the causes of the conflicts in the country and that the solutions to these conflicts lies in secession or the creation of independent states.

Instead, addressing the economic and political inequities in the system (which no doubt had been disguised and confused by ethnic labels), enlarging the economic base so that there are resources to share among various ethnic groups, opening up the political system so that everyone, regardless of his or her ethnic background, can have access to it, as well as creating a system of governance that is democratic and respects the political and human rights of all citizens, could go a very long way towards remedying the so-called "ethnic" conflicts in Ethiopia.

In conjunction with this, one should work at developing systems that could prevent ethnicity from becoming a cause for further cleavages and civil war in the various societies of the Horn. First, it must be established that the question of identity is not and should not be a zero-sum issue in human relationships. All people have multiple identities which are expressed differently in different circumstances. The freedom of an individual or a group to choose its own separate identity should not, therefore, be a threat to others as long as that individual or group also recognizes that there is common identity at another level with those from whom it is distinguishing itself. Thus, as much as people endeavour to articulate and enhance what is unique about themselves, an equal amount of energy should be invested in articulating and enhancing what binds them with other people.

A mechanism must be found to legitimize ethnic identity in the Horn of Africa without making it incompatible with the formation of a larger unit of identity based on mutuality and beneficial collaboration. A promising endeavour in this context might be to adopt a very loose federal system of governance supplemented by building infrastructures for regional integration. The loose federal system of governance would allow for the expression of ethnic identity. But the tendency towards fragmentation that might arise from legitimizing ethnicity would be balanced and tempered by providing incentives towards higher levels of integration and identification with the entire region. As the various ethnic groups become reassured of their identity and security, they would also be provided with incentives for a larger regional identity by highlighting the benefits that could emerge from higher levels of association and integration.

The fear and resentment which groups have of the current state systems in the region, as well as their tendency to view separation as a solution, can be tempered if the state is viewed as an intermediate institution rather than the institution of final resort to work out problems, as it has been to date. The creation of a supra-state regional structure, in which the various groups in the region have a say but which is capable of dealing with problems that cannot be dealt with at the state level, could have a salutary effect on the conflicts between the state and the various groupings within it.

This approach could enable the societies in the Horn to work at both ends of the identity problem. While people would be reassured about being what they are or cannot avoid being, they would also be encouraged to explore greater vistas of meaningful identity with greater entities, beyond the state. The disintegration and exclusive orientation of ethnicity would become more balanced by the synthesis and inclusiveness that comes from a sense of regional identity. Creating a regional framework with a move towards regional integration could permit the relaxation of strict boundary demarcations, allowing freedom of movement and interaction between peoples. It could reduce the pressure for the creation of new independent states by disaffected groups, since there would be a new regional forum to redress their grievances or address their interests and rights without their being forced to resort to secession.

The concept of a regional identity arising from a vision of regional integration could create a less threatening, consociational process where all the actors in the region could be engaged in building a more equitable and peaceful social contract that could lead to mutually enriching relationships.[8] Regional identity would not be an end in itself, but a step in a transition to more inclusive identities. It would challenge groups to recognize aspects of themselves that could they could share beyond the ethnic group and the state.[9]

Conclusion

The confusion revolving around the subject of ethnic conflict suggests that the problem has not been well grasped, at least as it has manifested itself in the Horn of Africa. The tendency has been, however, to take the phenomenon as given and to think of building mechanisms to deal with it. Unfortunately, the solutions generated under these circumstances have also been full of contradictions and anomalies. People who have been frustrated with the existing state systems in the Horn have advocated self-determination as a way of dealing with the problem. These proponents argue for the restructuring if not the dismantling of the existing states and the creation of new ones such as Eritrea, Oromia, Ogadenia, Somaliland, and Southern Sudan. But the proposed states in many ways resemble the ones being dismantled. As long as they are not completely ethnically homogeneous they will be faced again by an "ethnic" or "minority" problem or a "nationalities question," just like their predecessors. The problem of "ethnic conflict" then starts all over again. Alternatively, if there are no minorities there is no guarantee that the "homogeneous ethnic group" will not break up into subdivisions such as the disintegration along clan lines in Somalia. From that conflict we have observed that violence and animosity between clans is not necessarily any less intense than that between ethnic groups.

The logic of a separate ethnicity or nationality as a basis for the creation of a separate state forces us to seek the highest primordial common denominator between people, in order to determine the unit for whom a state is to be created. If we pursue this logic, it is not clear at what level of social organization we might be able to attain that common ground. In the Horn, ethnic and clan identification have not yet provided that highest common denominator. One might be forced to look at smaller and smaller units, such as the family. The search for such a primordial common denominator, which the logic underlying the ethnic state seems to demand, could lead us to very absurd conclusions.

The major problem with the notion of ethnicity or nationality as a form of identity is that it is a very exclusive concept. It is preoccupied with the identification of how one is different from others. Without denying that aspect of identity which is exclusive, an equal amount of energy must be put into exploring and articulating more inclusive conceptions of identity as well. The current preoccupation with exclusiveness must be counterbalanced by notions and visions of inclusiveness. In the current debate in the Horn, and for that matter in many other places where there has been a revival of nationalism or ethnicity, it seems that it is the narrow and exclusivist voices that have carried the day.

Simultaneously, there is a sense of resignation, even among the scholarly community, that the brutal slaughter and destruction taking place in the name of ethnic and national conflicts in the Horn of Africa region and other places, such as Yugoslavia or the former Soviet Union, are sordid aspects of human nature about which little can be done. Part of the challenge for human civilization is to tame those atomistic tendencies towards greater and greater disintegration based on exclusive identity. This should be done not by ignoring or denying the need for such identities, but by working at them from the opposite end, by fusing them with a more inclusive sense of identity, and by helping people to recognize and nurture their commonality with others instead of always glorifying and celebrating their differences and exclusivity. The approach discussed in this chapter is an attempt in that direction.

Notes

1. Greenfield makes this point from his observation in Harar: "In Harar today the term Amhara means little more than a Christian" (Greenfield, 1965: 57). In Wollo people used to ask: "Are you an Amhara or a Muslim?" in order to qualify a person's religion.
2. A new law in Ethiopia defines "nation" or "nationality" as "people living in the same geographic area and having a common language and a common psychological makeup of identity." See *Proclamation* no. 1, 1992, on the "Establishment of National and Regional and Woreda Council Members Election Committee," p. 2. This definition illustrates some of the difficulties identified earlier. How is the "common psychological makeup of identity" to be determined? How is it to be measured? What happens to those that speak the language but do not feel the "common psychological makeup of identity," such as the Wollega Oromo and the Wollo Oromo? Or have the same "psychological makeup of identity" but do not speak the same language, such as the Shoa Amhara and the Shoa Oromo?
3. But as we will see later, bearing an Amhara name does not necessarily signify having Amhara lineage.
4. Clapham, 1988: 24. Darkwah (1975) points out that the founder of the Shoan kingdom, Negassi, was a self-made Oromo war leader who made his own position but styled it after an Abyssinian model. Others point out that the Oromo language was used at court in Gondar and Shoa and that Oromo leaders controlled many of the emperors in the north, especially during the Gondar era (see, e.g., Greenfield, 1965: 56). Haberland (1963) points out that a Shoa Amhara is largely an Oromo as a Shoa Oromo is to a very large extent an Amhara. The boundary between those identities is very fluid. Gedamu (1972: 5) makes a similar argument about the relationship between Shoa Amharas and the Gurages, as well as between the Gurages and Oromos in Shoa.
5. Teske and Nelson (1974) indicate that acculturation and assimilation are separate processes, though they may be interrelated. Assimilation is unidirectional while acculturation may occur in both directions. According to Salole (1979), acculturation is the cultural changes which occur to two or more populations in close contact. Assimilation is the incorporation of individuals or groups into another culture.
6. Transitional Period Charter, 1991. Nationality was defined as "people living in the same geographic area and having a common language and a common psychological makeup of identity."
7. For an interesting discussion of how the ideology entertained by student activists in the 1960s distorted the understanding and analysis of historical situations in Ethiopia, see Marcus, 1992.
8. See North and Draimin (1990: 245–6) for similar examples in Central America.
9. For a more in-depth discussion of the regional approach as a mechanism of countering ethnic conflict and disintegration in the Horn of Africa, see Assefa, forthcoming (b).

References

Africa World Press. 1988. *The Horn of Africa, Conflict and Development.* Briefing Paper no. 1. Trenton, NJ: Africa World Press, March.

Anderson, Benedict. 1983. *Imagined Communities*. London: Verso.

An-Na'im, Abdullahi. 1989. "The Right to Self-Determination in the Horn of Africa: Perils and Promises." *Association of Concerned Africa Scholars Bulletin* 27 (Spring).

Assefa, Hizkias. Forthcoming (a). "Interest Based Approach to the Resolution of Conflicts in the Horn of Africa: Focus on the Eritrean Negotiations." In Kumar Rupesinghe (ed.), *Internal Wars and their Transformation*. PRIO.

———. Forthcoming (b). *Regional Approach to the Resolution of Conflicts in the Horn of Africa*. Washington DC: Brookings Institution.

Bhardwaj, Raman. 1979. *The Dilemma of the Horn of Africa*. New Delhi: Sterling Press.

Clapham, Christopher. 1988. *Transformation and Continuity in Revolutionary Ethiopia*. Cambridge: Cambridge University Press.

———. 1988/9. "The Structure of Regional Conflict in Northern Ethiopia." *Cambridge Anthropologist* 13, no. 2.

———. 1990. "The Political Economy of Conflict in the Horn." Paper presented to the Regional Security Conference, Cairo, 27–30 May.

Darkwah, Kofi R.H. 1975. *Shewa, Menelik and the Ethiopian Empire*. London: Heinemann.

Friedrich Ebert Stiftung. 1983. "Das Horn von Africa von 'Scramble for Africa' zum Ost-West Konflikt, Symposium in Bonn, Juni, 1982." *Analyser* 106/107, March.

Gedamu, Fekadu. 1972. "Ethnic Associations in Ethiopia and the Maintenance of Urban and Rural Relationships with Special Reference to the Alemgena Wolamo Road Construction Association." Ph.D thesis, London (LSE).

Gellner, Ernest. 1983. *Nations and Nationalism*. London: Basil Blackwell.

Gilkes, Patrick. 1991. "Conflict in Ethiopia: Roots, Status and Prospects." Unpublished paper.

Greenfield, Richard. 1965. *Ethiopia: A New Political History*. New York: Praeger.

Haberland, E. 1963. *Völker Süd Äthiopiens*, vol. 2: *Galla Süd Äthiopiens*. Stuttgart: Kohlhamer.

Halliday, Fred, and Maxine Molyneux. 1981. *The Ethiopian Revolution*. London: Verso.

Hymes, D. 1968. "Linguistic Problems in Defining the Concept of Tribe." In June Helm (ed.) *Essays on the Problem of "Tribe"*. Washington DC: Washington University Press.

Legesse, Asmeron. 1973. *Gada: Three Approaches to the Study of African Society*. New York: Free Press.

Levine, Donald. 1965. *Wax and Gold, Tradition and Innovation in Ethiopian Culture*. Chicago: Chicago University Press.

Marcus, Harold. 1992. "Does the Past Have Any Authority in Ethiopia?" *Ethiopian Review*, April.

Markakis, John. 1989. *Nationalities and the State in Ethiopia – An Interpretation*. Working Paper Series no. 63. The Hague: Institute of Social Studies.

———. 1990. *Nation and Class Conflict in the Horn of Africa*. New York: Zed Books.

Mayall, James. 1990. "The Roots of National and International Conflict in the Horn of Africa." Unpublished paper presented at the Regional Security Conference, Cairo, May 1990.

Moerman, M. 1968. "Being Luo: Uses and Abuses of Ethnic Identification." In June

Helm (ed.), *Essays on the Problem of "Tribe."* Washington DC: Washington University Press.

Nadel, S.F. 1947. *The Nuba.* London: Oxford University Press.

North, Liisa, and Jim Draimin. 1990. "The Decay of the Security Regime in Central America." *International Journal* 45, no. 2 (Spring).

Nyongo, Peter. 1989. "Crises and Conflicts in the Horn of Africa: Problems and Challenges for Africa." *Genève–Afrique* 27, no. 2.

Salole, Gerry. 1979. "Who are the Shoans?" *Horn of Africa* 2, no. 3.

Teske, R.H.C., and B.H. Nelson. 1974. "Acculturation and Assimilation." *American Ethnologist* vol. 1, no. 2.

Transitional Period Charter of Ethiopia. 1991. In *Negarit Gazeta*, 50th Year, no. 1, 22 July.

3

Ethnic conflicts in the context of social science theories

Valery A. Tishkov

Different social science approaches to the phenomenon of ethnicity and the methodologies of the discipline influence a rather wide spectrum of interpretations of ethnic conflicts. The problem is that what is usually categorized as an ethnic conflict quite often has a more complex nature. As an example, the national movements for independence in the Baltic region were considered by Soviet experts as an ethnic conflict developed in the former USSR.[1] But, in reality, the decisive factor of these events was political rather than ethnic: it was a movement of three Baltic polities comprising ethnically mixed populations for state sovereignty and for a complete secession from the Soviet empire.

The majorities of people in these republics consist of three distinct ethnic groups, and they were the ones who formulated the national idea and the programme of ethno-nationalism. Around this programme an overwhelming majority of the population, including non-natives, was mobilized. Half of the ethnic Russians living in these republics openly supported and participated in the national movements for independence. In this Baltic case, it is not so easy to distinguish inter-ethnic parameters from the predominantly vertical political struggle between the periphery and the centre. In spite of inter-ethnic tensions between titular groups and that part of the Russian-speaking population which showed solidarity with the agonizing all-Union structures, it would be an oversimplification to put these contradictions in a category and analyse the tension as an ethnic conflict *per se*. The Baltic experience was closer in nature to the political struggle of third world peoples for their national self-determination after the Second World War, when the leaders of this struggle were at the same time resolute opponents of ethnic and tribal separatism. It was only later on that Latvian and Estonian nationalist leaders took a resolute position of open discrimination towards the non-titular (or "Russian-speaking") populations of their republics, when the laws on citizenship, official language, and new constitutions were passed and elections to new parliaments were held (in Estonia and Latvia over a third of the population was disfranchised).

Equally, it is not quite correct to consider the political struggles and nationalist movements for sovereignty now taking place in the territory of the Russian Federation as ethnic conflicts. They often repeat the same logic of decentralization of large multi-ethnic state formations, and these movements of Russian autonomies also include strong ethnic and cultural parameters because their initiators and leaders are predominantly represented by titular groups. Meanwhile, there are not sufficient grounds to speak about the Russian–Tatar and Russian–Chechen conflicts as inter-ethnic conflicts in connection with the political strategies of the Tatarstan and Chechen republics. Among those who formulate and support these political strategies there are many individuals and activists of Russian and of mixed ethnic origins, such as the vice-president of Tatarstan, Vasilii Likchachev.

The same kind of reservation could be applied to the interpretation of the movement for the autonomization of the Crimea as a Ukrainian–Russian conflict; although one can easily trace behind this movement a feeling of threat on the part of the Russian majority in the Crimea regarding its status in a new geopolitical situation when the Ukraine became an independent state and kept the territory of the peninsula under its jurisdiction.

Because of the multi-ethnic composition of almost all major areas of the former Soviet Union (the only exception is Armenia after the exodus of the Azeris from this territory), practically all kinds of conflicts and clashes – social or political (from young men's fights in local discotheques to collisions at the highest levels of power) – easily acquire an ethnic manifestation and flavour, making these conflicts and contradictions deeper, more complex, and extremely hard to resolve. Thus, while avoiding the easy temptation to extend the category of ethnic conflict to encompass all conflicting realities in this region, we must state that there are more than enough serious reasons for inter-ethnic tensions and unrest, both on an individual and a group level. The list of crimes and persecutions against ethnic groups and cultures committed by previous regimes is so long, and the existing socio-political and cultural hierarchies of ethnic groups are so obvious, that it would be a naïve and irresponsible approach to reduce conflicting ethnicity to any other societal collisions and contradictions.

The ethnic factor in this region of the world often generates in its turn many critical situations which appear in the realm of politics, inter-community contacts, and federal–provincial relations. Precisely for these reasons, the borders between socio-political and ethnic conflicts in the territory of the post-Soviet states, including Russia, are fragile and hard to diagnose. The conflicts have multidimensional characteristics, and one form can easily convert into another or can have external, displaying façades with quite different internal contexts.

We can find a striking example of this kind of ethnic camouflage, with a political struggle posing as "national self-determination," in the case of the northern native people. This struggle, led by authorities of autonomous districts of Russia, is backed by the powerful interests of local élites recruited from the Russians and other non-natives who dream of building their Eldorado by exploiting the vast resources of the north. The most recent and striking example is the proclamation in 1992 of the new sovereign Chukchi Republic (the former "autonomous *okrug*") on behalf of Chukchi national self-determination. Meanwhile the titular group comprises only 7 per cent (12,000 people) of its population and does not have any significant representation in this formation. This Arctic people is suffering from aggressive and poorly-controlled entrepreneurs and from a collapse of state-supported social programmes, no less than they had suffered under the Soviet regime. An opposite example, where an ethnic conflict is camouflaged as a political one, can be seen in the fight of Moldovan nationalists against "pro-Communist bastions" in the Trans-Dniester and Gagauz areas: in reality these were (and still are) serious conflicts between Russian-Ukrainian and Gagauz minorities on the one side and pro-Romanian Moldovan nationalists on the other. There is also a serious conflict between ethnic and sub-ethnic clan-divisions in Tajikistan. This has involved indigenous Pamiri groups, which were behind the dramatic political clashes in 1992, and was represented externally as a fight between the "democratic opposition" of Islamists and the "corrupt party-based ruling élite" supporting the former President Nabiev and the current President Rakhmonov.

The difficulty of defining the notion of ethnic conflict in the context of the political realities of the former Soviet Union lies not only in the multi-faceted nature of ethnicity but in the region's diverse ethnic systems. Donald Horowitz (1985) defined two major categories, "centralized" and "dispersed" ethnic systems, existing within the limits of multi-ethnic states. One occurs when ethnic groups are so large and strong that problems of their interactions are constantly present at the centre of the political life of a state. These systems are mostly predisposed and potentially vulnerable to large ethnic conflicts, since dominant ethnic groups more often formulate demands for control and even for the exclusive possession of state institutions. These unacceptable demands become the reason for the polarization of societies along ethnic or racial lines, as in Sri Lanka, Burundi, Rwanda, or South Africa.

To a "dispersed ethnic system" belong states with a population comprising a large number of ethnic groups, each of them so small and weak that it is unable to control the centre. Such systems, according to Horowitz, are more prone to inter-ethnic harmony and consensus. Switzerland, Nigeria, and probably India could be categorized as such.

In which of these two categories do we place the former Soviet Union? Its ethnic system was a rather asymmetrical imperial type constructed by ideological doctrine and the political practice of ethno-nationalism, based on the following postulates:

- most ethnic groups were defined as "nations" comprising only titular nationalities living within the limits of their "own" republic, qualified as "national states";
- the whole population of the Union and autonomous republics was divided into categories of "indigenous" and "non-indigenous" or (Russian-speaking) living in the territories of a state that was not their "own";
- the a priori dominant status for titular nationality included undeni-

able rights to control republican centres in spite of the fact that in many cases these groups did not comprise a majority of the population.

An attempt in 1988 by President Gorbachev to replace Kunaev, the first Party secretary of Kazakhstan, by an ethnic Russian, Kolbin, brought resolute opposition on the part of the Kazakh population, aiming to destroy this long-functioning political formula. This formula of exclusive property of a state by a titular group has found new strength in recent years in spite of democratic reforms and ideological liberalization. Small concessions in favour of non-titular groups could be found recently in successor states and in republics of Russia. In independent Kazakhstan and in the Russian Republic of Tatarstan, for example, official titular-Russian bilingualism was proclaimed; Lithuania and Ukraine passed special laws on rights of minorities. The Georgian and Moldovan leaderships have started to discuss opportunities for developing federal systems for their countries.

But more often these steps carry a declarative form, and real political power is controlled by titular groups. In Tatarstan over 80 per cent of all major administrative positions were taken by ethnic Tatars comprising 49 per cent of the population in their republic. In Georgia, the ruling Provisional Council approved a new formula that Georgia is a "national state of Georgians and Abkhazians" – but *not* of Ossetians, Armenians, Meskhetian Turks, or other indigenous residents of the republic! Mentioning Abkhazians did not prevent their long-standing exclusion from central power and prestigious positions in Georgia. This very position justified a veto against the return of Meskhetian Turks to Georgia, as well as repression towards Southern Ossetian autonomy, initiated by the ultra-nationalist leader, Zviad Gamsakhurdia.[2] Events since August 1991 have shown that as soon as new state leaders acquired a weapon of mass destruction from Soviet Army arsenals it was very often used against local minorities; for example, against the Ukrainian-Russian population in Moldova in the Trans-Dniester region, or against Abkhazians in Georgia to prove the exclusive status of titular groups.

The same kind of asymmetrical imperial ethnic system, based on a special status for "indigenous nations" (or titular groups who gave a title to one's republic), is reproduced in the territory of the Russian Federation, where the titular nationalities of the former autonomous republics do not comprise a majority in 15 of 21 so-called "national states."

Judging by formal demographic characteristics, many CIS states and most of the Russian Federation republics could be considered as "centralized" ethnic systems with approximately equal titular and non-titular groups – Kazakhs and Russians in Kazakhstan, Tatars and Russians in Tatarstan, Russians and Latvians in Latvia, etc. – but in reality, because of deep-rooted legacies of the past and mental attitudes, the existing practice and ideology do not allow any non-titular groups to formulate claims to dominate the centre, or even to attain an equal status.

We can consider as a dispersed ethnic system in a more or less conventional sense that which exists in the republic of Dagestan (Northern Caucasus), the only one where no group was assigned a titular status. Even in this republic, however, non-official domination of the comparatively large groups of Avars and Dargins took place, and they controlled key power positions until recently. Only in spring 1992 was this situation challenged by smaller and less privileged groups, especially the Nogai and the Kumyks. This caused a serious ethnic crisis within a republic with an extremely diverse ethnic mosaic. The situation has been seriously aggravated by the nationalist organization "Sadval," representing ethnic Lezgins, a group divided by the border with Azerbaijan. Azerbaijani Lezgins were subjected to severe assimilationist policies, to the extent of denial of registration during Soviet censuses. In Dagestan Lezgins were underrepresented in political and cultural institutions.

Another remarkable characteristic of the former Soviet Union, making for an asymmetrical ethnicity, is the status of the dominant ethnic group, the Russians, who comprised 51 per cent of the USSR and now comprise 82 per cent of the Russian Federation. Officially, there was no "national state" for the Russians, and they did not have their "own" territory. Even now, the Russian Federation is not considered a "national state." But, in reality, this group used to be, and remains, politically and culturally dominant in Russia. The ethnic Russians, or acculturated non-Russians of Ukrainian, Armenian, Georgian, or other origin, are keeping control of the federal centre and of local regional administrations. The Russian culture and language serve as a referent (or "core") culture for the whole state. That is why the Soviet people in the past have often been referred to as "the Russians" by the outside world.

For a long time, this dominant status was so obvious and unchallenged that there was no need to fix it officially through the doctrine of "national state" and through the practical implementation of national self-determination for the Russians. Members of this group felt quite comfortable and protected in all regions of the USSR, and also, because of their higher professional and educational status, easily migrated over the territory including the Baltic and Central Asian republics, Ukraine, Siberia, and the north. At the same time, the Russians did not enjoy any privileges in terms of access to political power or to prestigious institutions in the republics. In Kazakhstan, for example, where Russians comprise 40 per cent of the population, they were not among the members of the Kazakh Academy of Sciences and were poorly represented in other prestigious positions, except as industrial personnel and specialists in agriculture. The living standards of the Russians were not significantly higher than those of the local population, and in Russia itself the standard was even lower compared with the living standards for the majority of other republics.

The demise of the USSR and the ethnic challenges in the Russian Federation made the status of the Russians one of the most serious problems, and it became a focal point in relations between the successor states. Although Russians did not become a subject of direct ethnic violence and were not involved in bloody conflicts, with the exception of military personnel, anti-Russian sentiments and actions in many regions became widespread and even became an element of official state policies, especially in relation to legislation on citizenship, ownership, and language.

The growing out-migration of Russians from these regions back to Russia demonstrates the most evident reaction to this changing climate. In Russia itself, the loss of its former comfortable status and a growing feeling of lost pride generated a powerful syndrome of Russian nationalism and patriotic movements, including political coalitions (see Carter, 1993; Drobizheva, 1992). These movements to prevent a further disintegration of Russia became especially strong after a manifest move to secession by two large republics, Tatarstan and Chechen. Moral projections and political accusations regarding injustices directed towards the Russians as a whole by other nationalities created a potential for dangerous conflicts involving the Russians.[3] Being previously politically inert and demoralized, the "Russian-speaking population" could easily in the near future choose self-organizing militant or political resistance in a situation when previously they preferred "to leave and not to stay," as in the Tuva or Chechen republics. In times of economic crisis and inflation, resettlement to other regions brings in practical terms a loss of personal property including apartments, houses, cars, and even personal belongings.

Thus, defining the systematic peculiarities of the former Soviet Union's ethnic characteristics, and making certain reservations against too broad definitions of ethnic conflict, we must, at the same time, accept a certain degree of conditionality among social scientists as to how to define this phenomenon. In spite of different approaches, there is a certain consensus that we consider a conflict as ethnic when it involves organized political movement, mass unrest, separatist action, and civil wars with opposing lines drawn along ethnic boundaries. As a rule, that is a conflict between minorities and dominant majorities, where the majority controls access to the power and resources of the state and the minorities, often without going into an open confrontation with the dominant group, could question the state structure as a whole and act violently when the society and the state are unable to suggest any mechanisms for regulating and resolving these contradictions (Stavenhagen, 1991; for an updated overview of recent approaches and work on the issue see Väyrynen, 1994).

Among the strongest theoretical approaches to the study of ethnic conflicts widely shared by Soviet and Western experts is a *sociological* one, explaining phenomena in categories of social groupings and socio-economic interest. Ethnic parameters of social stratifications, labour divisions, and class differentiations are the main focus of interest for proponents of this approach. Being mostly newcomers in the field of ethnic studies, sociologists consider as major discoveries the phenomenon of usurpation by members of one ethnic group of certain privileged social niches and also the effect of social discrimination based on ethnic and racial characteristics. It is hard to deny that basic social and class disparities exist and that hierarchy and discrimination based on them remain among the strongest impulses for inter-ethnic tensions and open conflicts. This has been proven by analysis of many case studies for different regions of the world (Rupesinghe, 1992).

In the case of the former Soviet Union, we have quite a few studies analysing serious disproportions and correlations between ethnic and social structures. For several regions, especially former Union republics, the proportion of Russians and Ukrainians among highly skilled industrial personnel, management staff, health professionals,

and educators was considerably higher than that of titular nationalities. The Russians and the Ukrainians possessed disproportionately large representation also among specialists in agriculture. The
reasons for this were quite obvious: it had been the policy and practice of the centre to construct large industrial and military projects all
over the territory of the USSR by bringing in personnel from central
areas of the country. For a long period, the Russians also played a
major role in educational policy. These factors all contributed to
making the industrial centres of the republics, including capital cities
like Riga, Alma-Ata, Tashkent, Minsk, Kazan, Ufa, and others, predominantly Russian (Guboglo, 1991).

This correlation between rural and urban structures along ethnic
boundaries could also be considered as conflict-generating, but it
cannot be presented as the main reason for open ethnic conflict – at
least, there are no serious research data or field observations which
could prove this thesis. In fact, some regions clearly show the opposite tendency. In Nagorno-Karabakh, for example, the social status of
the Armenians in the enclave was higher than that of the Azeris
inside and outside the territory (Yamskov, 1991). Nevertheless, it did
not prevent the *irredenta* movement and, later on, a devastating civil
war among two communities.

In the republics of Central Asia, where the Russians and the
Ukrainians enjoyed higher social status, the tolerance for Russian-
speaking people was motivated by an understanding of the important
economic and social role this group plays in the functioning of local
societies, and special efforts on the part of authorities to keep them
from leaving their homes and jobs were undertaken (Tishkov, 1995a).
However, this did not prevent a massive exodus of Russians from this
region, mainly because of internal insecurities, economic hardship,
and different adjustments to a new political order.

In Tatarstan, for example, the Russians are now the major labour
force and provide managerial personnel for the most important pro-
ductions in the automobile, gas and oil, and military industries. The
local republican authorities and leaders of the nationalist movements
understand the significance of converting Russian-speaking residents
into allies to achieve full sovereignty.

In sociological analysis, special interest is focused on trade and its
agents in multi-ethnic societies. There is a tendency to control the
trade and market activities by members of a certain group, usually a
minority.[4] This often causes a negative reaction on the part of the
rest of the population. A whole series of pogroms of the food markets

and cooperative kiosks run by non-natives took place in many large cities of Russia, including actions in Moscow in November 1991 against "faces of Caucasian nationality." Similar actions took place against Meskhetian Turks in Fergana and against Armenians in Uzen, Uzbekistan, in the summer of 1990.

Nevertheless, there is some evidence that rural and urban settlers accept mutually beneficial economic roles: different groups are tending to overcome their negative feelings towards more successful ethnic aliens who serve as trade mediators, since they have regular contact with them and receive useful services from them. For example, throughout the region of Central Asia and Kazakhstan, ethnic Uzbeks traditionally play the role of skilled agricultural traders, while Kazakhs, Kyrgyz, and Turkmens are more inclined towards traditions of nomadic horticulture and have negative cultural stereotypes of trade-related occupations (Polyakov, 1990). Over the whole territory of the former Soviet Union, traders from the Transcaucasus practically controlled the farmers' markets selling fruit and flowers, by this occupation providing relatively higher living standards for themselves. But for decades, the situations both with the Uzbeks and with the Caucasian people were peacefully accepted by the rest of the population.

Even in cases of aggressive behaviour towards non-native traders, it is more often the case that political motivations are hidden behind the actions. Thus, competitiveness in labour and trade relations based on mutually beneficial and accepted roles can only rarely be considered among the major reasons for large ethnic conflicts.

From our point of view, certain experts who analyse nationalist movements emphasize too strongly the role of economic sustainability as a precondition for "independent economic activities of the people" and for "reproduction of ethnos" (Shkaratan and Perepelkin, 1989). This represents a simplification or a reductionist approach towards regional economic forces pushing for self-management and freedom from the tyranny of Moscow central agencies. These moves are not simply a part of the process for self-determination. If they were, it would be impossible to understand why economic separatism became equally strong in practically all administrative regions of Russia. The thesis about "reproduction of ethnos" through acquiring economic independence contains a certain irony and myth, because, as pointed out earlier, major contributions to the economic basis of republican GNPs are provided by non-titular employees. Energy production in Estonia, electronics in Latvia and in Kyrgyzstan, mining and metallurgy in Ukraine and Kazakhstan, gas and oil in Tatarstan, gold and diamonds in the Yakut Republic are produced largely by the labour of non-titular groups.

We can conclude that the realization of separatist scenarios leads more often to economic losses than gains for their initiators, even when the economic aspects of separatism include a desire to maintain relatively higher economic standards and not to share in the burdens borne by the states of less advanced regions. This last statement could be illustrated by Eritrean separatism in Ethiopia and by the economic reorientation of the Baltic republics away from the USSR. The main conclusion is that the choice for ethnic separation is usually made against economic calculations. Probably there are more powerful factors in operation.

That is why some political science theories can help in explaining ethnic conflicts. One of the approaches is the élite-based theory of conflict. This approach sees the role of intellectuals and politicians in mobilizing ethnic feelings and inter-ethnic strife as key, and has been fruitfully applied in the analysis of a number of cases.[5] Unfortunately, this approach has been hardly used to interpret Soviet realities, because of the inertia of previously dominant methodologies and a lack of scholarly interest to the phenomenon of power. From our point of view, the question of power and the hedonistic predisposition to rule on the part of élite elements, the interaction between power and material rewards, are the key factors for understanding the causes of ethnic nationalism and conflicts in the regions of the former Soviet Union.

For many decades, the access to power in that country was strictly controlled by the party *nomenklatura*. The ruling élite in the centre, especially at the level of the high party apparatus and the government, was unconditionally loyal to the totalitarian and unitarian type of rule. This élite included representatives of different ethnic origin, and special seats in the Politburo were reserved for party leaders of the largest republics. But the actual power belonged to the dominant group of Russians. For example, in the spring of 1991, on the eve of the full collapse, after a few years of democratic changes the apparatus of the Central Committee of the CPSU did not include one single Jew or any representatives from many other groups (Tishkov, 1991a). The army officers and diplomatic corps consisted mainly of Russians and Ukrainians, with a few other nationalities represented in minor posts.

Even after the breakdown of the USSR, in spite of the danger of further disintegration, no radical changes took place in the power structures of the Russian Federation except a wider representation of Jews after Gorbachev openly brought forward accusations of anti-Semitic practices. As in the past, no proper representation has been given to such large ethnic groups as Tatars, Bashkirs, Chuvash, etc., in the federal governmental structures. At the same time, powerful and educated ethnic élites were formed among non-Russian nation-alities as a result of efforts by the centre. From the "nativization" policies of the 1920s to the 1980s, purposeful efforts were made to develop a system of preferences and affirmative actions to prepare non-Russian intellectuals, scientists, and cultural figures. In the repub-lics, the reproduction of intellectual and bureaucratic élites occurred on an unprecedentedly wide scale. The Institute Diploma and Ph.D. degrees became a symbol of prestige and the proportion of scientific degrees granted was not only equal but considerably higher among some groups, such as Georgians and Armenians, compared to the national average and to Western standards as well (see statistical data in Arutiunian and Bromlye, 1986). To support prestigious symbols of national statehood, extensive resources were put into institutions like Academies of Sciences and professional creative unions such as those of writers, actors, and cinematographers. At the same time, in the republics and autonomies powerful strata of local bureaucracy took shape, including members of the party apparatus, KGB, and militia.

As soon as the centre lost its control over ethnic élites, and as soon as a vacuum of power and ideology took place, these élites were ready to start a fight for real power in the polities which, according to the Constitution of 1977, were qualified as "Sovereign National States." The most powerful means of political mobilization and of providing popular support became a national idea. The intellectual élite changed its Communist ideology and was able to start effective struggle first against the centre and then against the local party apparatchiks. Professors, writers, dramaturges, and cinematographers became leaders of nationalist movements and even of military units. In most cases they played a decisive role in overturning the old guards from their power positions. After the republican elections in spring 1990, national élites of titular groups won the majority of seats in republican parliaments and local councils, pushing aside repre-sentatives of other groups. Even in republics such as Kazakhstan, Tatarstan, and the Yakuti Republic, where they were not the major-ity of the population, they were able to take control of legislative bodies (Tishkov, 1991b).

Intellectuals and other élite elements were among those who provided emotional and historical justification for participants of mass inter-ethnic clashes, starting with the Karabakh movement and spreading to the tragic events in Moldova and Central Asia. However, it would be a mistake to overestimate the generating and organizing role of élites as a reason for ethnic conflict. This approach cannot fully explain the phenomenon of mass mobilization itself, the intensity of emotion among participants in conflicts, nor the strength of group desire for autonomy and the readiness to sacrifice and to use the most violent methods to achieve goals formulated by activists. We can find a partial answer to these questions in political science theories about the logic of collective behaviour (see, e.g., Amirahmadi, 1987). These arguments deserve proper attention because they can explain how a phenomenon called "ethnic fever" or "mob power" can appear at a grass-roots level. Rank-and-file participants are often ready to follow their leaders out of a sense of collective solidarity, even when the leaders' appeal can cause the followers negative rewards and losses.

Probably, the aspects of *behavioural psychology* and *socio-psychological mechanisms* play a more significant role in ethnic conflicts than traditional interpretations have suggested. We have enough evidence to prove that groups with diminished status and who are subject to discrimination in dominated environments quite often express fears for their own existence, even when objective demographic, political, or cultural conditions would normally not lead to such conclusions. This "reaction of concern" comes from the exaggerated feeling of danger and leads to "extreme actions in response to rather moderate dangers" (Horowitz, 1985: 383).

In support of this thesis, we can mention the sensational and exaggerated notion of the "dying out" of nations, languages, and cultures which dominated public discourse during the first years of rising nationalism in the USSR, and also the strict protective measures taken by republican governments to safeguard the position of titular nationalities. An objective analysis of the demographic and socio-cultural data for most ethnic groups of the former Soviet Union does not prove the above-mentioned arguments. In spite of old crimes against the peoples and the deep crisis through which they are going now, not one ethnic culture has disappeared from the map of the Soviet Union. Indeed, a few rather small groups, such as the Baltic peoples, could be described as flourishing cultures even by Western European standards. The Estonians, who number less than one million, possess not only a strong ethnic identity but also more highly developed forms of culture – professional theatre, literature, music, science, education, and publishing – than any comparable group in Europe. In spite of this, the irrational fear of losing cultural integrity became a powerful political reality in Estonia and Latvia, for instance, which helped to formulate extreme ethnic claims and provided motives for the involvement of broad masses in the political struggle.

The same kind of reaction to hypothetical dangers, such as rumours of the division of land plots or providing apartments for ethnic aliens, could be traced in conflict-generating events in Central Asian republics. Psychologically speaking, ethnic conflicts can spring from irrational feelings of loss of collective worth and suffering from historical injustices. Ethnicity in its extreme, manifest forms often serves as a therapy for the trauma suffered by all nationalities of the Soviet Union, from the Russians to the small indigenous groups of the North.

Similarly, the problem of group legitimacy is connected with a sense of collective identity and with the fact of an existing political entity in the form of state. Among the ethnic groups we can trace the growth of an idea, and then a political programme, which holds that a state is an attribute and guarantee of preserving group entity. That is, the state, including its territory, institutions of power, and resources, must have an ethno-national character and be an element of a certain cultural system. The state must have an official language, that of the dominant referent group, which provides a moral basis for exclusive control of resources and power by one group. Arguments in favour of this position are usually taken from history and especially those historical periods that are more favourable to the territorial borders and the status of the group. The struggle for making its own state may be a goal *per se*, as a confirmation of status and the very fact of existence for the group, and also as a guarantee against both real and hypothetical challenges from alien environments. Through this state, the ethnic group tries to establish certain symbols of collective legitimacy and protection. Most often, such symbols are territory and language. The territory is considered not only as a source of subsistence, especially under contemporary conditions, where the market economy effectively fails to recognize ethnic and political boundaries. The struggle of Armenians and Azeris for Karabakh, the Japanese desire for the return of northern territories, or the feelings of Russians towards the Crimea, spring from symbolic rather than pragmatic interests. But these symbolic interests are not mere irrational mystifications; they can acquire a real strength. The behaviour of states towards territorial problems is often strikingly irrational: states are more ready to lose their own citizens as victims of violence and as emigrants than to make territorial concessions.

The same kind of symbolism lies behind language problems in ethnic conflicts. It is not coincidental that in the programmes of national movements the struggle for strengthening the status of native languages was not only a part of a general cultural strategy, or a question of enlarging opportunities for a certain nationality in the field of labour and education. The desire of ethnic groups to give their own language official status became also a means of proving their higher legitimacy compared with other members of polities. Language became one of the symbols of newly acquired group integrity and a symbol of the domination of one group over another.

Symbolic interests in a system of inter-ethnic relations are not only an illusion by which élites manipulate for mobilization of the masses to achieve pragmatic goals. Distribution and acquisition of prestigious symbols is a real and rational subject for ethnic conflicts. The problems of prestige and symbols are quite different from material interests. The latter more often lie at the basis of social and class conflicts and can be negotiated in quantitative parameters – salaries, pensions, payments, working hours, and so on. Symbolic demands are extremely difficult to negotiate and redistribute because they are expressed in moral and emotional categories and are not subject to quantitative characteristics. That is why ethnic conflicts, like religious conflicts, in themselves comprise unconciliatory irrationalism and often acquire a bloody character.

Acknowledgement

Assistance in the translation and typing of this chapter was given by Jan Helge Hordnes, PRIO.

Notes

1. See Prazauskas, 1991. For a more substantial study, see Clemens, 1991.
2. Eduard Shevardnadze has refused to restore autonomous status for Southern Ossetians, and his war minister, Tengiz Kitovani, when starting military sanctions against Abkhazia, stated publicly that in Georgia there will be only "cultural autonomy."
3. A sociological survey done in Moscow in 1991 showed that 40 per cent of Muscovites expressed a negative attitude towards refugees from non-Russian republics and 72 per cent expressed a negative attitude towards "traders from southern republics."

4. On ethnic business see Light, 1972; Pincus and Ehrlich, 1994: 237–72.
5. See, for example, on Quebec and Sri Lanka, Handler, 1988; Spencer, 1990.

References

Amirahmadi, H. 1987. "A Theory of Ethnic Collective Movements and Its Application to Iran." *Ethnic and Racial Studies* 10(4).

Arutiunian, Y.V., and Y.V. Bromlye (eds). 1986. *Socio-cultural Profile of Soviet Nations.* Moscow: Nauka. (In Russian.)

Carter, Stephen. 1993. *Russian Nationalism: Yesterday, Today and Tomorrow.* London: Pinter.

Clemens, Walter. 1991. *Baltic Independence and Russian Empire.* New York: St Martin's Press.

Drobizheva, Leokadia. 1992. "Perestroika and the Ethnic Consciousness of Russians." In G. Lapidus and V. Zaslavsky, *From Union to Commonwealth: Nationalism and Separatism in the Soviet Republics.* Cambridge: Cambridge University Press.

Elebayeva, Inura, A. Dzhusupbekov, and N. Omuraliev. 1991. *The Osh Inter-Ethnic Conflict: Sociological Analyses.* Bishkek; Znanie. (In Russian.)

Guboglo, M. 1991. "Ethnic Populations of USSR's Capital Cities." *Journal of Soviet Nationalities* 1, no. 4.

Handler, Richard. 1988. *Nationalism and the Politics of Culture in Quebec.* Madison: University of Wisconsin Press.

Horowitz, Donald. 1985. *Ethnic Groups in Conflict.* Berkeley: University of California Press.

Light, Ivan. 1972. *Ethnic Enterprise in America: Business and Welfare among Chinese, Japanese and Blacks.* Berkeley: University of California Press.

Pincus, Fred, and Howard Ehrlich (eds). 1994. *Race and Ethnic Conflict: Contending Views on Prejudice, Discrimination and Ethnoviolence.* Boulder: Westview Press.

Polyakov, Sergei P. 1992. *Everyday Islam: Religion and Tradition in Rural Central Asia.* Armonk, NY: M.E. Sharp.

Polyakov, Y. 1990. *Traditional Structures in the Central Asian Societies.* Moscow. (In Russian.)

Prazauskas, A. 1991. "Ethnic Conflicts in the Context of Democratizing Political Systems." *Theory and Society* 20 (5), special issue on Ethnic Conflict in the Soviet Union.

Rupesinghe, K. (ed.). 1992. *Internal Conflict and Governance.* London: Macmillan.

Shkaratan, O.I., and L.S. Perepelkin. 1989. "Ekonomicheski suverenitet respublic i puti razvitiia narodov" [The economic sovereignty of republics and ways of the peoples' development]. *Sovetskaya Etnografiya* 4 (Moscow): 581–602.

———. 1990. "Soviet Republics Are on a Move to Economic Sustainability." *Kommunist* 5.

Spencer, J. 1989. "Writing Within: Anthropology, Nationalism and Culture in Sri Lanka." *Current Anthropology* 31, no. 3: 283–300.

Stavenhagen, Rodolfo. 1991. "The Ethnic Question: Some Theoretical Issues." Paper presented at UNRISD Workshop on Ethnic Conflict and Development, Dubrovnik, 3–6 June.

Szporluk, R. 1989. "Dilemmas of Russian Nationalism." *Problems of Communism* 38, July/August (Washington DC): 15–35.

Tishkov, Valery. 1991a. "Nationality is a Communist: Political Anthropology of CPSU." *Polis* 1, no. 5.

———. 1991b. "Ethnicity and Power in the Republics of the USSR." *Journal of Soviet Nationalities* 1, no. 3: 33–66.

———. 1995a. "The Russians in Central Asia and Kazakhstan." In *Muslim Eurasia: Conflicting Legacies*, ed. Yaacov Roi, 289–310. London: Frank Cass.

———. 1995b. " 'Don't Kill Me, I'm a Kyrgyz!': An Anthropological Analysis of Violence in the Osh Ethnic Conflict." *Journal of Peace Research* 32, no. 2 (May): 133–49.

Väyrynen, Raimo. 1994. *Towards a Theory of Ethnic Conflicts and Their Resolution*. University of Notre Dame, Notre Dame, Indiana: The Joan B. Kroc Institute for International Peace Studies.

Yamskov, A. 1991. "Ethnic Conflict in Transcaucasus: The Case of Nagorno-Karabakh." *Theory and Society* 20(5): 631–60.

4

Settlement of ethnic conflicts in post-Soviet society

Emil Payin

1 Introduction

Following the collapse of the Soviet Union, the region's peoples have opted for a mode of national development common throughout Eurasia – they all want to have sovereign states of their own. But the rate of collapse of the former multinational Soviet state has been truly unprecedented, and this in itself is one of the reasons for mounting ethnic tensions. Surely no other country in living memory has been gripped at one and the same time by such deep economic, political, and also ethnic crisis. Social and ethnic tensions have been brought to a head by the plummeting living standards of the population. All this has paved the way, in most former Soviet republics, for the establishment of authoritarian-nationalist regimes which inflame nationalist passions even more. Conflicts flaring up as a result further exacerbate the plight of the people.

Prazauskas has termed the process precipitated by the collapse of the Soviet Union "division of the colonial legacy": the former colonies (the former Soviet republics) are dividing among themselves the country's territory and armed forces, its factories and plants, and other resources. Similar processes in Africa, Asia, or Latin America have often been accompanied by territorial and ethno-nationalist conflicts.[1] In the case of the former Soviet Union, such conflicts have flared up at a galloping pace. The Centre for Ethnopolitical Studies lists some 20 such conflicts from 1988 to 1991. According to the USSR Interior Ministry, a total of 782 people were killed and 3,617 wounded in such conflicts in 1991 alone.[2] The general toll of dead and wounded over those four years is estimated at over 10,000. According to the same statistics, the number of refugees had reached 710,000; a total of 1.0 to 1.2 million people had been forced to abandon their homes in areas of high inter-ethnic tension.[3]

2 Types of inter-ethnic conflicts and their distribution

Inter-ethnic conflicts of different types have been observed to interact with one another, producing a cumulative effect.[4]

Conflicts of "uncontrolled emotions"

Typical of this category are riots and pogroms. Their organizers usually pursue no clear-cut objectives. Thus, neither researchers nor police officials can explain the attacks on the Meskhetian Turks during the Fergana riots in the summer of 1989 nor on the other ethnic minorities in that area. Nor have there been any clear explanations for the anti-Armenian feelings at the start of the Dushanbe disturbances of 1990. In such cases the "scapegoats" were probably chosen at random, the real causes of massive unrest being of a socio-economic nature, such as an acute housing shortage in Dushanbe or a shortage of land in Fergana, Osh, and other places.

Conflicts like these are often triggered by mounting unemployment, so it was not accidental that all these riots occurred in the areas of highest unemployment. Such high-risk areas today include major multi-ethnic towns and cities, especially their industrial lower-class suburbs. If living conditions continue to deteriorate, there may be widespread riots, but the most explosive places of all will be areas with high concentrations of refugees.

Conflicts of "ideological doctrines"

These conflicts always have deep historical roots. The demands of the conflicting parties are formulated in the slogans and programmes of nationalist movements. Unlike those underlying ordinary riots, political demands bear a strong nationalist tinge and have been elaborated by theorists and ideologists of the movements involved. Worsening socio-economic and political conditions can promote the spread of such doctrines and determine the degree of violence of their manifestations. The champions of such an "ideal" are frequently ready to sacrifice not only economic benefits and personal comforts but even their own lives.

Regrettably, many politicians in the Commonwealth of Independent States (CIS) fail to take into account the "non-pragmatic" character of such ideological conflicts. Instead they assume that all these troubles are "rooted in our poverty," that a better economy is the key to solving inter-ethnic problems. The price of this political naïveté is the escalation in ethno-ideological conflicts of many kinds:

- Conflicts over historically disputed territories. Examples include the dispute between the Ingushes and the Ossetians over the Prigorodny Region and the civil wars in Nagorno-Karabakh and Southern Ossetia. The two latter examples demonstrate yet another variety of inter-ethnic confrontations.
- Conflicts over the administrative status of an ethnic territory (events in Abkhazia, Gagauzia, Trans-Dniester, the Chechen Republic, and many other areas).
- Conflicts produced by the changing ethno-demographic situation in various regions and a growing share of non-indigenous settlers. The ethnic majority is afraid of losing its privileged status, or is trying to re-establish its status by demanding that the rights of the indigenous nationality be "protected," for example by granting them certain privileges. As can be expected, such demands run into opposition with the "non-indigenous" ethnic groups, precipitating all kinds of inter-ethnic confrontations, such as in the Baltic region in Moldova, in several republics within the Russian Federation, and elsewhere.
- Conflicts of an ethno-territorial nature, arising as a "historical echo" of the deportation of peoples. Such conflicts take place in areas where deported populations have been forced to settle (as in the "Fergana pogrom" of the Meskhetian Turks), as well as in their historical native territories when the deported people return there. Thus, the call for "restoring historical reality" championed by the Crimean Tatars clashes with the idea of "preserving the historical reality" advocated by today's ethnic majority of the Crimean Autonomous Republic.

All these varieties of ethno-ideological conflicts have one thing in common: a veneration, often bordering on the irrational, of what the parties describe as their sacred "historical rights". This is in reality an attempt to substitute civil rights for those of a certain clan as sanctified by tradition. Such traditionalist, tribal ideology expressed in an ethnic or confessional form is typical of the whole of the post-Soviet world. Indeed, this tendency is actively encouraged and strengthened by the political élite in most of the newly independent states.

In recent times, new causes of inter-ethnic conflicts and their aggravation have also emerged on the scene. These include the abrogation of some ethnic divisions in Transcaucasus, the requirement of residential status for granting citizenship rights to people in the Baltic states, and a "merger" of riot-type conflicts with ideological ones.

Conflicts of "political institutions"

Confrontations of this kind are rooted not only in ideological doctrines; they also represent the conflicting political interests of different parties, political alliances, and institutions of government. In the early 1980s, a team of US researchers led by George Demko started to generalize and map territorial claims advanced by various national movements.[5] Their studies revealed that practically all former Soviet republics have some type of border dispute with their neighbours. Such disputes are especially acute between Azerbaijan and Armenia, Moldova and Ukraine, Russia and Kazakhstan, and Russia and Estonia.

With time, nationalist movements have turned from political opposition into a political base for the leadership of the republics; republics have turned into independent states and territorial claims have become elevated to the level of government policy.

We should also bear in mind the psychological complexion of the leaders of these newly independent states. Their obsessive usage of tautologies like "a sovereign state" and "an independent state" betrays a political inferiority complex in which a "shortage" of genuine sovereignty is made up for by verbal and other status symbols. Thus, the former republics want to have armies of their own, not because of any threat of internal conflicts, but simply as yet another symbol of genuine statehood. When, however, such symbols come into collision, then we must expect some far more serious conflicts.

Summing up the individual factors that lead to ethnic conflicts and assessing the real threat of inter-ethnic confrontation, scholars of the Centre for Ethno-political Studies have worked out a preliminary system of comprehensive assessment of ethno-political stability in various regions. Maps compiled on the basis of these studies show that nearly the whole of the post-Soviet territory is affected by conflicts of various types.

This "scale of ethno-political stability" developed by my colleagues and myself (and I wish to stress that these are only preliminary assessments which are constantly being refined and corrected) is based upon three kinds of factor:

(i) Factors of "potential conflicts"

This parameter represents what we have termed the historic-cultural alienation of ethnic communities. It includes factors such as historical territorial disputes; certain tragic historical memories which can lead to ethnophobia (such as the memories of the genocide of Armenians in 1915, which still cast their shadow on relations with Azerbaijan), linguistic and confessional distinctions. This general historical background to present-day inter-ethnic relations can lead to conflicts only under certain additional conditions. These may include, for example, worsening living conditions that prompt people to look for the "culprit," a sharp change in the proportion between the "indigenous" nationality and "settlers," or growing numbers of refugees and deported nationals. Taking into consideration all these factors, we constructed the second level of our "stability scale," then we turned to qualitatively different indices or factors.

(ii) Factors of a "conflict of ideas"

These may range from the most insignificant (like isolated nationalist statements in the press) to the most violent (the staging of rival rallies and demonstrations by conflicting national movements).

(iii) Factors of a "conflict of actions"

These are sporadic clashes without bloodshed; brief armed clashes; prolonged armed conflicts. Taking a look at a map which indicates degrees of ethno-political stability (or instability), we can see that the epicentre of inter-ethnic confrontation is the Transcaucasian region. Right next to it comes another belt of tension including parts of the northern Caucasus, areas along the Black Sea (the Crimea), along the

Dniester, and in Central Asia. There are high levels of inter-ethnic tension in Tatarstan and the Tuva Republic. There are also potentially dangerous conditions in many parts of Bashkortostan, the Yakut Republic, the Baltic states, and the border regions of Russia, as well as other regions of the Commonwealth of Independent States.

The conflict area continues to grow. In 1988 the only place suffering armed conflicts was Nagorno-Karabakh; in the following year there were several such conflicts in Transcaucasus and Central Asia. In the ensuing years the flames of bitter internal conflicts continued to engulf the northern Caucasus, the areas along the Black Sea, and along the Dniester and the Volga rivers. All this demonstrates the urgent need for comprehensive measures to prevent a continued escalation of ethnic conflicts and to try and settle existing ones.

The many notions of the principles and methods of resolving inter-ethnic problems can be grouped into three basic categories: **current**, **tactical**, and **strategic**.

Current settlements

Current settlements are of a practical nature and they envisage certain specific efforts either to curb a conflict (such actions as disarming militants or belligerent groups, or reinforcing the protection of vital objectives) or to overcome the tangible consequences of conflicts (accommodating refugees, restoring damaged buildings and communication lines, punishing race rioters, etc.).

By their very nature, current settlements of inter-ethnic problems are heavily dependent on the economy, the transport and communication systems, law and order, as well as on the stability and prestige of the government and its ability to manage the country. Today's economic and political crisis in CIS countries has a highly negative effect on organizations working for inter-ethnic regulation.

What urgent measures can be taken to settle a conflict, when simply making a telephone call from Moscow to nearby Podolsk is a problem and there is a great shortage of petrol and spare parts even for police cars? Equally great hindrances are caused by the lack of coordination between legislative and executive powers, federal and local authorities, the press and the government, and the like.

The main point is that the CIS countries lack a specialized network for the prevention and settlement of internal conflicts, and that impedes urgent decision-making. Most disastrous is the absence of agencies able to ensure monitoring of the ethno-political situation, early diagnosis and prognosis of conflicts, and a "rapid deployment" service which could protect people, prevent escalation and expansion of conflicts, and organize negotiations.

Such agencies never existed in the USSR, but prior to 1991 at least some of these mentioned functions had been fulfilled by the USSR Committee for Emergency Situations. After the disintegration of the USSR, its territory, and especially the junctions of several states, have been neglected because the new Commonwealth has no agencies which could coordinate the independent states' efforts to prevent ethno-social conflicts.

Tactical settlements

Tactical settlements are meant to cope with existing conflicts either by bringing all kinds of pressure, including economic, to bear on the parties involved or organizing negotiations between them. Former Soviet leaders preferred police methods for suppressing national movements and re-animating the unitary Soviet Union, as became clear during the well-known events in Tbilisi (1989), Baku (1990), and Vilnius (1991). Each of these police actions led to losses among both the army and the civilian population. In each case, the results were opposite to the desired affect: the national movements grew stronger and the disintegration of the USSR was accelerated. Economic blockades against national and separatist movements brought similar results – suffice it to recall the fuel blockade of Lithuania in 1990.

The mistakes of the Soviet government were repeated by the Russian leaders, who tried to stop Checheno-Ingushetia from seceding from the Russian Federation by threatening to send troops there. That threat only intensified opposition to the federal government among the majority of national movements in the northern Caucasus, especially those forming the Confederation of Nations of the Caucasus.[6]

Since 1988 various political forces in the USSR (and later in the CIS) have repeatedly tried to organize negotiations between various national movements involved in inter-ethnic conflicts, but in most cases they have failed. Strenuous efforts have been made to resolve the long and murderous conflict in Nagorno-Karabakh. As far back as 1988, Andrei Sakharov visited both Armenia and Azerbaijan on a goodwill mission followed by representatives of a political movement of the Baltic republics, the *Moskovskiye Novosti* newspaper, Russian MPs, and others. These efforts, however, have obviously failed to yield any notable positive results, and inter-ethnic confrontation has increased.

The causes of this failure should be analysed in detail elsewhere. Here I shall mention only a few – those which I find most typical of the USSR and the CIS.

First, all those efforts were made spontaneously, without proper preparation, without a special plan or a well-thought-out timetable. Secondly, no special attempts were made and no special professional methods were used to remove one of the main obstacles in any negotiations – the stubborn belief of each party that its decision is the only correct one.

Thirdly, there was no "information boom" in any of the cases; and the situation occurred when the negotiating parties used either unreliable or deliberately distorted information about the major circumstances of the conflict and the opportunities to settle it.

Fourthly, the political status of the negotiators did not guarantee a strict observance of agreements, if any. That was the case with the talks in Zheleznovodsk (1991) in which Azerbaijani and Armenian leaders took part and Russia and Kazakhstan acted as mediators; political forces directly involved in the conflict were not represented at all, though many of them acted independently and often contrary to decisions made by Armenian and Azerbaijani leaders.

This reveals a recurrent problem in organizing negotiations on inter-ethnic conflicts: to find the most authoritative representatives of the conflicting sides able to evaluate adequately the standpoint of each side and to restrain the parties from violating the agreements. The Zheleznovodsk talks provide an example of still another mistake: inviting major political figures to take part in negotiations which have not been properly prepared. As a result, the politicians lose face (as potential mediators in particular) and trust in negotiations as a means of resolving inter-ethnic problems is undermined.

A shortage of relevant specialists, conflictologists in particular, makes itself felt when negotiations are to be organized and when other means are to be used for inter-ethnic regulation. The CIS countries still lack a system of training professional conflictologists.

Speaking about minor imperfections of conflictology in both the former USSR and the present CIS, we must also recall the repeated attempts at trying to use methods elaborated for definite regions, say

Central Russia, to evaluate the inter-ethnic tensions in quite different historical and cultural conditions – Central Asia, for example. The main drawback of both current and tactical settlements of inter-ethnic conflicts is that they are poorly coordinated with general inter-ethnic strategy, both in individual CIS countries and in the Commonwealth as a whole.

Strategic decisions

These are meant to prevent ethnic crises by providing, in good time, the legal, political, economic, and socio-psychological conditions for a civilized development of these processes.

In the historical period commonly referred to as *perestroika* – a more accurate name for which would be "Mikhail Gorbachev's time in office" – no sensible ethnic policy was pursued, and no relevant strategy existed. Nor does such a strategy exist in the Commonwealth of Independent States today. At any rate, the fact that Russia has no such strategy has been confirmed by its government leaders.[7] At the same time, most politicians in the USSR and the CIS have had, and still keep, certain ideological preferences which prompt them to take certain lines of practical action to settle ethnic conditions.

Arkady Popov of the Ethno-political Research Centre has studied these ideologies, and reduced them to three basic doctrines:[8]

(i) The "might is right" doctrine
As applied to ethnic relations, this boils down to the theory that stronger nations and states have a "right" to assert themselves by ousting or subduing their weaker neighbours. In the former Soviet Union, the doctrine manifests itself in ethnic policy in its two basic varieties: **orthodox-imperial**, the adherents of which insist on all the peoples and ethnic groups of the former Union being subordinated to the centre; and **neo-imperial**, which recognizes formal independence of the states which have broken away from the Union but which reserves for Russia, as a great power, the "right" to dictate to them (not necessarily by force).

Today these varieties of the "might is right" doctrine are preached by representatives of the so-called "national-patriotic" forces of Russia. In all the other republics, however, this doctrine is rejected outright, in whatever form it appears. The organizers of the August 1991 putsch in Moscow would seem to have drawn their inspiration from it; an attempt to put the doctrine into practice would have been fraught with the danger of at least a dozen "Yugoslavia-type" wars breaking out in the former USSR.

(ii)   The traditionalist "historical right" doctrine
Here the underlying principle is as follows: "a particular land or region belongs to its indigenous inhabitants." There are two varieties of the "historical right" doctrine. The **"ethno-demographic"** variety gives priority to "the people which was the first to settle on the given land and is, therefore, indigenous to it"; according to the **"ethno-political"** interpretation of the doctrine, "the land by right belongs to the people which was the first to establish its statehood there."

The traditionalist doctrine is extremely popular with with ethnic movements today. Most of them have made it the basis of their political programmes; upon coming to power in the Baltic republics, the Transcaucasus, Moldova, Tatarstan, and other places, they have vigorously applied it in practice, thus triggering or fomenting a multitude of ethnic conflicts.

The main flaw of the "historical right" doctrine appears only too obvious: modern humanistic notions are incompatible with the absurdity of making the rights of a given territory's permanent inhabitants dependent on the hypothetical merits of their distant ancestors. History grants people no preferential rights.

(iii)   The legitimist "ethnic right" doctrine
According to this doctrine, the nation's right to state self-determination is a function of constitutionally legitimized legislation ("the nation which has the constitution and the law on its side is right"). Few people deny today the need for observing constitutional and legal succession; in a situation, however, where a union state has fallen apart and new independent states have emerged from it, there are negligible chances of such a legal succession remaining unbroken. In withdrawing from the USSR, each of the former Union republics deviated, in one way or another, from the former Union Constitution and from the law on the procedure of seceding from the Soviet Union.

Today, however, these newly independent states are fighting the separatism of their own ethnic minorities on the grounds that it is against their Constitution and their new laws. Naturally, this argument sounds unconvincing to those who champion the right of small ethnic groups to their national and state self-determination. On the

78

other hand, the arguments the ethnic minorities use to substantiate their claims are based on certain provisions of the Constitution of the now non-existent USSR, which makes them unsuitable for resolving ethnic conflicts; such arguments can only escalate ethnic tension even further.

All three doctrines – imperial, traditionalist, and quasi-constitutionalist – are defective in that they emphasize the collectivist forms of national self-determination only. They recognize only a state, a people, or a clan as a subject of law, whereas individual human rights are regarded as mere derivatives from the rights of a community and of a social system. This results in certain politicians sacrificing the interests of individuals (their compatriots included) and to those of "the people," "the nation," and "the motherland."

These doctrines are contradictory and based on different – often mutually exclusive – and discriminatory principles. For instance, the standards applied to the self-determination of autonomies differ from those set for the sovereignty of a former "Union Republic," now an independent state.

Each of these doctrines bears evidence of politicians clearly exaggerating the possibility of controlling ethnic relations by force – be it force of arms, injunction, or economic sanctions. Noting the record of abortive attempts made first by the Union authorities and now by the leaders of the CIS sovereign states to control ethno-political processes, we can conclude that the concepts and means used for the purpose are time-serving, usually geared to momentary political needs, and doomed to be soon out of date and unsystematic.

3 Ways to prevent ethnic conflicts

As a manifestation of Soviet society's overall crisis, the escalation of ethnic tensions cannot be arrested without radical socio-economic and political reforms. It would be a dangerous mistake to presume, however, that such reforms will automatically bring ethnic relations back to normal.

Moreover, any further worsening of the social and ethnic situation in the CIS will render these reforms impossible. Therefore, each of the Commonwealth's states, and the Commonwealth as a whole, are in urgent need of a special ethnic conflict prevention system.

In my opinion, such a system can be set up through a combination of three approaches: institutional, instrumental, and phasic.

The **"institutional approach"** presupposes the establishment of a network of organizations (i.e., a special infrastructure) for the prevention and adjustment of inner conflicts. Such an infrastructure should comprise institutions at the national, regional, and global levels, and have functions that will differ from level to level.

National conflict prevention systems must be responsible for solving both local problems which call for urgent action and national problems due to fundamental socio-economic causes not removable by external (foreign) intervention. At the same time, the people should be able to rest assured that other states will lend a hand in emergency situations where basic human rights are trampled underfoot, where a nation is on the verge of self-destruction, or where it is in danger of extermination or suppression by other nations.

Modern international legal practice rests on the principle of drawing international institutions into resolving ethnic conflicts stage by stage. In the initial stage of such a conflict, the leading role is assigned to the regional organization. The Organization of American States, for example, managed to resolve a conflict between Honduras and Nicaragua.[9] An organization of this kind ought to be set up in the CIS without delay. Of course, no one can prevent any state of the Commonwealth from using other effective mechanisms of adjusting ethnic conflicts – through the International Court of Justice in The Hague, for instance. If its verdicts are ignored, then the UN Security Council should be authorized to take measures of compulsion – in other words, global-level institutions should come into play.

The **"instrumental approach"** consists of selecting the right combination of specific measures (instruments) to resolve conflicts. Unfortunately, the role played by a certain individual instrument is often exaggerated in conflictology. The British-American tradition in conflictology, for instance, assigns the decisive role to the organization of talks, or rather to the psychological aspects of communication between representatives of the conflicting parties. This is only natural, considering that United States conflictology deals mainly (and quite successfully) with conflicts that arise in the so-called micro-groups: seller–buyer, management–union, municipality–community, and so on. In resolving such conflicts, negotiations can indeed play a crucial role.

However, massive ethnic conflicts caused by an all-round crisis of society are a different matter; such conflicts need to be dealt with in a comprehensive way using a multitude of different control levers.

Unfortunately, this principle has not yet been adopted by current political practice in the CIS. Politicians are prone to exaggerate the role of legislation. Recently, for example, a law has been passed in the Russian Federation on the rehabilitation of deported peoples and reinstating them in the lands once forcibly taken away from them. While supporting this law in principle, I am also certain that if the repressed peoples and those who have occupied their lands fail to reach an agreement, no decree can resolve the dispute between them. This is why the enforcement of this law without the preliminary organization of any negotiation process has caused escalation of ethnic differences in several regions, for instance the northern Caucasus.

On the other hand, the organization of the negotiation process will be ineffectual unless it rests on a firm legal basis and follows a clearcut agenda. A comprehensive approach consists in the optimal combination of various instruments meant to relieve tensions and prevent the outbreak and escalation of conflicts. Such instruments include: economic stimuli and sanctions; information, dialogue among the conflicting parties; creation and effective enforcement of laws in the sphere of ethnic policy, etc.

The typology of conflicts and an analysis of the stages of their development may provide the groundwork for various anti-conflict arrangements. The latter will make it possible to take action designed specially to bring the situation under control at any stage of a certain type of conflict. This is what the **"phasic approach"** is all about.

It is not my objective here to formulate an exhaustive conception of resolving ethnic conflicts. Many of the ideas I have put forward are of a tentative nature and may strike the reader as controversial. One thing is certain, however: the international scientific community must pool its intellectual efforts and resources to reach a comprehensive approach to the settlement of ethnic conflicts.

Notes

1. A. Prazauskas, "CIS as a Post-Colonial Space," *Nezavisimaya Gazeta*, 7 February 1992.
2. V. Mukomel, "Demographic Consequences of Ethnic Conflicts," *Vestnik*, 1992, no. 1.
3. Ibid.
4. This is followed by a typology of inter-ethnic conflicts as formulated by E. Payin and A. Popov, "Inter-ethnic Conflicts in the USSR," *Sovetskaya Etnografiya*, 1990, no. 1. The present paper contains excerpts from this study; some of the original definitions have been further specified.
5. George J. Demko, "Beginning from Typology," *Nezavisimaya Gazeta*. 25 July 1991.
6. By December 1994 the Russian leaders had turned from threat to military operation in the

Chechen Republic, causing mass resistance and numerous victims among the peaceful Chechen population.

7. Vice-Premier Sergei Shakhrai of the Russian Federation admitted this in a television appearance on 27 February 1992.
8. Arkady Popov, "The Ideology of Ethnic Conflicts," *News Letter*, Foreign Policy Association, vol. 1, February 1992.
9. V. Orlov, "How State Borders Are Redrawn," *Moscow News*, 16 February 1992.

5

Dynamics of the Moldova–Trans-Dniester ethnic conflict (late 1980s to early 1990s)

Airat R. Aklaev

1 Introduction

Assessment and study of the specific context in which inter-ethnic violence erupts are fundamental for a more adequate understanding of its nature and for the search for effective strategies to promote peaceful alternatives. The overwhelming majority of current violent ethnic conflicts in the republics of the former Soviet Union are predominantly political in nature. These are ethnic disputes over group status in the political structures of the ethnically-divided societies of these new nations, and intergroup struggles for the redistribution of power arrangements.

Rapid and turbulent socio-political change, the ongoing processes of state-building in these new nations, and transition to inter-state relations between these ex-Soviet republics, form another integral part of the context of present-day inter-ethnic violence within the borders of the former Soviet Union. This swift and vertiginous socio-political transition, amidst the complicated legacy of unresolved and deeply felt ethnic problems left behind after the collapse of the Soviet Union, provides both motivation and opportunity for ethnic groups to mobilize as political actors and to engage in militant struggles for power.

The burgeoning pressure of politicized ethnic assertiveness and the escalation of claims and counter-claims at every stage of socio-political change may lead to a crisis in inter-ethnic relations. With the crisis situation comes a special period in inter-ethnic conflict when a turning point is reached and a new, intense level of interaction between the conflicting groups becomes possible. Either escalation or de-escalation of conflictual behaviour may ensue. Under certain circumstances a crisis in inter-ethnic relations can become a transition point from non-violent to violent collective ethnic political action. Here, concrete case studies can help us understand the specific forms of current socio-political change which have produced crises in inter-ethnic relations, with some groups resorting to violence to achieve their demands for change.

This article will consider the major stages in the development of socio-political change and inter-ethnic violence in Moldova, discussing how the political nature of inter-ethnic disputes and the rapid political transformation of Moldovan society have led to recourse to violence in the Moldova–Trans-Dniester conflict since 1989. I shall also venture an assessment of the role played by ethno-political crises of legitimacy as transition points from non-violent to violent ethnic political action.

The pattern of conflict dynamics, as seen in the case of Moldova, seems fairly typical of current ethno-political conflicts in the post-Communist republics. That the sizeable Russian-speaking minority participated, as well as the fact of the considerable international implications of the violent ethnic disputes in Moldova, indicates that analysis and discussion of the Moldova–Trans-Dniester conflict can increase our general understanding of the nature and dynamics of ongoing inter-ethnic conflicts in new post-Communist nations. Moreover, it may contribute to the vital search for more effective techniques of conflict management in the modern world.

2 Historical background

Two major historical-territorial areas can be distinguished within contemporary Moldova: "right-bank" Moldova – Bessarabia proper – extending between the Prut and the Dniester rivers to the west of the Dniester; and "left-bank" Moldova – Transdniestria, or Trans-

Dniester – situated to the east of the Dniester. The larger part of modern Moldova's territory was included in the Russian Empire in the late eighteenth and early nineteenth centuries. After the 1787–91 Russian–Turkish war, the Yassy Peace Treaty (1791) allocated the southern part of left-bank Moldova (Tyraspol and Dubossary districts) to Russia. Two years later, the northern part of left-bank Moldova, previously under Polish control, passed to Russian rule. The Bucharest Treaty after the 1806–1812 Russian–Turkish war accorded the territory between the Prut and the Dniester (Bessarabia) to the Russian Empire. Under the terms of the Paris Treaty of 1856, Romania received southern Bessarabia, but this was returned to Russia two decades later at the Berlin Congress in 1878.

After World War I the territory of Moldova was divided once again. In October 1917, the collapse of the Russian Empire permitted the national liberation of the Moldovan people. Nationalist-democratic forces who came to power in right-bank Moldova proclaimed the independence of the Bessarabian People's Democratic Republic. The Bessarabian Parliament (*Sfatul Tserij*) appealed to the Western powers for recognition and assistance. In December 1917, Romanian troops marched into the Bessarabian republic. In 1918, the Sfatul Tserij voted for union with Romania. Left-bank Moldova, however, became a Ukrainian possession. By February 1920, civil war in the Ukraine had led to the establishment of a Soviet regime there.

After the formation of the Union of Soviet Socialist Republics in 1922, left-bank Moldova became an administrative region within the Ukrainian Soviet Socialist Republic, recognized as a Union republic within the Soviet federation. The Soviet government did not recognize the legitimacy of the inclusion of Bessarabia into Romania; in 1924, at the Soviet–Romanian conference in Vienna it demanded that a plebiscite be held in right-bank Moldova, a demand refused by the Romanian government. On 12 October 1924, the Moldavian Autonomous Soviet Socialist Republic (MASSR) was created as a national-territorial unit within the Ukrainian SSR, a Soviet protest against the recovery of Bessarabia by Romania.

The agreement reached between the Soviet Union and Nazi Germany in the Molotov–Ribbentrop Pact (1939) saw Romanian Bessarabia as being within the sphere of Soviet interests and guaranteed tacit German approval of eventual Soviet occupation of the territory. On 26 June 1940, the Soviet government presented Romania with an ultimatum to cede Bessarabia. Romania yielded and two days later Red Army troops entered right-bank Moldova. On 2 August 1940, the USSR Supreme Soviet adopted a law on the formation of the Moldavian SSR (MSSR), a new Union republic within the USSR, which included five western districts of the abrogated MASSR within the Ukraine (Grigoriopol, Kamenka, Rybnitsy, Slobodzeja, and Tyraspol districts) and most of the incorporated Bessarabia.

In June 1941, the Romanians, fighting as Germany's allies, reincorporated the whole of Bessarabia, but the Soviet Army reconquered it in the autumn of 1944 and the MSSR was restored. In February 1947 the Paris Treaty with Romania recognized the 1940 Soviet–Romanian frontier; thus, political control of the whole of Moldova remained in Soviet hands.

It is only natural to assume that historical developments have contributed not only to the mixed ethnic composition of the population but also to the aggravation of inter-ethnic tensions and grievances resulting from the perceived injustices of territorial attribution and ethnic coercion in Moldova.

Moldovans, the titular nationality of the MSSR and of the Moldova Republic after the collapse of the Soviet Union, constitute slightly less than two-thirds of the total population of the republic. Ethnic Russians, Ukrainians, and Belarusians in non-Russian republics of the former USSR are usually referred to as the Russophone minority because they either indicate Russian as their mother tongue or speak mainly Russian rather than the language of the titular nationality of these republics.

Demographically, Moldovans are the largest ethnic group in both right-bank and left-bank Moldova. However, while in right-bank Moldova the Moldovans predominate both among the urban and the rural population, in left-bank Moldova (Trans-Dniester) the ethno-demographic situation is considerably more complex. Here, the Moldovans, though numerically constituting the largest single ethnic group, represent only a relative numerical majority (39.9 per cent of the Moldovans against 53.3 per cent of the Russophones). The Moldovans predominate in rural areas, while the Russophones form an almost overwhelming numerical majority in the large industrial centres like Tyraspol, Rybnitsy, Bendery, and Dubossary. In Tyraspol, the Russophones comprise 87 per cent of the city population, in Rybnitsy 64 per cent. A similar situation is found regarding the ethnic distribution of the population in Southern Moldova, where the Gagauz, a Christian Turkish group which migrated to Bessarabia from Bulgaria in the early nineteenth century, predominate.

3   Linguistic disputes and growth of ethnic political activism in Moldova

The development of ethno-political disputes in Moldova appears closely connected with the dynamics of the rapid socio-political transition experienced by the republic since the late 1980s. These transformation processes in Moldova were largely the product of socio-political change in the USSR under *perestroika*. Democratization and *glasnost* proclaimed at the Union level by the Gorbachev leadership entailed a rise in political pluralism at the level of the Union republics. There came a surge of mass social movements, each pursuing its specific interests and advocating political objectives which differed from those officially endorsed by the Communist authorities.

The first stage of socio-political change in Moldova (summer 1988 to summer 1989) is connected with the formation of Moldovan and Gagauz voluntary associations of nationalist intelligentsia and activists. The initially proclaimed goals of these movements centred on the promotion of cultural and linguistic interests; very soon, however, these voluntary associations began to grow, becoming social movements numbering tens of thousands of activists and sympathizers. The ideological platforms of the movements (Popular Fronts), besides cultural goals, included ethno-political claims: the Moldovan Popular Front (MPF) was aiming at the political sovereignty of Moldova within the USSR federation, that is, for recognition of the priority of the Constitution of the Republic and its legislation over that of the USSR on the territory of Moldova; the Gagauz Popular Front (GPF) held that achieving national-territorial autonomy for Gagauzia (Southern Moldova districts) was one of its major goals, seeing this as the only way to ensure socio-cultural and socio-economic development for the Gagauz people.

Reacting to the growth of nationalist-democratic movements which challenged not only federalist but also basic Communist values, Communist leaders in industrial centres of left-bank Moldova mobilized supporters of "socialist internationalism" to form a counter-nationalist, pro-Communist movement of the Russophones loyal to the Union centre and to the "socialist choice" of "the Soviet multi-ethnic people." On 8 July 1989, the first institutional Congress of the so-called "Internationalist Movement" (IM) was held in Kishinev. (*SM*, 25 November 1989)

All three social movements proclaimed their support of *perestroika*, though each of them perceived the final objectives of these reforms in ethnic-political terms. Trying to enlarge their social bases, the leaders of the IM seconded the claims of the Gagauz for an autonomous status within Moldova. Competing social movements engaged in propaganda campaigns among the public. From the summer of 1989, mass rallies and demonstrations organized by activists of newly-formed movements – so unlike the previous public life of the society of "mature socialism" – became recurrent events on the political scene.

In May 1989, after the publication of the drafts of new republican legislation on the status and functioning of languages in Moldova, the issue of official language became the rallying cry of the competing social movements. The ethno-political nature underlying discussions of the status of languages was evident. The MPF claimed that the Moldovan language should receive the status of sole official language in Moldova, as an important symbol of the republic's aspirations to true sovereignty within the USSR. Without restricting the spheres of functioning of other languages in Moldova, this claim would mean that knowledge of Moldovan would become obligatory for all officers in republic level and local bodies of power, for the administrative personnel of industrial enterprises, and for employees in state-owned public services.

Previously, neither the USSR or Moldovan constitutions had envisaged any formally official language. At the same time, Communist propaganda had encouraged the molding of "the new historical community – the Soviet people" on the linguistic basis of the Russian language, and had proclaimed Russian as the only means of inter-ethnic communication between nationalities of the federation. Russian was an obligatory subject of study in all educational institutions of non-Russian republics, whereas knowledge of the language of the titular nationality was not required of the Russophone population in non-Russian republics.

With *perestroika*, such inequity became particularly deeply felt by the titular nationalities. Affirming the right of the non-Russian republics to have constitutionally proclaimed official languages other than Russian meant for nationalist-democratic forces not only a revolutionary cultural affirmation but an act of political challenge, a first step on the road towards asserting the political sovereignty of their republics within the USSR. Other demands advocated by the MPF included a return to writing Moldovan in the Roman rather than the Cyrillic alphabet and constitutional recognition of Moldovan as the main language of inter-ethnic communication in Moldova – the status previously enjoyed by the Russian language.

Russophones in Moldova saw these drafts of new legislation as linguistic discrimination, and became anxious that new policies might cause their children to become assimilated Moldovans. The IM exploited these fears, aiming to enlarge its political support. At rallies and in other propagandistic activities, IM leaders demanded that both Russian and Moldovan be legally recognized as the official languages, and that Russian should have the status of sole language for inter-ethnic communication.

Linguistic disputes over the draft legislation demonstrated the politicization of both Moldovans and Russophones and the cleavage between supporters of the values of republican sovereignty and defenders of the empire of Soviet nationalities. Recognition of Moldovan as the official language would necessarily imply a lower status for the Russian language, and thus, for parts of the Russophone population, a considerable drop in group ethno-political status.

The MPF also demanded a reassessment of the political and juridical interpretation of the historical events of 1918 and 1940 in Moldova, in official historiography which had defined them as "socialist revolution" and "fraternal liberation of the Bessarabian people from the yoke of bourgeois militaristic Romania." This demand was not met by the Moldovan authorities, but it represented another source of growing ethnic anxieties among the Russophones.

Confrontation between the MPF and the IM, as well as inter-ethnic tensions between Moldovans and Russophones in general, became particularly acute prior to the Moldova Supreme Soviet (parliament) session set to open on 29 August 1989 and to approve new republican legislation on languages. On 21 August, in the large industrial centres of Trans-Dniester (Tyraspol, Bendery, Rybnitsa, Dubossary), the Russophones went on a general protest strike, demanding that the adoption of legislation on languages in the republic be postponed until analogous legislation be taken at the Union level by the USSR Supreme Soviet. Over 80,000 workers at 116 factories and plants are said to have participated in the protest strikes in Trans-Dniester (*SM*, 30 August 1989). Sympathetic strikes were held in southern districts of Moldova populated by the Gagauz (Komrat and Chadyr-Lungi).

The MPF, in turn, counter-mobilized Moldovans to take part in mass rallies in support of the draft language laws. On 27 August in Kishinev, and in almost all centres of right-bank Moldova, some 400 rallies and demonstrations with approximately 500,000 participants were reported (*SM*, 29 August 1989). MPF activists picketed the Moldovan Supreme Soviet building.

On 31 August, after intense debate, the Moldova Supreme Soviet approved the new republican legislation on the status and functioning of languages, recognizing Moldovan as the only official language of the republic. A five-year term was established, however, for final introduction of the official language into office and clerical work in all state enterprises and bodies in zones where Russian was currently used in this function. Another concession to the Russophone deputies was the legislative recognition of both Moldovan and Russian as languages of inter-ethnic communication in Moldova. IM leaders and activists were not satisfied with the new legislation. Protest strikes in Trans-Dniester demanding the abrogation of the newly-approved language legislation and the arrival of the USSR Supreme Soviet Commission in Moldova went on till mid-September.

The August/September 1989 confrontation over the status of languages marked the first crisis in inter-ethnic relations in Moldova. Latent inter-ethnic political conflict had now become manifest.

4 First power shift and proclamation of sovereignty

The second stage of socio-political change in Moldova came with the period between September 1989 and June 1990, and was highlighted by a major shift in the power structures of the republic. The pro-Union Communist government of Moldova was succeeded by a coalition of nationalist-democratic forces, which won the democratic elections in February 1990 and proclaimed the political sovereignty of Moldova within the USSR. In September 1989 the MPF had advanced republican political sovereignty as the major objective of its political struggle. Criticism of the Communist-controlled republican government included appeals for an official re-evaluation of the historical events of 1940, and for the priority of republican legislation over the Union legislation in Moldova.

A spectacular rise in mass political activism, fuelled by the Moldovan ethnic movement, began after 17 September 1989, when the new republican draft law on parliamentary (Supreme Soviet) elections was published in the press for discussion. The MPF held a series of rallies and meetings to air its pre-election political programme, which combined affirmation of republican sovereignty and ethnic revival with anti-federalist and anti-Communist demands.

The October 1989 rallies staged by the MPF are reported to have gathered tens of thousands of participants in Kishinev alone. In November, two violent clashes were reported between the police and the MPF demonstrators. On 7 November in Kishinev, several thousand protesting demonstrators stopped the Communist Party celebrations of the anniversary of the 1917 Revolution by climbing onto tanks and forcing the Communist Party leadership of the republic to leave the review stand (*SM*, 8 November 1989). In addition, an MPF rally held on 10 November 1989 ended in rioting. After the rally, some 10,000–15,000 demonstrators demanding immediate dismissal of the Moldovan Communist Party leadership are reported to have attacked several official buildings in the centre of Kishinev. An attempt was made to set fire to the republic's Ministry of Internal Affairs building. The police struck back by beating and arresting the protesters; 40 civilians and about 100 policemen were reported to have been injured during the violent clash (*SM*, 12 November 1989).

On 16 November, Moldovan First Secretary of the Communist Party, K. Grossu, was dismissed after the weekend clashes and was replaced by P. Luchinsky, known to be reform-oriented and liberal. On 21–24 November, the Supreme Soviet of Moldova approved a new democratic electoral law and fixed new parliamentary elections in the republic to be held on 25 February 1990.

The success of the anti-Communist revolution of December 1989 in Romania had an important impact on the growing radicalization of the Moldovan nationalist movement and non-Communist commitments of large masses of the Moldovan population in general. At the February 1990 elections, the majority of the seats in the new Moldova Supreme Soviet were won by candidates supported by the MPF and by nationalist-oriented Communist candidates who expressed support for sovereignty for the republic.

On 27 April 1990, the newly-elected Moldovan Parliament approved constitutional amendments changing the flag of the republic from the red banner with socialist symbols to the Romanian ethnic three-colour (blue, yellow, and red) flag. (*SM*, 1 May 1990). On 23 June, the Moldovan Parliament adopted the Declaration on the Sovereignty of Moldova, which proclaimed the priority of the Moldovan Constitution and legislation over the USSR Constitution and legislation on the territory of Moldova.

The same day, the Parliament approved the conclusions of the parliamentary commission on the political and legal evaluation of the 1939 Molotov–Ribbentrop Pact's consequences for Bessarabia and North Bukovina. The commission had concluded that it was illegal for the Soviet Union to incorporate Bessarabia in 1940. With these acts the Moldovan Parliament was following the example of the Baltic nations in challenging the constitutional principles and established practices of the Soviet Union federation (*SM*, 25, 28 June 1990).

In this period, inter-ethnic conflict between the Moldovans and subordinate ethnic minorities of the Russophones and Gagauz manifested themselves in legislative confrontation between the Moldova central, republican, and local bodies and authorities, and in escalating protest actions by the minorities against Moldovan attempts to affirm the proclaimed sovereignty of the republic.

Although the protest strikes in Trans-Dniester against language legislation had stopped by the end of September, that did not mean compliance. Russophones opted for the tactics of non-recognition at the local level. On 7–8 September 1989, the deputies of Tyraspol City Council voted to ignore the new language legislation by all bodies and offices on territory under the authority of the Tyraspol local government. On 14 September, similar decisions were adopted by the sessions of Rybnitsy and Bendery city councils, adding a demand to the USSR Supreme Soviet to abolish the Moldovan Republic laws on languages.

In legal terms, such decisions taken on the part of the local authorities to oppose republic-level legislation were, in fact, anti-constitutional, for the local bodies were exceeding their authority (*SM*, 10, 19 September 1989). In their propaganda, the IM and Communist Party leaders alleged that electoral victory for the MPF at the republican level would entail the ascendancy of Moldovan domination over the minorities; loyalty to the Union centre and "socialist internationalism" were held out as the only guarantees against extinction under these conditions of burgeoning Moldovan nationalism.

As parliamentary elections approached, Trans-Dniestrian leaders presented their demand for national-territorial autonomy for the Russophone-populated districts within Moldova. In Rybnitsy (3 December) and Tyraspol (28 January) local referenda were held in support of granting these towns the status of autonomous self-governing and self-supporting territories. These referenda also supported the formation of the Trans-Dniester Autonomous Soviet Socialist Republic within Moldova (PASSR). On 12 December 1989, a mass rally organized by the GPF in Komrat proclaimed itself the

First Congress of the representatives of the Gagauz people, and petitioned the Supreme Soviet of Moldova for the establishment of the Gagauz Autonomous Soviet Socialist Republic within Moldova (*SM*, 9 December 1989; 30 January, 3 February 1990).

Spring 1990 saw new aggravation of inter-ethnic symbolic disputes. Sessions of the city councils of Tyraspol (30 April), Bendery (3 May), and Rybnitsy (8 May) abrogated the constitutional amendments concerning the new republican flag on their territories. The Moldovan Parliament reacted by amending the penal code of the republic to stipulate stricter punishment for non-observance of the legislation on republican state symbols (*SM*, 4, 7, 15 May 1990).

The critical challenge to the legitimacy of the Moldovan central government came in June 1990. On 2 June, Russophone deputies from legislative bodies of all levels elected from the territories of five districts of left-Bank Moldova convoked the "First Congress of People's Deputies of Trans-Dniester." This Congress adopted a resolution demanding the creation of an economically independent Trans-Dniester region and political autonomy within Moldova. The Congress called on the Russophone population to hold local elections to the Supreme Soviet of Trans-Dniester, which was to proclaim independence or autonomy within Moldova unless such political autonomy be granted by the central Moldovan authorities to the Russophone districts of Trans-Dniester (*SM*, 5, 7 June 1990).

5 From declaring sovereignty to declaring independence

The third stage of political transformation in Moldova comprises the period between June 1990, when the Declaration of Sovereignty was adopted by the Moldovan Supreme Soviet, and August 1991, when Moldova proclaimed its complete independence from the USSR. On 25–26 July, the Moldovan Supreme Soviet approved new laws on the economic self-support of the republic and the procedure for ratification of USSR legislative acts by the republican Parliament (*SM*, 26, 27 July 1990). The latter act institutionalized the principle of the supremacy of republican legislation over the federal legislation of the USSR.

The creation of republican institutions not subordinate to the central Union structures began in autumn 1990, with the establishment of the republican guard and republican police, not envisaged by the Union Constitution. In January 1991, the Moldovan Supreme Soviet backed the confederation approach towards the new Union Treaty and joined the position of the Baltic republics, Armenia, and Georgia in non-participation in the USSR referendum on the preservation of the Soviet Union federation.

On 23 May, the Moldovan Supreme Soviet struck the words "Soviet" and "Socialist" from the official name of the Republic of Moldova. In the period between June 1990 and August 1991, inter-ethnic disputes in Moldova culminated in the first crisis of ethno-political legitimacy, which erupted into violent clashes that were to claim human victims.

On 1 July 1990, a local referendum in Bendery supported the creation of the Trans-Dniester ASSR on the basis of association between the towns of Bendery and Rybnitsy. One week later, the Moldovan Supreme Soviet declared the results of the Bendery refer-endum illegal and anti-constitutional. On 22 July 1990, the Second Congress of representatives of the Gagauz people, held in Komrat once again, called on the central authorities of Moldova to review the petition of the First Congress demanding national-territorial autonomy to the Gagauz districts, declaring the intention to proclaim such autonomy unilaterally if necessary.

On 27 July, a special session of the Moldovan Parliament, through a special act of the Supreme Soviet, confirmed the guarantees for free cultural autonomy of the Gagauz community in Moldova and prom-ised state assistance to Gagauz cultural institutions. However, the Moldovan Parliament refused to grant territorial autonomy to Gagauz districts, and objected to demands for autonomous bodies of power (*SM*, 29 July 1990). On 2 August, large protest rallies were organized in Komrat and Chadyr-Lungi. On 19 August, the Congress of the Gagauz deputies to the Soviets of various levels proclaimed the formation of the Gagauz Autonomous Soviet Socialist Republic (GASSR) as independent from Moldova and a subject of the USSR federation. The Congress set 28 October 1990 as the date for local elections to the Supreme Soviet of their unilaterally proclaimed auto-nomous republic (*SM*, 22 August 1990).

The Moldovan authorities reacted by declaring such separatist decisions illegal, banning the GPF as a subversive movement. On 2 September, in Tyraspol, the Second Congress of Russophone depu-ties of all levels elected in Trans-Dniester declared the establishment of the Trans-Dniester Moldavian Soviet Socialist Republic (PMSSR) as independent from Moldova and a subject of the USSR federation. The PMSSR was announced as the legal successor to the Moldavian ASSR, which had existed within the Ukraine prior to 1940.

The secessionists argued that, just as Moldova did not recognize the supremacy of USSR legislation over the republic, Trans-Dniestrian autonomy would not recognize the supremacy and authority of Moldova. The Congress further declared that USSR legislation and Moldovan legislation pre-dating 31 August 1989 (the date of the adoption of the language laws) could be considered invalid on the territory of the proclaimed PMSSR. The population of Trans-Dniester was invited to participate in elections to the Supreme Soviet of the PMSSR on 25 November (*SM*, 4 September 1990).

On 16 September, the Second Congress of the Gagauz deputies of all levels of Soviets recognized the independence of the PMSSR and, in turn, declared the establishment of the Gagauz Soviet Socialist Republic (GSSR) within the USSR but independent from Moldova. The Congress confirmed 28 October as the date of elections to the Gagauz Supreme Soviet, to be held in southern districts of Moldova and organized by local Soviets (*SM*, 19 September 1990).

The claims of these unilaterally proclaimed new republics were perceived by the Moldovan majority as an encroachment on their territorial integrity and caused intense escalation of inter-ethnic tensions. Large-scale rallies involving tens of thousands of demonstrators were organized by the MPF in Kishinev and all major centres of right-bank Moldova, demanding that the Moldovan government should take urgent, decisive measures to suppress the separatists.

By 23 October, when Moldovan Prime Minister M. Druk, under pressure from MPF radicals, signed a decree legalizing the organization of detachments of Moldovan volunteers subordinated to the republican Ministry of Defence, the situation had grown beyond the control of the Moldovan government. As numerous formations of volunteers mobilized by the MPF radical activists started to arrive in the Gagauz districts of Southern Moldova, Gagauz local bodies initiated a counter-mobilization of volunteers into self-defence groups.

Trans-Dniestrian authorities promised their support to the Gagauz and called for the mobilization of self-defence groups of the Russophone workers. Thousands of Trans-Dniestrian workers were reported to have been sent from Tyraspol in support of the Gagauz. Barricades, barrages, and control posts on the roads leading to Southern Moldova were set up by Gagauz self-defence formations. Civilian self-defence formations blocked the Dubossary Bridge connecting right-bank Moldova with this nearest Trans-Dniestrian city. On 27 October, the concentration of opposing formations of volunteers in the Komrat, Chadyr-Lungi, and Vulkanesht districts of the

Gagauz area reportedly reached 80,000 people on either side (*SM*, 27, 28, 29, 30, 31 October 1990).

On the eve of the 28 October Gagauz elections, the Moldovan Parliament declared a state of emergency in Southern Moldova and called for USSR central government troops to help the republican police in maintaining social order. Moldovan police and internal troops managed to separate the opposing formations and to prevent major outbursts of inter-ethnic hostility in Gagauzia. Then, on 28 October, the elections to the Gagauz Supreme Soviet were held. Tension in Southern Moldova seemed to subside, and volunteer formations started to leave the area. At the same time, however, the confrontation in the Dubossary district reached such a height that three people were killed and nine wounded in a violent clash between the Moldovan police and Russophone civilians on 2 November, near the Dubossary Bridge over the Dniester (*SM*, 27 October, 4 November 1990; *Dialog* nos. 19, 20).

Realizing that further escalation could assume the Nagorno-Karabakh pattern and provoke the Union central authorities to apply force and impose martial law in the republic, both conflicting parties undertook to search urgently for a compromise. An extraordinary session of the Moldovan Parliament, held on 3 November, passed a resolution demanding complete withdrawal of volunteer formations of all parties from Southern Moldova and from the Trans-Dniester area, as well as the removal of road barricades and control posts (*SM*, 4 November 1990). A special parliamentary commission of reconciliation, headed by Moldovan Communist Party First Secretary, P. Luchinsky, was formed to negotiate with the Trans-Dniestrian and Gagauz leaders. Both parties responded to the mediation offered by the Union President, Mikhail Gorbachev, who then held talks with Moldovan and Trans-Dniestrian leaders on 3–4 November in Moscow (*IZ*, 4, 5 November 1990).

A special commission of the Moldovan Supreme Soviet was constituted, containing representatives of all ethnic minorities, and given the task of elaborating draft amendments to the Moldovan law on the status and functioning of languages. On 24 November, the Moldovan government abrogated the decree on legalization of the Moldovan volunteer formations and called for their disbandment. No decision concerning the destiny of the Moldovan republican guard was taken, however (*SM*, 15, 25 November 1990; *Dialog* no. 21, 1990).

Despite appeals made by the USSR central government to the local authorities and to the IM leaders of Trans-Dniester to waive their decision to organize elections to the Supreme Soviet of the self-proclaimed PMSSR, such elections were held on 25 November. The first session of the Trans-Dniestrian Supreme Soviet recalled from the Moldovan Supreme Soviet all deputies elected from the left-bank Moldova constituencies (*SM*, 30 November 1990).

On 22 December 1990, the Union President, Mikhail Gorbachev, issued a decree in which he attempted to call Moldova to order by threatening presidential rule from Moscow. The decree declared the unilaterally proclaimed Gagauz and Trans-Dniester republics and the elected bodies illegal and juridically invalid. The same decree insisted that the central government of the Moldovan republic repeal or revise numerous laws and decisions. Such "objectionable" laws included the creation of a separate republican guard, a language law supposedly giving preference to Moldovan speakers, and a denunci-ation of the Union annexation of Moldova under the 1939 Molotov–Ribbentrop Pact (*SM*, 22 December 1990).

One week later, the Moldovan Parliament agreed to comply by disbanding its national guard and revising the law on languages, which the Union President alleged restricted minority rights. The Supreme Soviet of Moldova rejected, however, any modifications to the republic's Declaration of Sovereignty, and refused to recognize the supremacy of USSR legislation over that of the republic on the territory of Moldova (*SM*, 30 December 1990).

On 21 January, the Third Extraordinary Congress of Trans-Dniester deputies was convoked to discuss the Gorbachev decree. The Congress repeated its demand to the USSR Supreme Soviet and to the Union President to recognize the independence of the pro-claimed PMSSR and GSSR and to let representatives of those re-publics sign the Union Treaty independently from Moldova.

6 The August 1991 coup attempt and the transition to independence

The failure of the August 1991 coup in the USSR can be regarded as the landmark of the fourth stage of socio-political transition in Mol-dova. Two events of major significance mark this period: Moldova's declaration of complete independence in August 1991, and world-wide recognition of the new republic after the definitive disintegra-tion of the Soviet empire and the resignation of Gorbachev in late December 1991.

Together with the Baltic states, Moldova was among those few

Union republics to condemn the organizers of the Communist putsch in Moscow from the outset. On 21 August, an extraordinary session of the Moldovan Parliament called for active resistance against the Union structures and against the putschists. After the failure of the Moscow coup, on 23 August, the Moldovan Parliament banned all activities of the Communist Party in Moldova (*ST*, 28 August 1991).

On 27 August, the Declaration of Independence and the secession of Moldova from the USSR was adopted by the Parliament. On the same day, Moldova's independence was recognized by Romania; two days later, diplomatic relations were established between the two states. On 23 October, the government of Moldova declared republican ownership of all industrial enterprises formerly under Union structures. In November/December 1991, the Moldovan Parliament adopted legislative acts on the creation of a national army, internal troops, frontier guard, and special police detachments (OPON). Nationwide presidential elections were to be held on 8 December.

As in other ex-USSR republics, the removal of the Union centre and the process of state-building were accompanied by growing differentiation and rivalries within the élite of the titular nationality. The radical wing of the Moldovan nationalist movement, headed by Moldova's former Prime Minister M. Druk, called for the restoration of Greater Romania within the 1940 borders, through reunion of independent Moldova with Romania and presentation of territorial claims to the Ukraine. A large group of Moldovan intellectuals, followed by some of the rank and file, left the MPF, disapproving of Druk's radicalism. The majority of the Moldovan élite backed the moderates, headed by Moldovan President Snegur, whose policies envisaged strengthening Moldova's independence, preserving economic ties with other ex-USSR republics, and joining the Commonwealth of Independent States.

On 14 October 1991, the MPF declared its transition into opposition to the Snegur government (*NM*, 24 October 1991). After that, the MPF leaders called a boycott of the forthcoming presidential elections. On 1 December, a rally of the coalition of radical nationalist parties declared the formation of a "Pan-Romanian National Council of the Reunion," for Greater Romania within the borders of 1940. This Council consisted of radical nationalist Moldovan Parliament deputies and their colleagues from the Romanian Parliament who belonged to right-wing opposition parties in Romania (*NM*, 4 December 1991).

At the nationwide elections held in Moldova on 8 December,

Snegur won the presidency, receiving 98 per cent of the vote. Voter turnout was high, at 83.9 per cent (*NM*, 13 December 1991). The failure of the MPF boycott and the victory of Snegur demonstrated the popular support and legitimacy enjoyed by the moderate nationalist leaders.

The same period between August 1991 and December 1991 was marked by a new crisis in inter-ethnic conflict between the Moldovan majority and the Russophones of left-bank Moldova. Since the very beginning of the August coup attempt in Moscow, Trans-Dniestrian and Gagauz leaders had supported and expressed allegiance to the putschists. After the failure of the coup, on 25 August, the Supreme Soviet of the PMSSR proclaimed Trans-Dniester independent from Moldova. The Moldovan Parliament did not recognize this proclamation, and on 27 August the Moldovan central authorities issued an order authorizing the arrest of separatist leaders of Trans-Dniester and Gagauzia. The next day, a special decree of President Snegur abolished or suspended the publication of almost all local Russian-language newspapers, accusing them of Communist propaganda and support of the coup junta (*ST*, 28 August, 4 September 1991).

On 1 September, the Russophone population of Trans-Dniester began a railway blockade of Moldova demanding the release of the arrested leaders and threatening to interrupt electricity and gas supplies to right-bank Moldova, populated predominantly by Moldovans. On 2 September, the outlawed Supreme Soviet of the PMSSR approved the Constitution of the republic, adopting the former socialist Moldovan state emblem and flag as symbols of the Republic of Trans-Dniester (*IZ*, 2, 3 September 1991; *ST*, 7 September 1991).

From 9 September, in the towns and cities of Trans-Dniester, armed formations of so-called "forces of self-defence of Trans-Dniester" and "detachments of people's militia" (people's volunteer corps), subordinated to staff headquarters in Tyraspol, came into being. On 21 September, the Trans-Dniestrian "parliament" approved a "law" on the creation of Trans-Dniestrian republican armed forces (the republican guard) and announced military mobilization of Russophone males aged 20–40 (*IZ*, 10, 11 September 1991; *ST*, 14, 21 September 1991). Sentries and control posts were stationed by Trans-Dniestrian guardsmen and militia on all roads and on the Dubossary Bridge.

A particularly explosive situation arose in Dubossary, with its mixed Moldovan and Russian population. The city police and executive power were controlled by Moldovans, while the legislative local bodies were controlled by the Russian majority. On 25 September, after five Russian civilians were arrested by the police and accused of non-compliance, Russian citizens attacked the central office of the city police and the building of the Dubossary branch of the Moldova State Bank. The ensuing police control action resulted in three casualties. Groups of Moldovan peasants from nearby villages arrived in the city to support the police (*IZ*, 27 September 1991; *ST*, 2 October 1991).

A delegation of deputies of the Russian Federation Supreme Soviet arrived in Moldova to assist in settling the conflict. On 1 October, an agreement was signed between the Moldovan govern-ment and representatives of left-bank Moldova. It provided for the liberation of the arrested separatist leaders, mutual withdrawal of additional Moldovan police forces and Trans-Dniestrian guards from Dubossary, and an end to the railway blockade of right-bank Mol-dova. However, control posts stationed by Trans-Dniestrians on the roads and on the Dubossary Bridge remained (*NM*, 4 October 1991).

Inter-ethnic conflict did not abate, however. Russophone leaders insisted that Moldova should recognize the independence of Trans-Dniester as an indispensable precondition for initiating negotiations on Trans-Dniester's entering Moldova as an ethno-territorial auton-omy with the right of free secession. The Moldovan central author-ities, however, rejected direct bilateral negotiations with the leaders of separatist parliaments and refused to recognize the legitimacy of these bodies, demanding their dissolution and the return of deputies from Trans-Dniester and Gagauzia to the central Moldovan Parlia-ment as a precondition for examining the minorities' demands.

In October 1991, the Supreme Soviets of Trans-Dniester and Gagauzia called for local referenda to be held on independence and presidential elections on 1 December 1991 (*NM*, 17, 31 October 1991). Starting in November 1991, Trans-Dniestrian Russophones made attempts to subordinate local organs of social control to the authority of the Trans-Dniester republic. The decree issued by the head of the Trans-Dniestrian Department of Internal Affairs envisaged the establishment of a Trans-Dniestrian militia instead of Moldovan police officers, and required dismissal of any policemen dis-inclined to swear allegiance to the PMSSR (*NM*, 15 November 1991).

On 1 December 1991, two separatist leaders, I. Smirnov and S. Topal, were elected president at the local elections held in Trans-Dniester and Gagauzia, respectively. The referenda held the same day supported independence from Moldova. On 3 December, the

Supreme Soviet of Trans-Dniester approved the creation of the Trans-Dniestrian Ministry of Defence and Security. G. Yakovlev, Commander-in-Chief of the 14th Soviet Army, located in the region, expressed his support for the PMSSR (*NM*, 4, 7 December 1991).

In mid-December 1991, a new crisis in inter-ethnic disputes erupted, with violent clashes in left-bank Moldova. On 16 December, Russophone militiamen attacked and occupied the local offices of Moldovan police in the Grigoriopol and Slobodzeja districts, which had refused to recognize the legitimacy of the Trans-Dniestrian republican authorities (*NM*, 17 December 1991). The Dubossary Bridge was once again reported to be seized by Trans-Dniestrian guardsmen, and the town of Dubossary cut off from the neighbouring Moldovan villages. On 7 December, about 700 armed guardsmen and three armoured personnel carriers under Trans-Dniestrian "Dniester" formations of guardsmen were reported to be gathering in Dubossary district (*NM*, 14 December 1991). The Russophone Dubossary City Council and the local radio called on citizens to blockade the city police office, and presented Moldovan policemen with an ultimatum to leave the city. The policemen rejected this and staged a defence, calling for support from Kishinev.

Moldovan peasants from neighbouring villages who hastened to help the besieged policemen were stopped at the Dubossary Bridge by shots from Trans-Dniestrian guardsmen. Additional police detachments from Kishinev made an attempt to enter Dubossary. Exchanges of fire and clashes between the Moldovan OPON detachments and Trans-Dniestrian guardsmen resulted in five killed and twelve wounded (*NM*, 17 December 1991). Minor armed collisions were also reported in Kamenka and Grigoriopol districts.

In late December came reports of potential trouble. The command of the 14th Soviet Army promised support to the Russophones in the event of new intervention from the Moldovan police. On 25 December, the first semi-armed groups of Russian Cossacks from the Don region of the Russian Federation were reported to have arrived as volunteers in Tyraspol, to swear allegiance to the PMSSR as a sign of solidarity and support to their Russian ethnic brethren in Trans-Dniester (*MN*, 21, 26 December 1991).

7 Large-scale inter-ethnic violence

A new socio-political transition began in winter 1992 after Moldova had gained international recognition. In early March, the new republic became a member of the United Nations. Between March and June 1992, domestic conflict between Moldova and Trans-Dniester escalated into large-scale organized violence with international implications. By late July 1992, only a fragile inter-ethnic peace seemed to have been reached.

On 9 January 1992, the Trans-Dniestrian authorities decreed that the ex-USSR armed forces located on the territory of left-bank Moldova be placed under the command of the PMSSR government. The CIS armed forces ignored this demand and declared the neutrality of the former Union army in internal conflicts in the ex-USSR republics. In January–March 1992 came reports of armed assaults made by Trans-Dniestrian guardsmen and Cossacks at military depots of the 14th Army and ex-USSR internal troops.

New signs of polarization of the Moldova–Trans-Dniester conflicts were reported in February 1992. In late February hundreds of Cossacks from the Don region of Russia began to arrive in left-bank Moldova in response to appeals made by the Trans-Dniestrians to their Russian ethnic brethren. Their arrival served to heighten ethnic tensions. Soon afterwards, groups of Romanian volunteers were reported arriving in right-bank Moldova expressing their solidarity with the Moldovans in the struggles against separatists (*KU*, 2 March 1992; *IZ*, 5 March 1992).

At its third Congress, held in Kishinev on 23 February 1992, the MPF renamed itself the Christian Democratic Popular Front (CDPF), underlining its political linkage with right-wing Romanian parties, which also sought further reunion of Moldova with Romania and the restoration of Greater Romania (*NG*, 26 February 1992).

On 1–2 March, Trans-Dniestrian guardsmen attacked the Dubossary City police office and arrested Moldovan policemen, demanding the closure of Moldova loyalist organizations in Dubossary. Moldovan OPON detachments sent to restore order were blocked at the Dubossary Bridge control post. After an exchange of fire with the guardsmen and Cossacks, one person was killed and one was wounded. On 3 March, the Moldovan police office in Dubossary was closed down and transferred to Kochiery, a Moldovan-populated village nearby. The same day, during a violent clash in Kochiery, six Trans-Dniestrian guardsmen were reported killed and 11 wounded. On March 3, Trans-Dniestrian leader I. Smirnov declared a state of emergency in left-bank Moldova and called for resistance to the Moldovan police. New Cossack detachments were reported arriving in

Trans-Dniester through the territory of Ukraine. Hostilities assumed the character of daily exchanges of fire and minor combat in the suburbs of Dubossary and in neighbouring villages with ethnically mixed populations (*IZ*, 2, 5 March 1992; *NG*, 4 March 1992).

On 6 March, the city police office in Bendery was besieged by Trans-Dniestrian guardsmen who demanded that it be closed and all city police disbanded. Violent attacks and exchanges of fire were reported on highways in Bendery and Grigoriopol districts. During the armed raid on a military depot on 15 March, the Cossacks, reportedly numbering 600, took possession of firearms, guns, machine and submachine guns, mortars, grenades, and ammunition (*KU*, 7 March 1992; *IZ*, 16 March 1992). In mid-March, hostilities spread to the rural areas of Dubossary, with hundreds of people participating in violent combat. On 16–17 March, over 600 Moldovan policemen and Trans-Dniestrian guards with a dozen armoured carriers were reported engaged in fighting near Kochiery village. In the combat near Koshnitsy village, the Moldovan side alone was said to number 3,000 policemen (*IZ*, 17 March 1992; *KU*, 18 March 1992).

Flows of refugees leaving *en masse*, both Moldovans and Russians, were the product of the escalating hostilities. On 20 March, 6,000 refugees had to flee to the Odessa region of the Ukraine after having been threatened or attacked. By 26 March, the total count of both Russian and Moldovan refugees was estimated at over 10,000 (*KU*, 21, 25 March 1992; *IZ*, 26 March 1992). The flow of people in opposite directions aroused anger and hatred on both banks of Moldova.

On 17 March, an armistice agreement was reached. Trying to promote a compromise, the Moldovan Parliament agreed to grant economic and taxation autonomy to left-bank Moldova and to introduce new amendments into the law on languages. The Trans-Dniestrian leaders did not find these concessions satisfactory, however, and insisted that Trans-Dniester be granted, if not political independence, then at least politico-territorial autonomy within Moldova and the right to free secession if Moldova should reunite with Romania.

By mid-March the Moldova–Trans-Dniester conflict had acquired international implications. On 17 March, the Romanian government demanded that the Russian Federation undertake urgent measures towards a peaceful settlement of the conflict in Moldova (*IZ*, 18, 20 March 1992). Moscow was hesitant and gave ambiguous signals. On the one hand, the Russian government had recognized the principle of non-interference in the domestic affairs of the CIS countries. On the other hand, protection of the rights of Russophone minorities had also been declared an important objective of Russia's foreign policy toward ex-USSR republics. Political opponents of the Yeltsin government accused it of ignoring the alleged violation of human rights of Moldova's Russophone inhabitants and of betraying their ethnic brothers. Ukrainian president L. Kravchuk, reacting to a note from Snegur, issued a decree for the creation of a 50-km special zone on the frontier between Moldova and the Ukraine, aimed at preventing any further influx of Don Cossacks from Russia through Ukrainian territory (*IZ*, 18 March 1992).

On 18 March, the command of the 14th ex-Soviet Army (composed mainly of Russophones) issued a declaration expressing the intention to provide military support to Trans-Dniestrians, even without orders from Moscow, should armed hostilities again begin to escalate. On 19 March, Moldova's President Snegur declared he did not exclude the possibility that his country might turn to Romania for military help: Don Cossacks from Russia had already intervened in the conflict on the side of the Russophones and there were good reasons for not trusting the promises of the CIS United Armed Forces Command that the 14th Army would stay neutral (*IZ*, 19, 20 March 1992).

On 19 March, during his emergency visit to Moscow, the Romanian foreign minister repeated Romania's appeal to Moscow to initiate four-way, peace-seeking talks. On 20 March, the Russian Federation Supreme Soviet appealed to the Moldovan Parliament to seek a peaceful solution to the inter-ethnic disputes. At the same time it expressed the opinion that the economic autonomy granted to Trans-Dniester by the Moldovan central authorities should be supplemented with recognition of political status, guaranteeing the right of left-bank Moldova to self-determination if Moldova should lose its independence through reunion with Romania (*RG*, 21 March 1992).

On 24 March, four-way negotiations between Moldova, Romania, Russia, and the Ukraine started in Kishinev at foreign minister level. Russia and the Ukraine agreed to the Moldovan demand that Trans-Dniester should not be present at the talks as an independent party.

A new outburst of violence in Dubossary region broke the armistice and complicated the negotiation process. On 30 March, an attack by Trans-Dniestrian guardsmen on Koshnitsy village resulted in one Moldovan policeman being killed and five wounded. A counter-response attack by policemen on the Dubossary highway resulted in one guardsman being killed and three wounded (*KU*, 31 March 1992).

On 31 March, the Moldovan Parliament enacted President Snegur's decree introducing a state of emergency throughout Moldova. A resolution passed by the Moldovan Parliament repeated the demand that illegal armed formations of Trans-Dniestrian guardsmen be disbanded, that the Cossacks return to Russia, and that Moldovan power structures be restored in left-bank Moldova as preconditions for further negotiations on the future political status of the region (*IZ*, 2 April 1992).

In April, hostilities spread to Bendery district as well. Another armed attack on the Bendery city police office on 1 April resulted in four days of combat between Moldovan OPON forces and Trans-Dniestrian guardsmen, which led to the division of the city into two sectors, each controlled by an opposing group. As a result of this violence, 19 were killed and 18 wounded (*KU*, 10 April, 1992). Officers of the 14th Army unit located near Bendery threatened to break the neutrality and to intervene in the conflict unless the hostilities stopped. From 2 April, Trans-Dniester mounted a new railway blockade of right-bank Moldova. Starting on 8 April, new violent clashes in Dubossary district escalated into rocket fire exchange, armed raids and assaults, fighting, and terrorist acts along the whole frontier in Trans-Dniester.

This lasted till 17 April, when a new cease-fire agreement was reached. The official figures issued by Moldovan and Trans-Dniestrian sources as of 17 April stated that since the beginning of violence in December 1991, 42 people had been killed (including 19 policemen and 23 civilians) and 130 wounded (including 72 policemen and 58 civilians) on the Moldovan side; and 60 killed, 100 wounded, and 60 missing on the Trans-Dniestrian side (*IZ*, 17 April 1992).

Between 12 and 28 May 1992, there was yet another new eruption of inter-ethnic hostilities, when Trans-Dniestrian guardsmen attempted to drive out Moldovan OPON and military detachments from the positions they had occupied on left-bank Moldova in April. Numerous attacks, raids, and acts of hostage-taking and pillage were reported in Dubossary and Grigoriopol districts. Trans-Dniestrian guardsmen and Cossacks were reported to be using tanks and armoured carriers stolen from units of the 14th Army. During the combat in Grigoriopol district, 27 tanks and 12 armoured carriers were reported to have been used by the Trans-Dniestrians. At least 54 persons were reported killed and 113 wounded in May. Officially registered refugees from left-bank Moldova numbered 20,000 in right-bank Moldova and 11,000 in the Odessa region of the Ukraine (*KU*, 22 May, 4 June 1992; *IZ*, 5 June 1992). By the end of May a new agreement on a 30-day-long armistice was reached, and new attempts were made to resolve the conflict through negotiations.

In early June, at the negotiations held in Moscow between the foreign ministers of Russia and Moldova, it was agreed to establish three working groups. Their tasks were to monitor the cease-fire agreement and to have consultations on the modalities of withdrawal of the 14th Army from Moldova and on the political and legal aspects of resolving the Moldova–Trans-Dniester conflict. (*IZ*, 12, 19 June 1992).

On 3 June, the Supreme Soviet of Trans-Dniester forwarded to the Moldovan Parliament a proposal to separate the armed formations in the zone of conflict and to stipulate a treaty of federation between Moldova and Trans-Dniester. The latter was to constitute a new status for Trans-Dniester as a politically autonomous republic within Moldova with the right to free secession.

Following debates held in the Moldovan Parliament on 9–11 June, the Parliament rejected the federation demands of Trans-Dniester but agreed to a special resolution promising reconsideration of the political and juridical status of left-bank Moldova (*IZ*, 15, 19 June 1992). After consultations with military leaders it was agreed to start the withdrawal of troops from left-bank Moldova on 16 June. However, dramatic events in Bendery were to check the peace-seeking process once again.

8 Bloodshed and conflict settlement in Bendery

On 19 June, a new armed attack by Trans-Dniestrian guardsmen on the Bendery city police office provoked the Moldovan government to send formations of their national army to restore Moldovan control in Bendery. For two months the town had been divided into two sectors, controlled by opposing armed groups. Moldovan troops (reportedly some 2,500 soldiers and officers) attacked the northern sector of Bendery, which was controlled by the Trans-Dniestrian guardsmen. Trying to check the rapid arrival of additional guardsmen in support of the Trans-Dniestrians, Moldovan aircraft bombed the bridge connecting the town of Bendery with the highway leading to Tyraspol. Artillery was used by both sides. The command of the 14th

Army garrison near Bendery declared its neutrality, but, according to the reports of the Moldovan press, several officers with their soldiers participated on the side of the guardsmen.

The next day, groups of Trans-Dniestrian guardsmen and Cossacks, outnumbering the Moldovan forces, arrived in Bendery district. The use of tanks in combat and the support of some officers of the 14th Army determined the outcome of the Bendery battle in favour of the Trans-Dniestrians, who regained control over the larger part of the city. The Moldovan forces withdrew into the suburbs. The three-day combat resulted in 20 killed and 200 wounded on the Moldovan side, and some 300 killed and 500 wounded on the Trans-Dniestrian side. Almost all the city buildings were destroyed by artillery fire (*KU*, 21, 22 June 1992; *IZ*, 22, 23, 24 June 1992).

On 22–23 June, leaders of the opposing parties reached an agreement on a cease-fire in Bendery. However, developments became out of control, unleashing a potent wave of inter-ethnic hostilities. Violent clashes were reported in the Dubossary, Bendery, Rybnitsy, Parkany, and Grigoriopol districts. Human losses as of 24 June amounted to 500 dead and 3,500 wounded on both sides since the Bendery battle. The number of Russophone refugees to the Odessa region of the Ukraine totalled 30,000 – three times as many as during the previous months of warfare (*IZ*, 25 June 1992; *KU*, 27 June 1992). The number of armed members of military formations reported to be participating in the hostilities was estimated at 15,000 persons from each side, with approximately 400 tanks and armoured carriers and 300 artillery guns and mortars being deployed. By July the total number of refugees exceeded 100,000 (*KU*, 2, 8 July 1992).

When officers of the 14th Army threatened to ignore the orders of the Russian authorities and to take an active part in the violent conflict on the side of Trans-Dniester, this danger of larger-scale violence compelled the political leaders to search with greater urgency for a way to settle the conflict and restore peace. On 25 June, during the Istanbul conference of the Black Sea countries, a special round of talks was held between the presidents of Russia, Romania, Ukraine, and Moldova. This yielded an agreement to halt the armed confrontation in left-bank Moldova and to undertake effective measures to ensure separation of the opposing armed factions.

The four presidents called on the Moldovan Parliament to reconsider once again the political and juridical status of left-bank Moldova. The same day, the Moldovan Parliament replied that recognition of Trans-Dniester as a separate politico-territorial unit was not for discussion, but it did approve a special act envisaging for Bendery the status of "free city" within Moldova and new legislative guarantees of wide-ranging economic and cultural autonomy for Trans-Dniester within Moldova (*IZ*, 26, 27 June 1992).

On 8 July, the negotiations between Moldova's deputy minister of defence, the commander of the Trans-Dniestrian guard, the commander-in-chief of the 14th ex-USSR Army, and representatives of the Russian Federation Defence Ministry ended with the signing of a mutual order on cease-fire and disarmament along the entire frontier-line of left-bank Moldova, and the introduction of the CIS armed forces (*IZ*, 8 July 1992).

A political settlement of the Moldova–Trans-Dniester conflict would appear to have been reached in the course of intensive Moldova–Trans-Dniester talks, with active participation of the Russian Federation, in late July 1992. On 21 July, in the presence of the Trans-Dniestrian delegation headed by President I. Smirnov, the Russian and Moldovan presidents signed the Moscow Agreement on the principles of peace settlement of armed conflict in Trans-Dniester districts of the republic of Moldova. This accord envisaged the creation of a dividing line in left-bank Moldova between the opposing parties, to be supervised by military observers from Russia, Moldova, and Trans-Dniester. It further stipulated gradual withdrawal of all armed formations, military equipment, and machinery from Trans-Dniester; withdrawal of the 14th Army to the territory of Russia; and the establishment of a special control commission on security in Bendery.

Moldova assumed the obligation to determine and to fix the legal and political status of left-bank Moldova within Moldova and to grant to its population the right to express self-determination if the political status of the independent republic of Moldova should be changed. This compromise may not have resolved the Moldova–Trans-Dniester conflict completely, but it appears to have been successful in suppressing violence and in providing peace, at least for the time being (*IZ*, 22 July 1992).

9 Socio-political change and inter-ethnic violence

The above review shows the significant impact of socio-political transformation in Moldova 1988–92 on the politicization of inter-ethnic disputes and the escalation of ethno-political contentions to the highest degree of militancy. Each new stage of socio-political change entailed political crises in inter-ethnic relations, accompanied by an escalation of anxiety-laden demands concerning the political status of ethnic groups with zero-sum perceptions of power issues.

We may identify five major critical points in the inter-ethnic political struggles in Moldova between late 1988 and mid-1992:

(1) August–September 1989: crisis resulting from the adoption of new republican legislation on the status and functioning of languages;

(2) October–November 1990: crisis prior to local elections to the Supreme Soviets (parliaments) of unilaterally proclaimed separatist Gagauz and Trans-Dniester republics;

(3) September 1991: crisis following the failure of the coup in the USSR and the arrest of leaders of the rebel ethnic groups in Moldova;

(4) December 1991: crisis after presidential elections and referenda on independence in Gagauzia and Trans-Dniester;

(5) March 1992: crisis after the separatist authorities of Trans-Dniester attempted to subordinate local police offices by force, while using other means of official mass coercion.

Three major patterns and stages can be singled out in the development of disruptive inter-ethnic confrontation between Moldova and Trans-Dniester:

 (i) November 1990 and September 1991: transition from non-violent to violent ethnic political action as manifested in clashes between the Moldovan police and civilians in Dubossary;

(ii) December 1991: transition to recurrent violent interaction in ethnically-mixed urban and rural areas of left-bank Moldova; Moldovan police and special OPON detachments, Moldovan peasants on the one side engaged in violent interaction with specially created formations of Trans-Dniestrian militia and semi-organized self-defence Russophone civilian groups on the other;

(iii) March–July 1992: transition to warfare – large-scale, organized, and sustained inter-ethnic violence pervaded the whole border area between right-bank and left-bank Moldova, culminating in the Bendery bloodshed of June 1992. Organized armed military formations (Moldovan OPON, police and armed forces against Trans-Dniestrian guardsmen and militia) representing established populations of opposing ethnicities engaged in warfare employing a vast range of conventional weapons. Paramilitary formations of adversaries (Moldovan and Romanian volunteers, Trans-Dniestrian self-defence groups and Cossack detachments from Russia) added a guerrilla dimension to the civil war.

Resort to violence in the Moldova–Trans-Dniester conflict appears to have been highly instrumental and related to the issues of political contention. Violence seems to have been closely connected with the political nature of ethnic disputes in the changing Moldovan society. Comparing the timing of violence with the course of non-violent ethno-political disputes in Moldova, we can see that the points marking the transition from non-violent to violent ethnic interaction correspond to the ethno-political crises of legitimacy which marked the peaks of inter-ethnic struggles for power (reallocation of power arrangements, or establishing a new set of power arrangements).

The theory of collective action and social organization elaborated by Charles Tilly and his colleagues provides important insights in accounting for inter-ethnic violence in the Moldova–Trans-Dniester conflict. Tilly's research on the materials provided by a century of civil strife in European countries has shown that collective violence has regularly flowed out of the central political processes in a country or region, and can be better understood as growing out of the inter-action of organized groups carrying out sustained collective action.

A general rise in collective action can be almost always be observed during periods of political transition, when various groups in society become more highly politicized as they press their claims and counter-claims. Tilly observes that where there is a high volume of such collective action, there is also a higher likelihood that some of the events will turn into violent encounters. Highly mobilized groups and the rapid acquisition or loss of power by groups have usually resulted in a disproportionate number of violent conflicts (Tilly et al., 1975: 243–7, 281–8; Tilly, 1978).

Applying Tilly's propositions concerning inter-ethnic political strife more specifically to the consideration of inter-ethnic political disputes can help us assess those peaks in the development of an ethno-political conflict, as well as those stages of non-violent change in inter-ethnic political relations when transition from non-violent to violent collective ethnic action is likely to occur. One of Tilly's major conclusions is that collective violence peaks at times of political activity, and especially when fundamental changes are taking place in the distribution of power among the self-aware groups which constitute a society (Tilly et al., 1975: 247–51, 280–3). Hence, in the case of ethno-political conflicts in a multi-ethnic society, we may expect high levels of militant collective ethnic action at those stages of change in inter-ethnic relations when the stakes are high in terms of threats to and opportunities for objective political interests and subjectively perceived group-political status.

Socio-political change in multi-ethnic societies implies significant changes in how ethnic groups become organized. Owing to political changes in society, groups will actively press their interests, mobilize themselves and available resources, and engage in various forms of collective ethnic action. What is sought can be either a larger share of the power available through the political system, or a re-allocation of power arrangements – ranging from inclusivist to exclusivist terms, from territorial autonomy to ethno-secession.

"Times of transition are also times of ethnic tension" (Shibutani and Kwan, 1965: ch. 14). The atmosphere of uncertainty generated by rapid socio-political change is a factor of paramount importance for the politicization of ethnic groups. In this atmosphere of uncertainty, major group anxiety concerns the anticipated consequences of political transformation for the status and interests of the ethnic group in a multi-ethnic polity and/or the perceived threats emanating from other groups. After the collapse of the Union centre, in ethnically-divided societies of the ex-USSR republics, the transfer of power raised the cardinal question of who would rule. Activated fears of ethnic domination and subordination may become particularly salient and provide the rationale for militant politicization of groups.

Characterizing the processes in modernizing societies, D. Horowitz notes: "Power is sought to prevent the emergence of dire but distant and dimly perceived consequences," and "so critical and dangerous are those feared consequences that it is deemed vital to take steps to avert them in advance" (Horowitz, 1985: 186–7). At some point this quest for power will provoke a repressive reaction from the already established centres of power or from the majority group which aims at establishing its own exclusive dominance in the process of state-building. From the interplay between collective action by the ethnically aggrieved and repression by established organizations of the ethnically dominant may come ethno-political violence.

10 Ethno-political legitimacy crisis as transition to violence

Non-violent proactive action by a disadvantaged and aggrieved ethnic group seeking a revision of the established ethno-political order poses a challenge to the constitutional order if, as in the former

USSR or Yugoslavia, a multi-ethnic state includes ethno-territorial principles in the foundation of its political organization. Challenges to the constitutional order mean, of course, challenges to regime legitimacy. Such legitimacy issues are likely to be especially severe in newly establishing or newly established political systems, since such systems lack a past performance on which to base their legitimacy. Any perceived inequities in the system are particularly likely to be deemed unacceptable. The situation in the state then approaches anarchy, because there is no adequately legitimate authority capable of resolving disputes among ethnic groups. Moreover, the government controlled by the ethnically dominant group does not enjoy full legitimacy even among the dominant ethnicity, due to rivalries among ethno-nationalist leaders and sub-élites.

Under such circumstances, virtually every issue of ethnic cleavage and dispute (language, religion, culture, official versions of the historical past, and the like) will often acquire a salient political dimension, and will generally turn into contests for power or become instrumentalized as such. When power conflicts between ethnic adversaries are particularly likely to become extreme and to be viewed as questions of survival, the likelihood of violence will increase dramatically.

Tilly places special importance on the argument that there is no sharp division between violent and non-violent collective action: there exists a close connection between the two (Tilly et al., 1975: 248; Tilly, 1978: 172–88). In this perspective, collective violence is seen as a by-product of group political interaction, of the struggle for power and of its repression. Tilly stresses that agents of government play a major role in such interactions, not only because governments often make claims which groups within their jurisdiction resist, but also, and primarily because, agents of government play a crucial role in collective violence as repressors of collective action. (Tilly et al., 1975: 243, 257, 283).

Let us now apply these propositions to the consideration of ethno-political disputes. It would appear that the stage of an ethno-political conflict when the central (ethnically dominant) government resorts to violence to repress the collective action conducted by the ethnic subordinates in their struggle for ethnically relevant redistribution of political arrangements, is most likely to become the point of transition from non-violent to violent collective ethno-political action.

This gives rise to an important question. At which stage of an ongoing ethno-political conflict is the central government most likely to repress the disadvantaged ethnic group contending for power? This stage – the ethno-political crisis of legitimacy – appears to occur when the (ethnically dominant) government calculates that the challenge cast by the aggrieved ethnic group jeopardizes the regime's legitimacy *in toto*. No matter how tolerant and disinclined to repression the dominant ethnic group and its governing élite may be, there still exists a point in the escalation of ethno-political conflict which, once reached, is almost destined to entail reaction and repression from the agents of the central government.

This critical point can be called the ethno-political crisis of legitimacy – as the culmination of non-violent ethno-political interaction. Such a point has been reached when the aggrieved group has become, or is on the verge of becoming, so highly mobilized as a political actor that the central government comes to realize that the anticipated next step of the disadvantaged ethnic group will not only pose another challenge to the legitimacy of the regime but may also bring about complete delegitimation of the current order.

It is during such an ethno-political crisis of legitimacy that inter-ethnic power contention becomes extreme. The stakes in terms of threats to and opportunities for the objective political interests of the groups involved are particularly high; zero-sum perceptions become widely shared and the likelihood of violence peaks. (For a more general discussion in legitimacy issues and politicized ethnicity, see Rothschild, 1981.) The outbreak of an ethno-political crisis of legitimacy means that a turning point in the power conflict has been reached and a new, intense, and different level of political interaction between the conflicting ethnic groups becomes possible. Violence then appears as a likely resultant mode of further conflict behaviour.

The dynamics of the Moldova–Trans-Dniester conflict indeed indicate that the ethno-political crises of legitimacy which occurred at different stages of the rapid socio-political transformation in Moldova, each time entailed violence. As demonstrated by the Moldova case, fast-paced socio-political change appears to be a major factor in shaping the dynamics of inter-ethnic violence. This influence can be assessed in at least three ways:

(1) It was the rapid character of the transformation of political life in Moldova which created an intricate superimposition of political struggles on inter-ethnic cleavages, and the escalation of ethnic disputes to the stage of ethno-political crisis of legitimacy. The unresolved issue of power allocations between Moldova and

Trans-Dniester and the salience of ethnic anxieties contributed to the reoccurrence and reproduction of legitimacy crises at each stage of socio-political transformation.

(2) Each new legitimacy crisis was more acute than the previous one, resulting in an ever-increasing scale of ethno-political violence. The overall pattern passed from the small-scale sporadic violence of single violent clashes between government agents and rebel civilians to large-scale organized and sustained warfare.

(3) Each new stage of socio-political transformation, with old patterns of ethno-political arrangements being broken and new issues arising, encouraged the growth of group organization and militant, politicized ethnic assertiveness. This is turn raised the level of political ethnic mobilization.

Acronyms and abbreviations

ASSR	Autonomous Soviet Socialist Republic
CDPF	Christian Democratic Popular Front
GASSR	Gagauz Autonomous Soviet Socialist Republic
GPF	Gagauz Popular Front
GSSR	Gagauz Soviet Socialist Republic
IM	Internationalist Movement
MASSR	Moldavian Autonomous Soviet Socialist Republic
MPF	Moldovan Popular Front
MSSR	Moldavian Soviet Socialist Republic
OPON	special police detachments created by Moldovan government
PASSR	Trans-Dniester Autonomous Soviet Socialist Republic
PMSSR	Trans-Dniester Moldavian Soviet Socialist Republic
SSR	Soviet Socialist Republic

IZ	*Izvestiya* (USSR Supreme Soviet newspaper).
KU	*Kuranty*
MS	*Moldova Suverana*
NG	*Nezavisimaya Gazeta* (Independent Newspaper)
NM	*Nezavisimaya Moldova* (Independent Moldova)
RG	*Rossiiskaya Gazeta*
SM	*Sovetskaya Moldavia* (Soviet Moldavia)
ST	*Sfatulo Tserij* (Weekly paper published by the Moldovan parliament)

References

Dialog (Tyraspol local newspaper), nos. 19, 20, 21, 1990.

Horowitz, D. 1985. *Ethnic Groups in Conflict*. Berkeley: University of California Press.

Rothschild, J. 1981. *Ethnopolitics: A Conceptual Framework*. New York: Columbia University Press.

Shibutani, T., and K.M. Kwan. 1965. *Ethnic Stratification: A Comparative Approach*. New York: Macmillan.

Tilly, C. 1978. *From Mobilization to Revolution*. Reading, Mass.: Addison-Wesley.

Tilly C., L. Tilly, and R.T. Tilly. 1975. *The Rebellious Century: 1830–1930*. Cambridge, Mass.: Harvard University Press.

6

Ethnic conflict in the Osh region in summer 1990: Reasons and lessons

Abilabek Asankanov

The territories of the former Soviet Union have experienced several inter-ethnic conflicts, particularly in Sumgait, Fergana, Noviy Uzgen (Kazakhstan), and Tuva. The bloody war in Nagorno-Karabakh is still going on. Here, I shall focus on the Osh conflict in the summer of 1990, which involved the large Kyrgyz and Uzbek ethnic groups of Central Asia. This conflict shares several common features with conflicts elsewhere, but differs also. Furthermore, as elsewhere, in this "Turkic self-genocide" the ethno-territorial interests of the people were aroused. This tragedy was prompted by the difficult socio-economic conditions and under-utilized labour resources in the region. The conflict is also connected with the struggle for access to power. A certain part of the population was seeking power and "greater liberty."

As we shall see below, this conflict was characterized by the cruel forms which it took: murder, rape, arson, and massacre. This report is based on statistical material, periodicals, research, observations, and analysis of our own sociological observations. Nearly 2,000 people – Kyrgyz, Uzbek, and Russian – of the towns Osh, Uzgen, Jalal-Abad, and Kara-Suu, where the tragic events happened, were interviewed in a survey carried out in May 1992.

The population of the Osh region of Kyrgyzstan is composed of Kyrgyz people (54.6%), Uzbeks (27.1%), Russians (about 10%), Tajiks (1.5%), Ukrainians (1.3%), and many others.[1] The polyethnic population has increased through immigration from other republics, particularly neighbouring Uzbekistan, at the expense of natural increase in the native population.

In Uzgen, the main conflict took place on 5–7 June 1990, with sporadic outbursts of criminality on other days as well. Both sides committed arson, killed horses, and plundered shops and offices. They were armed with small-bore guns, pistols, sticks, and rods. Murders in Uzgen, Osh, and other regions were committed by strangulation with wire or rope; torture and beating; assault and battery using axes, stones, and other hard objects; and guns. There were cases when the victim was burnt, to make identification impossible. Rape was characteristic of both sides, as were various forms of humiliation and torture, such as parading women naked in the street.

It is still early to draw any final conclusions as to the results and lessons of these bloody events. We may only sum up the number of victims and the material damage caused to the inhabitants of the region and the state, and venture some preliminary remarks. During this "self-genocide," according to official data, more than 300 people were killed, including about two dozen people who could not be identified. Three dozen disappeared. The material damage, according to preliminary data, runs to about 100 million roubles.

A number of different economic, social, and political factors can be adduced as reasons for the ethnic conflict in the Osh region. In economic terms, Kyrgyzstan had been developing one-sidedly, serving as a source of raw materials for industrially developed regions of the Soviet Union. In the region, industry developed at a slower pace in small towns where the mining and processing branches of industry were predominantly under Union control. The population had been mainly engaged in agriculture with its hard manual labour, cultivating tobacco and cotton and breeding sheep and cattle. By the late 1980s, the Soviet Federation of Trade Unions calculated that more than 80 per cent of the population had incomes lower than the living wage and were on the verge of poverty.[2]

The Osh region, where over half of the population of the republic lives, has been lagging behind the average level for the republic in most respects. Among those interviewed, 57 per cent pointed to the backwardness of the economy in the region, low wages, and low living standards as the main causes of the tragic events in Osh. All those interviewed, whether Kyrgyz, Uzbeks, or Russians, mentioned these as the main causes of this Turkic "self-annihilation." To be more precise, 51.9 per cent of the Kyrgyz respondents identified these as the main causes, as did 57.3 per cent of the Uzbeks and 75.1 per cent of the Russians.

The existing economic structure, weak socio-cultural structures, and a high birth rate among the native population, led to a situation in which nearly 150,000 people in the republic (or every sixth inhabitant) were engaged in industry, of whom three-quarters were young people.[3] This social group is the main destabilizing force in the republic. The bulk of the crowds committing excesses were youths. Thus, 78.7 per cent of those interviewed said that young men aged 20–29 took the most active part in the conflict. This was also confirmed by the militia.

The advent of a market economy undoubtedly brings unemployment, especially among young men. This could significantly aggravate the situation in the future. The population of the Osh region is expected to number three million in 18–20 years, making Osh, especially the areas near the Fergana Valley, the most densely populated area not only in the republic and in Central Asia, but in the former Soviet Union. The population is by and large concentrated in the plains – conveniently for agriculture and industry – in areas near the Fergana Valley in the south of Kyrgyzstan. Here, the density of the population requires changes in the economic structure. The republic needs to build plants and factories to process raw materials.

Mobility among the native population is relatively low. The policy guidelines that dictate that all school graduates are required to work on the farms are ill-suited. Such a call leads in some places to a surplus of labour resources, thus complicating the situation. It is necessary to enrol village women, especially young women, to work in industry and to stimulate their involvement in society.

The housing problem became one of the most important factors in the tragic events in Osh. Statistically, 47 per cent of the Kyrgyz, 49 per cent of the Russians, and 48.3 per cent of the Uzbeks surveyed thought that one of the main causes of the tragedy was the housing shortage. In Osh region nearly 60,000 families, or every sixth family, was on the waiting list for housing.[4] In ethnic terms, the bulk of these still waiting were young native men. For years they have been waiting for dwellings and plots of land, while living in hostels. Among their actions, they formed the informal organization Osh Aimagi.

It was a criminal error for the authorities to give plots of land for housing on the *kolkhoz* (collective farm) named after Lenin, without the prior consent of its leaders. The bulk of the population in this district is Uzbek. The situation changed radically after opposition to this move developed into inter-ethnic conflict.

One of the causes of the 1990 tragedy was the collusion of the *nomenklatura*, the militia, and the business sector, who forgot about the elementary social conditions of workers and thought only of personal gain. As President Akaev put it, in the South social and property differentiation was taking place between poor and rich, those who had power and those who did not. When the situation erupted into violence, the corrupt leaders had no control.[5] Indeed, they themselves brought on the conflict. Of those interviewed, 43.7 per cent said that the mafia's activity was one of the main reasons for the Osh tragedy (by "mafia" we mean the criminal collusion of business people and the authorities of the district, the city, and the regions.

This problem is closely connected with that of training of national cadres. Especially during the post-war period, it was thought in the former Soviet Union that a precondition for a correct national policy was the training and representation in the organs of power of all the ethnic groups living in the country or in the republic. This was often done to the detriment of the professions, business, and other sectors. It was assumed that any excessive clustering of representatives of one ethnic group in a particular sphere of public life or power would cause discontent among another ethnic group.

In 1990, Kyrgyz constituted 66.6 per cent in the executive committee of the Osh Regional Soviet of People's Deputies, Russians 13.7 per cent, and Uzbeks 5.8 per cent.[6] At the same time, however, Uzbeks constituted 71.4 per cent of all those working in the trade system of Osh. These disproportions were also characteristic of the militia. Ethnic disproportion in the training of cadres caused discontent among Kyrgyz and Uzbeks alike.

At the same time, these people, working in the service sector *nomenklatura*, lived in peace and friendship for a long time. Uzbeks in the service sector fed and served the party workers, the workers of Soviets, and militia workers "at the highest level." The latter provided the workers in the trade sector with sucess in collecting their capital. Such "mutual aid" among the corrupt upper strata of a region, a city, the militia, and in the service sector guaranteed a smooth social and inter-ethnic façade for a long time.

But this could not go on forever. At the same time the majority of the population – Kyrgyz and Uzbeks – was living in misery and poverty. With greater democratization of the society, activity among the people was growing. People with "trade capital" who had amassed fortunes lacked only power and independence. To gain these, they raised the question of "Uzbek" autonomy within Osh region. They were the inspirers in 1989 of the Adalat Union, consisting of nationalistic Uzbeks, including those favouring separation.

These events coincided with the removal of the Osh Regional Executive Committee leaders. The new leadership began by dismissing Kyrgyz with close ties to the regional commercial mafia, thus causing discontent among the latter. Removed from power, the representatives of the mafia turned to the people for support, inflaming nationalist and separatist sentiments. More than one-third of those interviewed stressed that one of the causes of the Osh tragedy were mistakes in the selection of the cadres.

For the future, the authorities should try to use the existing structures to serve the interests of the people, instead of destroying or dismantling them. Time is needed for the transition of people from one historical occupation to another. Excessive "percentomania" in the placing of national cadres in the public structures of power, without taking into account their professional qualities, damages the national economy. It is necessary to rise above the difficulties of narrow national psychology and interests. However, some local authorities have taken the wrong path in the forming of cadres. Thus, in the Kara-Suu district, after the tragic events, the authorities began mechanically changing the national composition of the militia, recruiting young Uzbeks without paying any attention to their moral, political, or physical training. Although young Uzbeks were reluctant to work in the militia, the local authorities promised them all kinds of possible and impossible social guarantees in order to bring the ethnic composition of militia into conformity with the ethnic structure of the district.

The socio-cultural aspects of the Osh region are weakly developed, compared to other regions of the republic. Strictly speaking, there is no effective system of medical care in the South. Kyrgyzstan ranks lowest among the former Soviet republics in the number of its doctors. As a result, infant mortality is very high in the Osh region; in fact, it is the highest in the republic.

The republic, especially the rural areas of the Osh region, needs far more educational and cultural institutions. For example, only 25 per cent of children in the Osh region attend kindergarten; in the rural areas only 16 per cent.[7] The number of schools constitutes only 65 per cent of what is actually needed. Furthermore, the south of Kyrgyzstan lags far behind the rest of the republic in the number of cinemas, clubs, theatres, museums, and libraries. As for everyday repairs and other services, the Osh region ranks lowest in the republic. Every second respondent expressed dissatisfaction with the work of the service institutions. All these factors lead to social tension and discontent among the population.

National concord depends by and large on the culture of relations among nations and groups. Inter-ethnic conflicts usually take place when general culture is low, and the traditions, interests, languages, and customs of some nations are neglected in favour of others. Thus, 20.7 per cent of respondents said that the cause of the tragedy was the low cultural level of the population: 16.3 per cent of Kyrgyz and 20.1 per cent of Uzbeks mentioned the low cultural level as the cause of the inter-ethnic conflict, whereas 40.3 per cent of the Russian respondents pointed to this factor.

From the middle to the late 1980s, there was considerable growth in political activity and national self-consciousness among all the peoples of Kyrgyzstan, and indeed the whole Union. A gradual liberation from totalitarianism in the republic, as elsewhere in the former Soviet Union, was marked by the active growth of informal public unions: national movements, national and cultural centres, associations, societies, and the like. The "National Democratic Front of Kyrgyzstan," consisting of Kyrgyz, and Adalat, consisting exclusively of Uzbeks, appeared in the Osh region in 1989. Later, Osh Aimagi, which was exclusively Kyrgyz, emerged. In these two informal groups, nationalistic Osh Aimagi and separatist Adalat objectives took shape.

Osh Aimagi undertook mainly the social tasks, such as getting plots of land for individual housing for the Kyrgyz. It demanded the territory of the Lenin *kolkhoz* of the Kara-Suu district, planning to create a Kyrgyz village there. In this *kolkhoz*, however, the bulk of the population was Uzbek. Discontent among the *kolkhoz* inhabitants swiftly became inter-ethnic opposition.

Representatives of the Adalat group submitted 20 claims, including Uzbek autonomy in the Osh region and recognition of the Uzbek language. More than one-third (35 per cent) of the Kyrgyz respondents considered the Uzbek aspiration for autonomy in the Osh region to be the cause of the Osh conflict.

In fact, such demands for autonomy were raised not only by separatist groups like Adalat. In the late 1980s the awakening of the national consciousness was characteristic of the greater part of the Uzbek population in the Osh region. The idea of national separatism also was typical of educated, well-to-do Uzbeks in high posts and Uzbek *aksakals* (elders), who were held in high respect. They were the inspirers and sponsors of Adalat, but at the same time they preferred to keep in the background, as we will see below. In March 1990, a petition signed by 23 Uzbek inhabitants of Jalal-Abad town – including 16 communists, two Heroes of Socialist Labour, and one Hero of the Soviet Union – was sent to the Supreme Soviets of the USSR and of the Kyrgyz SSR, where the creation of the autonomous republic was declared.[8] Such declarations also appeared in Uzbekistan, for example in the Tashkent Institute of Microbiology.

These claims put forward by various leaders of the informal unions became a principal cause of the Osh tragedy. If only the regional party committee, the regional executive committee, and the leaders of the Central Committee of the republic had acted more resolutely, this tragedy could have been prevented. The party leaders in the republic and in the Osh region did not change their approach, nor display any resourcefulness in this matter, but worked in an old command-administrative style. They either prohibited informal movements or gave them free rein.

The confession of the leaders of the republic that they did little to keep ahead of events is really striking. The former First Secretary of the Kyrgyz Communist Party, the Chairman of the Supreme Soviet, A. Masaliev, admitted in an interview with *Pravda* that the conflict was quite unexpected.[9]

Sometimes criminal errors were committed. The decision of the leaders of the Osh region to allot fertile lands of the Lenin *kolkhoz* for housing for the Kyrgyz youth was one such blunder. This is reflected in the fact that 6.9 per cent of the Kyrgyz, 18.1 per cent of the Uzbeks, and 16.7 per cent of the Russian respondents said that the actions of the local authorities and the party organization caused the Osh conflict. Furthermore, 12.5 per cent of the Kyrgyz, 34.8 per cent of the Uzbeks, and 28.9 per cent of the Russians stressed that the conflict began with the allocation of plots of land for housing. According to 53.4 per cent of those interviewed, the local authorities knew about the coming conflict and failed to take adequate measures to prevent it. This was confirmed by the report of the head of the regional KGB, Colonel A. Mameev.[10]

Between January and June 1990 the leadership of the Osh region KGB delivered nine reports to the regional committee and to the regional executive committee about the potentially explosive situation between Kyrgyz and Uzbeks. These reports also contained concrete recommendations. But neither the reports nor the recommendations were given any serious attention.

The "rumour syndrome" played a major part in the inter-ethnic conflict. In answer to the question "What was the cause of the fight between Kyrgyz and Uzbeks?", 43.4 per cent of respondents said that it was the allocation of plots of land. However, 39.4 per cent of those interviewed answered that they began to fight after hearing that "our folk are being beaten and killed." But actually, there were no murders and conflicts in those places. Lack of objective information, weakly developed mass media, the low level of education among both Uzbeks and Kyrgyz, and the inexperience of the militia aggravated the situation.

The reports of the KGB pointed out the great role of trade and service workers in the inter-ethnic conflict. As mentioned above, the disproportions in the cadre arrangement and in trade and commerce were one cause of the tragedy. Of those interviewed 40.9 per cent said that trade and service workers were neutral in the conflict, 15.2 per cent thought that they were leaders and that they instigated the conflict, whereas 25.4 per cent answered that they only sponsored the actions.

Our ethno-sociological investigations confirmed the report of the KGB, according to which the opposing sides, especially Uzbeks, had long been preparing for this conflict. The Uzbeks had probably begun preparations in February 1990. Some of the Uzbek population in Osh began to drive out Kyrgyz tenants from their lodgings, prompted by the threats of Uzbek extremists to set fire to their houses if they did not expel their Kyrgyz tenants. The result was the appearance of some 1.5 thousand young Kyrgyz men in Osh who joined Osh Aimagi.

Of those interviewed, 63.9 per cent thought that the confrontations were premeditated, 24.6 per cent did not respond, and 8.7 per cent said that they did not think the violence was premeditated. More than a quarter of those interviewed answered that the Uzbeks had been preparing for the violence, 17.6 per cent that the Kyrgyz had been preparing, and 15.5 per cent that both sides had been doing so.

What was the attitude of other peoples toward this conflict? Besides Kyrgyz, Uzbeks, and Russians, there are Ukrainians, Tatars, Turks from Meskhetia, and others living in southern Kyrgyzstan. Of those surveyed, 59.6 per cent replied that other peoples were neutral observers and 21.3 per cent that they tried to conciliate two fraternal nations; only 2.4 per cent replied that the others sided with the Uzbeks, and 6.1 per cent that they took the Kyrgyz part.

To normalize the situation enormous forces were drawn in: the armed forces of the Soviet Army militia and KGB from other union republics. Three-quarters of those interviewed answered that the Soviet Army normalized the situation, 38.6 per cent that it was the militia that did so.

All are anxious about the problem of averting inter-ethnic conflicts in the future. Solutions to economic and social problems are also of interest to people. Nearly two-thirds (64%) of those interviewed answered the question "what measures should be taken to prevent national conflicts?" by saying that "it is necessary to improve living conditions"; then came such factors as "strengthening of friendship between nations" (48.7%), "the correct arrangement of cadres" (38.4%), and "improving the work of the militia" (38.6%).

For that reason, we may conclude that solving socio-economic problems will help bring about a normal state of inter-ethnic relations in the Republic of Kyrgyzstan.

Notes

1. Results of All-Union Census on the population, 1989 (*Naselenie SSSR: podannym vse-voiuznoi perepisi naseleniia, 1989*), Moscow, 1990.
2. *Sovetskaya Kirghizia*, 19 June 1991.
3. *Sovetskaya Kirghizia*, 15 January 1991.
4. *Sovetskaya Kirghizia*, 15 August 1990.
5. *Sovetskaya Kirghizia*, 15 January 1990.
6. *Sovetskaya Kirghizia*, 15 August 1990.
7. *Ala-too* (literature and feature magazine) no. 2, 1991.
8. *Pravda*, 25 September 1990.
9. *Sovetskaya Kirghizia*, 23 September 1990.
10. *Kaplya-Express*, supplement to *Literaturnyi Kyrgyzstan* no. 1, October 1990.

7

From centre–periphery conflict to the making of new nationality policy in an independent state: Estonia

Klara Hallik

Having been subjugated by strong neighbouring countries, Estonia has had the status of being a borderland to others. At one time it was the easternmost province of an empire: at another time, the westernmost. In both cases Estonia was a peripheral entity whose existence depended on powerful centres beyond its own borders. During the eighteenth and nineteenth centuries, Estonia was in fact a double borderland. In religion and culture it was dominated by German culture as a Baltic-German subculture. Administratively and politically it was dominated by Russia. During the final decades of the nineteenth century, Russia started tying Estonia to the empire also through its policy of flagrant "Russification." This was pursued even more vigorously after the incorporation of Estonia into the Soviet Union.

There was, however, one exception: the short period of Estonia's national independence (1919–1940). That period saw the reorganization of Estonian society, during which time Estonia's own administrative, political, economic, and intellectual centres were developed. The principle of the nationalist movement, "Let's stay Estonians, but become Europeans," was the dominant idea of Estonia's cultural policy during this period. A main thrust of the cultural and educational policy was aimed at liberation from the overbearing influence of German and Russian cultures. There was a notable approach to the Scandinavian countries and cultural centres recognized by Europe. The international ties of ethnic culture proceeded from the inner needs of Estonian development, including a need to withstand "foreign" cultures. This major change in cultural orientation stopped resettlement and put an end to the provincial status of Estonia's young ethnic culture.

Possessed of an independent ethnic culture system, Estonia was then able to preserve its cultural identity even under the later pressure of Sovietization. Looking at the broader implications of the Estonian experience, it is worth noting that during the 1920s and 1930s Estonia became a part of a multi-centred Europe, and this favoured the preservation of its own identity. As today's united Europe remains culturally and intellectually multifarious, the example of Estonia suggests that other small nations may also be able to find an equal place there. There is also a reverse argument: as economic and political integration standardizes cultures, it is primarily the small post-socialist nations who will fall into Europe's cultural periphery.

This article deals with ethnic relations in the Estonian republic during the period of Soviet rule as well as when it gained its independence. It also takes up questions of ethnic relations and conflicts.

From country to borderland, from nation to minority

Taking into account international or even global tendencies of development, it may seem inappropriate to speak of a "nation-state" nowadays. The term has become an anachronism, an atavistic remnant of the last century, and a phenomenon of exaggerated ethnic narrowness. This criticism is definitely justifiable if a "nation-state" is considered to be an "ethnically pure" or one-nation country.

Methodologically, of course, we need to distinguish between specially systemized communities (the state as a system of political community).[1] As a rule, nation and state do not coincide empirically. But, no matter how big the multinational state is, the ethnic centre will still be formed by one group – the dominant nationality in number or in strength. With independent statehood, nationalities have been able to develop multifunctional socio-cultural systems to guarantee their stability, their ability to adapt to changing circumstances and inter-

126

national impulses of development. In contrast, ethnic groups that lack a state-oriented organization have often become "building material" for the multinational state, frequently leaving no visible traces in the culture of big nations. In this sense, all European state entities can be typified as nation-builders. The fact that they are not ethnically "pure" does not lessen the share of the state in the consolidation of an ethnic sense. Empires never managed to create a single nation state with a single religion, language, and mentality. At first glance, it seems that the cause lies in an immanent undemocracy, because a "democratic empire" is a contradiction in terms.

Experience to date, including that of the Soviet Union, indicates that a new democracy may be achieved in relations among nationalities through the state or statelike institutionalization of ethnic life. That is especially the case if ethnic separatism is also influenced by specific cultural differences: regional underdevelopment; ethnic history; competition among social groups (particularly the intelligentsia); and an ethnically discriminatory policy.[2] Such factors force nationalities out of larger multi-ethnic communities, as has been pointed out by Anthony D. Smith.[3] Here, we may note a vigorous nationality's structural and institutional incompleteness, which unavoidably leads to national separation in the creation of structural integrity.

Turning to Western culture, we must presume that Western democracy can, in the process of integration, create relationships and institutions which allow limitless freedom of development to local cultures and ways of life. This idea was not unknown among various Estonian-born scholars in the West, who thought it possible to guarantee the existence of nationality by primarily changing the character of relations with the central government of the Soviet Union. To quote Hain Rebas: "More important than gaining statehood is getting free from colonial exploitation ..."[4] Tõnu Parming has expressed a similar attitude in stating: "In principle there is no reason why the Estonian nation could not live in the Soviet Union, or in some other federal state. But only if it is not accompanied by danger to the endurance and development of the national identity ... A nation state, the other extreme, often leads to the stagnation of identity."[5]

Such a version of development may seem difficult to accept at first, not least for the Baltic nations, burdened by a different experience. The abolition of their national independence endangered the very existence of their nationality. The Soviet government started eliminating the country by breaking up the integral structures of local societies. In the course of a few months after annexation, the Soviet authorities got rid of the local army and the elected organs of local authorities were dismissed and replaced by officials appointed by the new regime. The legitimacy of statehood and local government ceased to exist with the abolition of the legal order of the Estonian Republic and the enforcement of the Russian Federation's code of law in September 1940.[6] The enforcement of the laws of the Soviet Union (actually Russia) upon a sovereign Soviet Republic destroyed the last vestiges of Estonia's statehood, its distinct citizenship, and control over its territory and its foreign relations.

Pre-Soviet Estonian society had an admittedly brief experience of national and political democracy. But this was largely compensated by a well-developed, many-faceted civil society which played a leading role in the nation's self-organization from the 1860s onwards. Many-sided economic relations between producers and consumers, culture, educational and religious clubs – all this formed a stable foundation which protected society from the shake-up of the political power of the young republic. In 1940, everything was shut down. Almost 16,000 clubs and organizations were subordinated to the Communist Party and the new government.

The break-up of civil society in Estonia broke the intranational connections and interrupted the organic social process of reproduction of nationality. Traditional social structures were replaced by a rigid state-oriented structure, which was given the task of interpreting the superior authorities' directives and guaranteeing their implementation.

To enable the centre's influence to reach as far "downward" as possible, Estonia's traditional territorial-administrative divisions were abolished, while the number of administrative units was increased threefold and that of the first rank (parishes) two and a half times.[7] In pre-Soviet Estonia, local authority, national culture, and sports had been based on the support of voluntary cooperation, a very strong factor of national identity. Its positive and constructive role was clearly perceptible and understandable in forms which appealed to individual involvement. State control, regulated from the centre of an alien culture, killed off public life for a long time and led to alienation from broader social objectives. Only in the late 1950s, when the danger of direct repression came to an end, did the traditional substratum of Estonia's cultural life gradually start to reawaken from totally state-oriented forms of life.

Since, in the situation of international crisis in the 1940s, the Soviet Union's occupation of the Baltic countries did not provoke any demands for explanations or sanctions, it could start "rewriting" history without any hindrance. This touched the whole cultural heritage of the nation. Written documents were mercilessly destroyed. For example, out of the books that had appeared in Estonia from 1918 to 1940, ten thousand publications, plus five thousand issues of magazines and newspapers, were removed from public libraries and mostly destroyed.[8] The history of the Estonian nation was henceforth to reflect only the empire's history. The 1918–1920 war of independence (in which every tenth Estonian carried a weapon) was degraded to the status of a civil war and Estonia's 20 years of independence were depicted as a period of socio-economic deterioration, ceaseless class struggle, and political dictatorship. A thorough revision also befell the earlier history of the Estonian nation, which attributed a certain messianic role to the Russian empire. Identifying the Russian conquest with the ancient lands of the Russian nation is among the most consistently used Soviet myths, kept alive by official ideology and propaganda till the last moment.

With this kind of geopolitical thinking, there could be no acceptance of the independence of nations which had been under the control of the empire, but only the established status of borderland. The abolition of Estonia's national independence for almost half a century changed the place of Estonians in the surrounding ethno-cultural area. The year 1940 saw the severance of cultural communication with the Europe toward which the young professional culture had become oriented and under whose influence it had modernized. Those of the intelligentsia who did not manage to emigrate in 1944 became victims of repression.

Estonia was transformed into a periphery of Soviet Russian-centred cultural hierarchy. One vivid example in this case is the "geography" of translated books. Of the books printed in Estonia from 1945 to 1955, translations from Russian made up over 94 per cent, with works from other languages (not Soviet nations) accounting for only 3.6 per cent. From 1945 to 1985 over 80 per cent of translated books printed were Russian.[9] A similar development affected mass communication; the repertory of theatres and hobby clubs was Russian-directed as well. Thus, the Estonian ethno-cultural system lost its natural mechanisms of associating with other cultured nations and was instead forced to accept the transplantation of the elements of another culture system.

Estonia's fall into subordination to the most centralized great power was accompanied by a major demographic denationalization.

Ethnic composition of population in Estonia

Nationality	1959	1989	% of total population 1959	% of total population 1989	Rate of growth 1959–1989 (%)
Estonians	892,653	963,269	74.6	61.5	7.9
Russians	240,227	474,815	20.1	30.3	97.6
Finns	16,699	16,622	1.4	1.1	−0.5
Ukrainians	15,769	47,273	1.3	3.0	199.8
Belarusians	10,930	27,711	0.9	1.3	153.5
Jews	5,436	4,613	0.45	0.3	−15.1
Latvians	2,888	3,135	0.24	0.2	8.5
Poles	2,256	3,008	0.18	0.2	33.3
Lithuanians	1,616	2,568	0.13	0.16	58.9
Tatars	1,535	4,058	0.13	0.26	164.4
Germans	670	3,466	0.0	0.2	417.3
Others	6,112	15,124	0.56	0.96	147.4
Total	1,196,791	1,565,662	100.00	100.00	30.8

Sources: *Itogi fsesojuznoi perepisi nacelenja SSSR 1959 goda. Estonskaya SSR.* p. 94; *The Population of the Counties, Cities, and Market Towns of the Republic of Estonia.* 1: *Collection of Statistics* (ESA, Tallinn, 1990), p. 32.

During the last century, Estonia had traditionally about one million inhabitants. In 1939, 83.2 per cent of these were Estonians. Naturally, this number of inhabitants has influenced the balance of social and natural environment, the ways of communication between individuals, and their adaptation to one another. In 1945 there began a period of unprecedented colonization, which led to fundamental changes in the ethnic situation in Estonia. Suddenly, Estonia was inhabited by a large group of people who knew nothing about the indigenous people, their history, or their culture. Especially when we recall the fact that in the 1940s and 1950s, more than 40,000 people were deported from Estonia,[10] while the immigrant flow from the Soviet Union was as much as 200,000 (1945–1958),[11] the colonist character of such a population turnover is incontestable. In the course of 45 years of Soviet rule, the relative proportions of native Estonians to newcomers fell from 97.3 per cent to 61.5 per cent.

With the annexation of land for the establishment of Soviet military bases in Estonian military areas, the native inhabitants began leaving. For nearly half a century, much of the Baltic coastline and the islands were off limits to civilian inhabitants, or a so-called permit into a border zone was required. Denial of access to the sea and the ban on fishing meant the death of the centuries-old coastal culture and way of life, which had been a factor in the traditional "horizontal" ties between the different parts of the nation's territory and the units of local subcultures.

Nowadays, immigrants of other nationalities inhabit strategically important areas. Half of them are centred in and around the capital; over one-third are in the metropolitan area of north-east Estonia; while in the "border towns" of Narva and Sillamae (in several workers' settlements there, as in the town of Paldiski) practically no Estonian population has remained.[12] The result is that three-quarters of the non-Estonian population are concentrated in towns, where they make up an ethnic majority. This fairly compact alien enclave has pressed the Estonian republic's little settled area between "palisades" and forced it to draw closer to regions bordering Russia and away from the western border, away from areas rich in natural resources and important centres of communication.

Research still in progress may indicate whether this breakup of the ethnic territory of Estonia was in line with the conscious aims of the Union centre's policy. But surely it is not coincidental that the biggest concentration of immigrants was in places forcibly occupied by the Soviet military as demanded in the ultimata of 27 September 1939 and 16 June 1940.[13] The units of the Soviet army in Estonia have methodically adopted the civil structures of alien inhabitants, in some cases organically uniting into closed micro-societies.

No matter what the pragmatic aims of the Soviet Union's central powers were – directing the inhabitants of other Soviet republics into Estonia or favouring migration – the result was typical settlement-colonization. Foreign immigration supplemented the urban population (and over 90 per cent of the immigrants are townspeople). Almost three-quarters of the aliens live in either multifunctional or industrial towns with more developed urban facilities, for these towns have enjoyed priority in social policy. By contrast, almost 40 per cent of Estonian town-dwellers live in small towns with relatively limited functions. The heavy concentration of non-Estonians has meant a fundamental change in the ethnic mosaic of cities. As a result, over half of the townspeople of Estonian nationality became a minority in their own areas.[14]

Estonia has actually never been closed to other nations, not even while under Soviet rule. Its geographical position kept Estonians in the stream of development of the neighbouring nations – whether voluntarily or forcibly. But the events from 1940 onwards marked such an abrupt turning point, indeed a return to pre-civilization, that overcoming their consequences is tantamount to establishing a new society.

An ethnically divided society

In stable industrial societies, class integration should dominate ethnic integration. But, as has been noticed in countries with active immigration, the boundaries between ethnic and social differentiation very often coincide, especially with the first generations of migrants. Estonia's employment system bears the clear stamp of ethnic differentiation. The main reason is typically Soviet: namely, the subordination of nearly 90 per cent of the industrial economy to an all-Union department. Even though Estonia does not have industrial raw materials and has scant labour reserves, several labour- and material-intensive enterprises were constructed. From the beginning, the authorities planned for the use of foreign labour.

Within the Soviet Union there was a general practice of dispersing millions of people from different groups among different regions. Ethnic variegation of labour groups was seen as a measure for internationalism and friendship among nations. For Estonia, however, this policy conclusively destroyed the country's ethnic balance and created the economic basis for colonization. This is not to deny the importance of an industrial economy for the socio-economic development of Estonia. However, we need to point out the very contradictory consequences which Soviet industrialization has had in the social and ethnic spheres. In a rational economic system, capital is seen to move to areas of relatively lower-level development, where opportunities for growth are greater. This has been the case in the capitalist countries of Europe, where, in some instances, uneven technological progress has been compensated for by capital flows to less developed regions. This has a tendency to increase development in less-developed regions and to speed up the growth of new technologies and of a highly qualified labour force.

In the Soviet Union, these processes were very often the opposite. From more developed regions in Russia, economic sectors were relocated into the periphery, while retaining their administrative adherence to all-Union departments. Once in place, these units became alternative social structures and "pumps" drawing in constant migration. At the same time, in Central Asia, Moldova, and Kazakhstan, this kind of cultural division of labour acquired a hierarchical – and in the Baltics, at first, "segmental" – character. Estonian society was able to withstand this structural expansion for 10 to 15 years, but not after the abolition of the Councils of National Economy in 1965 and after the polarization of employment among groups of nationalities became more pronounced. Thus, by 1988, the share of Estonians in industry had fallen to 40–42 per cent (in 1948, it had been 69 per cent), railway transport to 20 per cent, shipbuilding to 0.12 per cent. However, in agriculture, culture and the arts, the percentage of Estonians was 85 per cent, and in state leadership over 70 per cent.[15]

In principle, such a distribution of labour among nationalities does not necessarily represent a source of conflict. That, however, presupposes that the economy constitutes an integral entity situated in one territory, with all the enterprises performing according to uniform rules of management. In Estonia the situation was different. The segmental division of labour grew into a hierarchical division of labour between two language groups because of the preferences exercised by all-Union enterprises, especially in the military-industrial sector. Incidentally, between 1945 and 1985, capital investments in Estonia of industrial plants closed to the public made up nearly 40 per cent of the basic investment in enterprises under the jurisdiction of the central authorities. Large-scale enterprises engaged in the defence industry have for decades been such collectives, where Estonians are either totally absent or their share is infinitesimal. These are branches of the economy requiring relatively high craftsmanship, where, in general, a greater number of engineers, technicians, and professionally educated workers are employed than the average in civilian industry.

The drop in the number of Estonian nationals in main branches of industry was caused by the imbalance of economic life as a whole, as well as its isolation from local sources of labour. Also relevant were the adaptational difficulties Estonians experienced in labour collectives with heterogeneous cultural and communication structures. Labour was recruited throughout the Soviet Union. As a consequence, the near-total ex-territoriality of the central departments brought about a situation where even some specialists of trades and professions taught in Estonia were recruited from outside Estonia under the central scheme of distribution of cadres from the other Soviet republics.

Furthermore, Soviet ideology promoted the preferential development of basic branches of industry. Industrial workers and particularly workers in large-scale industry and industry of basic branches were granted, a priori, the role of bearers of the main political values of socialism. This was reflected in the streamlining of the composition of the Communist Party, which was carried out up to the quite recent past. Thus, the workers at such enterprises became representatives of public interests, and people were under the tutelage of the state and the central power. All this meant that the ethnic communities in Estonia occupied different places in the social system; hence, the difficulties now involved in consolidating ethnic groups and achieving a rapprochement of interests on the basis of an Estonian-centred concept of further development.

The language issue

The national language has been of great importance for Estonian society. Historically, this derives from the fact that for centuries Estonians were disenfranchised, both economically and politically. To Estonians, the preservation of their own language and national culture has meant the preservation of the viability of the people. This awareness accounts for the rapid rise of national culture and the heightened cultural activity in the 1920s and 1930s. During the Soviet era also, regardless of the changes in the content of culture, the national tongue of that culture generally persisted.

This situation started to change in the late 1970s and early 1980s, when official schemes for the forced development of Estonian-Russian bilingualism threatened the integrity of the national tongue. The resolution of the Communist Party of Estonia Central Committee dated 19 December 1978, in reaction to the all-Union regulations "On further improvement of mastering and teaching Russian," became pivotal for local language policy in Estonia. This not only planned an improvement in Russian language instruction but also envisaged extensive measures to promote the propagation of Estonian culture. As a corollary to its move to spread the Russian tongue, the central government issued a decree raising the salaries of Russian instructors, as well as the grants offered to students of Russian philology.

All these developments took place in a situation where the official language policy of the Soviet Union and the ideological conditioning of the people were unambiguously oriented towards Russian-ethnic bilingualism, with the unlimited privileged expansion of the functions of Russian. Command of foreign languages has always been held in great esteem in the Estonian cultural tradition as an indicator of a high level of general culture and a necessary business asset. However, the over-politicized and ideologized propaganda of Russian, aggravated by administrative excesses, created widespread antagonism. The campaign was seen as a step back to the worst Russification practices of the Tsarist regime. Indeed, these fears were justified, because there had already been such a differentiation of the functions of the Estonian and Russian languages that the Estonian language had been relegated to a position of secondary importance. At a certain level of one's career it was essential to master Russian, whereas the ability to speak Estonian was not required. As a result of territorial localization, the Estonian and Russian languages were in different situations in the urban areas and in the countryside, compared to 100–150 years ago. Finally, these languages had become quite different in functional terms. Science, much official management and documentation, and the railway, trade, medical, and communication services used mainly Russian. The Estonian language started to recede into the sphere of traditional ethno-cultural usage and everyday life. This discrimination against Estonian is the main reason why Russians and other nationalities who had migrated have not picked up the local language. Second-rate and doomed to perish gradually, Estonian was not prestigious in either Russian schools or in the Russian community as a whole.

The situation of languages in Estonia today is anything but satisfactory. According to statistics gathered in the 1989 referendum, the Estonian language is spoken by 67.1 per cent of the whole population, but the share of those who have mastered the language shows a tendency towards a constant decline (72.8 per cent in 1970, 69.4 per cent in 1979, 61 per cent in 1989). Finnish immigrants have integrated with the Estonians most of all (33 per cent speak the language), then Jewish and Gypsy immigrants (26 per cent). Among Latvians and Hungarians, one-fifth state that they speak the language. The majority of the members of the small groups of nationalities have acquired Russian. There are, in fact, two rival languages in Estonia's language system, while the integrating force in alien-tongued groups is nearly three times stronger than that of Estonian.[16]

The dominant position of Russian throughout the Soviet Union as the so-called language for communication between nationalities was established in every republic and even in private communication. Only 13.7 per cent of the Russians who live in Estonia have mastered Estonian. This situation is changing very slowly because of the difficulties in learning and teaching, as well as negative attitudes. For decades, people had been used to the complacency of Estonians regarding their own language. The language barrier was always crossed from the Estonian side.

Estonia was the first of the then Soviet republics to enforce a language act and give the native language the status of an official language. That step was conditioned by the necessity of protecting the national language. But attempts to reinstate the Estonian language strained relations among the various nationalities, leading to an unprecedented campaign in the Soviet press. After Estonia's independence, one of the most complicated problems in regulating language relations has been how to start "joining" the divided halves of society. Without this, it will be difficult to stabilize society and democratize state powers. "A society divided into two hostile classes is presumably ripe for a revolution, but a society divided into two hostile status groups – nations, for example – is threatened by secession."[17]

Who has been the minority since August 1991?

Estonian society is leaving behind a situation in which Estonians were a minority of a great power without the legal protection afforded minorities in contemporary Europe. It is interesting to note that until recently, nations have competed with other nations for dominance or at least equality of status, whereas today the number of pretenders to the position of "minority" has increased suddenly. This indicates that the immanent qualities of *all* groups of peoples and the pluralism of culture are finding increasing acceptance. However, translating this phenomenon into the language of laws and standards demands more precise formulation – and this is no simple task, as is shown by discussions on defining the term "minority" in the Commission on Human Rights' Sub-Commission on Prevention of Discrimination and Protection of Minorities.[18] For Estonia this problem is of great importance, since the condemnation of settlement colonization – the UN General Assembly resolution of 8 December 1987 – has not yet been enacted. The European Convention on Minority Rights (Article 1) has defined minorities as "any group in a numerical minority within the population of the given state that is not in a leading position, whose members differ from the rest of the population by their ethnic characteristics, and who demonstrate a sense of solidarity oriented towards preserving their own culture, traditions, and language."

As in all countries where there has been extensive immigration, in

Estonia it is important to distinguish between "settled" minorities and "recent immigrants" – especially since the republic had a chance to regulate immigration beginning on 1 July 1990. Another important factor needs consideration: in international practice migrant workers, refugees, non-nationals, and stateless persons do not belong to the category of minorities. But Estonia, like other former Soviet republics, lacked a legally-determined citizenry of its own. This explains many of the tensions between the two nationalities – Russian and Estonian – from the start of the movement of liberation in 1988.

The state of Estonia, having regained its independence, is only now starting to form its own citizenry according to the act of citizenship of the Estonian Republic of 1938, which was re-enacted on 26 February 1992. Only after determining a citizenry can one solve the problems of national minorities. On the psychological level, however, everything proves to be much more complicated.

Political developments during the past three years have increased the opposition of the two national-language communities, and that will have influence also in the near future. These clashes were generated by Estonian attempts to get rid of the status of a reigning minority in their own country, while on the other side much of the Russian-speaking community sought to maintain its position. The struggle against Estonia's regaining its independence was, in fact, directly led by the central power, especially the Communist Party of the Soviet Union. This is no longer secret. The sad part of it is that through advantage being taken of the uncertainty, through the prejudices characteristic of great powers, and simply through ignorance, many non-Estonian residents were drawn into action against Estonia. Here we should stress the dependence of the Russian labour force on the administration of the enterprises, because several all-Union enterprises were the last ones to be reached by democratization. Although the Communist Party lost its actual power over Estonia in 1989–1990, in the local all-Union units it remained valid until the August 1991 coup d'état.

The "monolithic behaviour" forced upon the Russian community and weak differentiation enabled all-Union-minded movements and Communist parties to speak demagogically in the name of the whole Russian population, the working class or the "minority." In formal terms, the counter-Estonian movement was organized as an alternative to the Estonian National Front's *perestroika*-minded programme, but in essence it revealed the strategy of the central power of the Soviet Union towards the Soviet Republics in the arena of political competition. Estonia's striving for sovereignty was publicly set against the non-Estonian population for the first time.

This was expressed very clearly in the documents of the International Movement of Estonia. In autumn 1988 came a re-organization of the Estonian Supreme Soviet into a bicameral system – a House of Representatives and a House of Nationalities, where the number of Estonians and aliens would be equal and where both houses would have a right to veto.[19] Parallel to the International Movement another movement emerged – a structure promoting all-Union interests. All-Union enterprises belonging to different authorities formed the Joint Council of Work Collectives of All-Union Enterprises in Estonia. Together with its declared economic tasks, this council started to play the role of a political organization right from the start. One of its demands was the creation of a two-chamber body for self-government – with deputies from enterprises forming a separate chamber with equal rights to a chamber chosen through territorial elections.

This was the first time in the history of Soviet Estonia that the all-Union industrial enterprises came openly into the political arena and exposed their political functions in the national republic. From then on, the all-Union enterprises were the ones that enacted new local laws and steps towards decreasing the power of the central authorities in Estonia. The so-called militarized brigades of workers operated under the aegis of the Joint Council.

Why were tensions in Estonia never accompanied by physical violence? Perhaps because, relying on the well-known forbearance of Estonians, people built their hopes on the idea that the experiences of Lithuania, Latvia, and Moldova would not be echoed in Estonia. The Estonian scenario seems to have provided mainly organizational forms of silencing. The preliminary work had been done in Tallinn's enterprises of citizen-insubordination campaigns, and the period saw the creation of the Deputies' Inter-regional Soviet for all levels. This Soviet declared on 14 September 1990: "Until the Union contract is concluded and ratified by the new constitution of the Soviet Union, the Inter-regional Soviet will not observe the legislative acts ratified by the Estonian Republic, which violates the constitution of the Soviet Union in force, and the UN's 1948 Universal Declaration of Human Rights."

On 7 September 1990, the Soviet claimed that the policy of the Estonian Republic's political leadership was aimed towards liquidating the socialist social order, workers' socialist achievements, and the political rights and freedoms of the citizens. Therefore, the Soviet proclaimed itself ready to perform the will of those inhabitants of Estonia who saw their future and that of their children in a socialist Estonia, sovereign and of equal rights, in a family of fraternal republics united into a new Union.[20] The alternative power founded in Estonia received unofficial recognition from the central authorities of the Soviet Union. This is evident in the fact that Soviet deputies took part in the all-Union sitting of the Deputies' Congress, as well as in the informal discussions that generally preceded the talks between the official delegations and experts of the Soviet Union and the Republic of Estonia (from autumn 1990 till July 1991). The important step of institutionalizing this alternative power was made at the 20th Congress of the Communist Party of Estonia, which had by then declared itself independent. This step also received acceptance from the Central Committee of the Communist Party of the Soviet Union, with the secretary being elected as a member of the Politburo of the Central Committee of the Communist Party of the Supreme Soviet.

These steps combined to provoke the mutual alienation of the Estonian and Russian communities within Estonia. However, the Estonian democratic movement for independence, including the National Front, could not unite the considerable number of democratic and Estonian-friendly non-Estonians. Thus, much of the Russian community in Estonia found itself aligned with those supporting the unitarian centre. It is worth noting that although 69 per cent of the "Estonian-minded" were born in Estonia (according to the census of 1989), only 37 per cent "identify themselves" with Estonia.[21] It is understandable, therefore, that the prospect of the breakup of the Soviet Union or the secession of Estonia increased uncertainty and solidarity with the central power. A public opinion poll taken in 1990 showed that only 16 per cent of non-Estonians supported complete national independence for Estonia. This proportion held good during the independence referendum on 3 March 1990, where only one-fifth voted in favour of re-establishing the national independence of Estonia. When we add to that the fact that in the Supreme Council of Estonia on 20 August 1991, all the deputies of the so-called Russian faction voted against national independence, the picture of the cleavage within Estonian society is clear.

Conclusion

Estonians have always realized more acutely than Russians the discord resulting from changes in the ethnic environment; but, in an undemocratic situation, this uncertainty was internalized. The Russian population neither heard nor realized Estonian national problems, nor comprehended their own interests on the ethnic level. This situation changed dramatically when the Estonians could start speaking publicly about national injustice, occupation, and their existential fears for the future. This national awakening took most Russian-speaking inhabitants of Estonia by surprise. They were shocked by the multiplicity of the problems that seemed to appear out of nowhere. The criticism of imperial abuse, demands to revive the historical truth, defence of the stability of Estonian society and Estonians – all these were first taken as something directed against non-Estonians.

The inter-ethnic relations of Estonia have now started to assume new qualitative features. The main shift can be accounted for by the fact that the Russian-speaking part of the Estonian population, first and foremost the Russians, has now begun to see its interests as related to a range of its national interests. In other words, the ideology of differentiation between Estonians and Russians has been transformed into a two-way nationalism.

In the shifts taking place in Estonian society in this sphere, there are many analogies to relations between Canada and Quebec. Let me draw on Raymond Breton's concept of two kinds of nationalism, in which he distinguishes between ethnic or ethno-cultural nationalism and civic nationalism.[22] The changes that have taken place in the development of Estonia's national ideology involve two phases. In the first phase, preceding the Estonian national liberation movement, Estonian nationalism had a strongly self-defensive character. This was induced by the exercise of alien authority by a great power, as well as the existential uncertainty caused by an unfavourable demographic situation. Since Estonian society and local authority lacked self-governing rights, the mechanisms which persisted in the Estonian national identity were forced into the ethno-cultural sphere. The leitmotif was to maintain the Estonian language and culture and to obtain strength from traditions. The tragedy that befell the nation favoured the preservation of a romantic image of the past. In contrast, Russian nationalism was state-centred (state nationalism) and valued the merits of being a great power, pragmatism and being future-oriented. In this concept, Russian culture and language lacked any special emotional potency. The notion of ideal national relations meant an internationalist and inclusive approach, which conflict with the Estonians' strong exclusive standpoint towards foreigners.

In the second phase, the ideology of both national-linguistic groups becomes more marginal. We may note that, psychologically, Estonians are having great difficulties in adapting positively to their refound legal status as a "majority." This orientation towards the past is even stronger because Estonian independence has been re-established, not proclaimed for the first time. Together with the re-establishment of the state, a process of restoration (renewing of pre-Soviet ownership, compensation for repression, the reinforcement of several laws, the revival of organizations and symbols, adaptation of exile culture, etc.), has partly begun. The presence of the Russian army, as well as the unchanging demographic situation, has kept alive the "state of defence." Ethnic exclusiveness is supported by the anti-Communism related to the restoration of ideology. That, in turn, excludes certain groups, and is not an integrating factor. Estonian society would appear to need time to rid itself of the ideology of the minority, so that it can move from ethnic nationalism towards civic nationalism and acceptance of a multi-cultural future.

Local state-centred nationalism has also lost its fulcra, and the changes taking place are dramatic. Overnight the citizens of a great power became inhabitants of a foreign country, whose relations with the new state as a former homeland are unclear. The dominant nationality has become the ethnic minority of a small state. This transformed situation has inevitably transformed the nationalism of the local Russian community and shifted it towards ethnicity. Perhaps Russian nationalism will start acquiring some of the features that had been characteristic of Estonian nationalism. Time will tell whether Estonia will be divided by ethnic conflict, or whether it can develop into a cooperative society which accepts ethno-cultural differences. The crisis in relations between nations has developed in close connection with the socio-economic, political, and moral crisis of Estonian society. To begin rebuilding society and the state, Estonia first needs to create a pluralistic democratic society, free of today's polarization.

Notes

1. Karl Aun, "A Critique of Nation-State – United in Diversity," in A. Nyri and T. Miljan (eds.), *Proceedings of the Interdisciplinary Research Seminar* (Waterloo, Canada: Wilfrid Laurier University Press, 1980), vol. 2, pp. 70–1.
2. Anthony D. Smith, "Towards a Theory of Ethnic Separatism," *Ethnic and Racial Studies* 2, no. 1 (January 1979): 22–3, 33.
3. Ibid. p. 31.

4. Hain Rebas quotes Anatol Renning in "Decisive Factors in the Formation of the Estonian Nation," in Enno Klaar (ed.), *Metroo teine raamat* (Stockholm: Metroo-trükk, 1979), p. 13.
5. T. Parming, "The Communist Party and the Estonians," in Enno Klaar (ed.), *Metroo teine raamat* (Stockholm: Metroo-trükk, 1979), p. 89.
6. V. Maamagi (ed.), *The History of the Estonian SSR* (Tallinn: Eesti Raamat, 1971) vol. III, pp. 503–4.
7. Op. cit., vol. III, pp. 595–6.
8. *Looming* 5, Tallinn, 1988.
9. K. Hallik, *On the Features of the Development of Estonia's Socialist Nation* (Tartu: Tartu Riikliku Ulikooli Toimetiset, 1989), p. 144.
10. *Rahva Haal* (daily newspaper), 19 October 1991.
11. Kalev Katus, "Demographic Development in Estonia Through Centuries," *Population Studies* (Estonian Inter-university Population Research Centre) 3 (1989): 16.
12. Rein Taagepera, "Size and Ethnicity of Estonian Towns and Rural Districts 1922–1979," *Journal of Baltic Studies* 8, no. 2: 105–27.
13. "Estonia v godu," *Estonian Express*, Tallinn, 18 October 1991.
14. *Joint Plenary Meeting of the Estonian Creative Societies*, 1–2 April 1988 (Tallinn, 1988), pp. 53–4.
15. *Trud v. SSSR, Statisticheskii zbornik* (Moscow, 1988), pp. 22–3.
16. The number of those speaking the Estonian language exceeds the number of Estonians by 9%; for the Russian language, the corresponding figure is 25%.
17. Michael Hechter, "Group formation and the cultural division of labour," *American Journal of Sociology* 84, no. 2 (1978): 294.
18. Hurst Hannum, *Autonomy, Sovereignty, and Self-Determination: The Accommodation of Conflicting Rights* (Philadelphia: University of Pennsylvania Press, 1990), pp. 60–3; MN Doc. E/ON 4/Sub. 2./1990/46 page 8; *Protection of Minorities*, Progress report submitted by Asbjørn Eide.
19. *Sovetskaya Estonia*, 12 October 1988.
20. *Mezregionalnoi Sovet Narodnoh Deputatov i Delegatov Trudyanskoi Estonskoi SSR. Rinfo #3* (Tallinn, 1990), pp. 2, 4.
21. Andrus Saar, "Inter-ethnic Relations in Estonia," *The Monthly Survey of Estonian and Soviet Politics* (Tallinn), December 1990, pp. 13–14.
22. Raymond Breton, "From Ethnic to Civic Nationalism: English Canada and Quebec," *Ethnic and Racial Studies* 2, no. 31 (January 1988): 85–102.

8

Conflict management in the former USSR and world experience

Victor A. Kremenyuk

1 Introduction

There are several important aspects to the comparative analysis of conflict management patterns and approaches which has emerged in the international community and in the former USSR. First, there is the general value of comparative analysis which reveals interesting differences or similarities which have developed in totally different social environments. In modern society, conflict management mechanisms acquire special importance, for they are regarded as safeguards of peaceful change, as a guarantee against violence which may disrupt normal evolutionary development. Such a comparative analysis can give additional support and evidence for those aspects of conflict management which have proved efficient, or can cast additional doubts on those which have yielded mixed results. Second, this is a problem for further sociological research, since comparative analysis has to explain where and why different methods and approaches were effective, and how in each case the results of conflict management efforts were different. Finally, comparative analysis should enrich our overall understanding of the role of ethnic conflicts in multi-national states.

We shall begin by analysing the notion of "conflict management" as it is treated in this article and as it has long been understood in European and non-European tradition. The specifics of "conflict" in various political and social cultures, and attitudes toward conflict, are studied further as a part of the whole problem of managing multi-ethnic societies under conditions of devolution of power. These stages of analysis permit us to describe typical approaches to conflict management in the former USSR and in some major Western nations. Comparative analysis may help us to see how the process of conflict management is connected with the process of nation-building, depending upon historical development, types of political culture, the nature and type of conflict, and the effectiveness of conflict management.

2   On the notion of "conflict management"

Decision-makers may approach conflict in a variety of ways. The initial and classic approach has been described by Schelling in his *Strategy of Conflict*: "We all are participants in international conflict, and we want to 'win' it in some proper sense." [1] This description needs no comment. Since ancient times, it has been assumed that the natural goal of any party in any conflict is (and should be) to win a victory. This basic notion is deeply entrenched in thinking and in practice.

However, even when winning the conflict was considered the only logical goal, there were doubts based on primitive cost-benefit analysis. It was realized that if the cost of victory exceeded the benefit of winning ("Pyrrhic victory") it could be more rational to avoid the confrontation and engage in other ways of managing the conflict. More detailed analysis of this approach, typical of the ancient Chinese tradition, is described in Lao-Tzu. [2] It is also interesting to observe that in the literature of ancient India, at least in some texts, the notion of conflict management comes closer to the "winning" theory than in the Chinese approach. [3]

The "winning approach" to managing conflicts has dominated European thinking since the days of the Roman Empire, and much of Roman law was built on this understanding. The legal heritage of the Romans, later entrenched into the legal systems of some European nations, established that in conflicts there is only one "right" side; the essence of law becomes to facilitate finding who is right and who is wrong. Such a system, reflecting the nature of Roman thought, could hardly accept that there could be conditions when both sides would be equally right (or equally wrong) and where victory would reflect only the balance of forces of the actors rather than the justness of their causes.

The "common-law approach" was an independent method of conflict management in the European tradition, reflecting the realities of small communities of German tribes. It focused less on winning and more on accommodation, on appeasing both sides in conflict. It is hard to say whether this was a way of survival for tiny communities (since this approach has later been found also in the primitive legal systems of African tribes[4] as well as of some tribes in the Pacific) or a reflection of a more sophisticated thinking which basically rejected the notion of "just cause" in conflict. Important for our present analysis is the idea that European tradition has somehow incorporated both Roman and "common-law" approaches to conflict management. Indeed, for many centuries both were developing as parts of the same political and legal tradition.

Instead of passing moral judgment on either of these approaches, we must understand that both were directed at managing conflicts in order to avoid disintegration of the existing social environment and the entropy of the social order. In this sense, even the violent winning approach, although it was oriented towards using brute force to achieve the victory of one side (and as such very often provoked further conflicts), could play a stabilizing role. This was usually reflected in the tradition of empire-building, where the empire acquired the role of the supreme arbiter, governing with an iron hand the relations between its different parts as well as between an individual and the state.

The common-law approach played a rather marginal role in history. It is only in the writings of Hugo Grotius in the seventeenth century that some principles of this approach were applied to the norms of international conflict. The basics of this approach have appeared more favourable to the stability of the system of relations both within separate countries and in their relations with the other nations. The historical evolution of the common-law approach, finally formulated as a global doctrine in US President Woodrow Wilson's "14 points" declaration of 1917, appeared far better suited for creation of the stable world and social order, and an adequate method of conflict management.[5]

A certain parallel may be drawn between this evolution of the European tradition of conflict management and the approach to

145

conflict management in Christianity. In the Bible the attitude to conflict is based upon divine judgment (e.g. the Ten Commandments), with neither moral and ethic imperatives allowing any compromise and both inclined towards winning the conflict. This is also reflected in the present-day attitude of the Israeli government towards the conflict with the Arabs. But in the New Testament a further evolution of Christian thinking found a way to avoid forcefully solving the conflict between a sinner and the teaching. "Let him who is without sin cast the first stone," Christ told the crowd that had congregated when a woman was sentenced to be stoned for her ,sins. This was regarded by religious orthodoxy as moral relativism, but it meant a way of reconciling two opposed structures.

The conflict management tradition which prevailed until recently was a blend of "winning" and "common-law" approaches, with the former dominating. It was strengthened by the lessons of Munich 1938, and thereafter tended to emphasize the necessity of winning the conflict when it had a moral dimension. This rhetoric was also part of John Foster Dulles' approach to Soviet–US relations in the 1950s.[6] Only with the advent of nuclear weapons did there come a new vision of the cost-benefit side of conflict. This contributed to the formation of a totally new academic theory of managing conflicts – "conflict resolution."

First developed by figures like Rapoport, Boulding, Singer, and others at Ann Arbor, Michigan, where the Center for Conflict Resolution was established, this approach has since acquired a large constituency both in the USA and abroad. Special attention has been given to this approach at the United Nations and other international bodies whose principles of management are based on consensus.

The essence of the conflict resolution approach centred on several assumptions: first, that conflicts, once started, may be solved without violence to the satisfaction of either side; second, that the resolution of conflicts is a special field of knowledge and experience to be studied along with other "peace science" disciplines; and, third, that there should be a set of normative prescriptions which, if introduced into behaviour of both sides, can lead to a satisfactory end of the conflict. Furthermore, on the value scale, its supporters have held that there are no unsolvable conflicts: everything depends upon shared values and the relevant will of the parties.[7]

Importantly, the foundation for the whole theory was a cost-benefit analysis of conflict in conditions of Mutual Assured Destruction (MAD), which provided solid proof of the futility of using force as an *ultima ratio.* The further evolution of the conflict resolution approach has brought a focus on conflict prevention and conflict avoidance as another means to settle conflicts in the early stages of their formation. Conceptually, these were off-shoots of the "mother theory," but they have had a major impact on attitudes towards conflict, strengthening the belief that it is possible to solve conflicts without letting them grow into wars.

Thus, from this brief overview we may sum up our use of the term "conflict management." Managing conflict means, first of all, keeping it under control, preventing the possibility of its unpredictable development; second, it means providing a framework which can incorporate both "winning" and "compromise" approaches as part of a single theory which stresses the need to manage conflict irrespective of the outcome; third, it may also envisage resolution, prevention, or indeed avoidance of conflict as a preferable outcome, as has been stressed by adherents of "conflict control" policies.

3 Two cultures of conflict management

Conflict management forms part of a larger social framework built by the general political process in a nation. Specific mechanisms of conflict management – courts of justice and appeal, arbiters, intermediaries, special government agencies – may be very similar in different countries. Contemporary civilization has already worked out some model institutions which are duplicated widely, sometimes even without proper understanding of why these institutions exist and what function they really play in maintaining the social order.

Basically, these institutions have been copied from developed Western democracies. It is the evolution of such states, especially in the nineteenth and early twentieth centuries, which brought into existence various institutions with the purpose of managing domestic conflicts between classes, large social groups, political movements, and ethnic minorities, in order to preserve the social order from major disruptions. Their emergence was partially a reaction by Western societies to atrocities of the French Revolution, the European upheavals of 1848–50, the Paris Commune, and, finally, the October Revolution in Russia. The experience of all these major social outbursts, as well as the lessons of social conflicts of lesser magnitude, spurred democratic societies on to work out mechanisms for coping with social unrest.

The last and largest impact on this institution-building came in the wake of the tragic experiment of the Nazi regime in Germany. After World War II, an institution-building process became universal, in developed European nations and in Japan, and in the developing states of Asia, Africa, and Latin America. This was a process largely encouraged by the findings of the theory of political development.

The scope of ideas behind this historical evolution was laid down by French thinkers of the Enlightenment, specifically by Rousseau's "social contract." The normative approach of their works was based upon a conclusion that through education and learning, humanity could make moral and spiritual progress, creating a "harmonious" society capable of maintaining the necessary balance between its main social groups on the basis of justice and equity. Although these ideas were at the time received with widespread scepticism, further evolution has given much more emphasis to the idea of "contract," which, together with the traditions of common law, has appeared as a sound basis of social organization. The traditions of contract and negotiations have become an important alternative to violence and power. One example of this type of development may be found in former US President Roosevelt's "New Deal."

On the basis of this evolution, concepts and theories of conflict resolution have been studied and developed. Knowledge backed up by numerous examples of social and international conflicts has shown that in the long run no violent conflict has ever brought success to the winner. The only stable result of such conflicts has been the perpetuation of the controversy, its reproduction over several generations, or even centuries. For example: the radical Tatar movement for independence insists that the Tatar people are still at war with Russia, ever since the days of Ivan the Terrible, when the Kazan and Astrakhan Khanates were conquered by the Russians in the 1550s and forcibly incorporated into the Russian tsardom. Tatar extremists maintain that the conflict between Russians and Tatars has continued through all these centuries and has never been ended.[8]

In this respect, conflict resolution theory holds that a durable solution to a conflict may be achieved only if and when the totality of variables which form the conflict situation is studied; the variables which can perform the main function in putting an end to conflict must then be activated through political decisions. This can provide a sound basis for a negotiated solution which will exclude the possibility of reactivating the conflict.

This view contrasts with the other approach found in the USSR and even today in the independent states. The latter approach assumes that violence is a midwife of history, and sees revolutions as a manifestation of violent conflict between classes who are the "locomotives of history." It assumes, further, that revolutions and armed struggles are generally the most efficient and desirable means of social change; hence, they should be regarded not as a deviation from a "normal" way of things, but rather as something to be encouraged and set as a goal of the political party which heads the mass movement of the working class. This goal consists in taking power through violent overthrow of the existing government and enforced change of the social order along the lines of Communist ideology.[9] It further insists that even after the successful overthrow of the old regime the new social and political order must continue to suppress opposition with the whole might of the state.[10] The contribution of this revolutionary process consists in promoting violent change of the social and political order in other countries where similar conditions exist.

This approach regards conflict as something natural, which provokes the existing contradictions of the society to their extreme. Only when they reach that extreme and conflict erupts can there be a possibility for genuine change, making revolution possible. This is not Schelling's "we all are party to the conflict" (where conflict is something alien to the will of the actors): on the contrary, the purpose of these actors in promoting change is perceived as conflict itself, which has to be promoted in order to "win." Conflict in this case is desirable because it is regarded as the best (if not the only) means to achieve progress and change.

Correspondingly, these two approaches differ in how they treat conflict management. The first, the Western liberal approach, considers conflict as unnecessary, as damaging to the society, and hence as something to be put down. The preferable solution is compromise, a mutually acceptable agreement to be worked out by both sides, sometimes with the participation of an intermediary or a third party, sometimes without it, and voluntarily accepted. Such a solution has two distinct assets: first, it tends to be optimal, since it has been achieved through negotiations where different positions are compared, analysed, contested, and finally brought together; second, it is usually more durable because the way it has been achieved minimizes the possibilities of challenging the agreement after it is signed. Thus, this approach prefers a non-normative, experimental way of forging a solution; it moves to the "cone" of agreement from beneath, searching for an acceptable solution.

The second approach, the Marxist, violent approach, treats conflict management in a totally different manner. First, it generally associates "winning" with management, stressing that to win in a conflict means to keep it under firm control; and, vice versa, that complete control of the conflict may be achieved only through a victory. Second, this approach does not exclude the possibility of negotiating in conflict, but regards this as an "auxiliary" method which may be used when there is an impasse in a forced solution, or when cost-benefit analysis shows that using force is counterproductive. Otherwise, negotiation is not preferable to conflict. Third, this approach does not exclude a compromise achieved through mediation, but it acknowledges only an authoritative intermediary, one possessing the necessary power. In a hierarchical society, it sees conflict management as the coercion exerted by a higher authority in relation to a lower one.

These two approaches to conflict management indicate how and on what principles a state can operate government in a multi-ethnic society in the midst of social upheaval caused by ethnic conflicts. Ethnic conflicts come into existence because the ethnic minority is dissatisfied with its position in multi-ethnic society: thus, ethnic conflict always means a challenge to the power of the central authority which keeps the nation together. In trying to control ethnic conflicts, the central authority does this in order to maintain its power, well aware that in the opposite case it would inevitably lose power and become the loser in the conflict. When we bear in mind the psychology of the relevant actor, it becomes evident that in this case losing power would mean political death.

4 Ethnic conflicts as objects of management

Ethnic conflicts may be found in various societies: developed and underdeveloped; liberal and authoritarian; democratic and totalitarian; Western and Eastern; Northern and Southern. Nor are they solely a product of contemporary times; ethnic conflicts have occurred throughout human history. The essence of these conflicts has been the desire of the ethnic minority to defend its identity, either through national liberation or through achieving national autonomy. This desire has always been prompted by the fear of losing one's own cultural traditions, ethnic heritage, and language to a larger and more developed nation which could swallow and ingest smaller groups. Indeed, this is what happened, for example, to Luzhichan Serbs in Germany, as well as many other minorities elsewhere.

Though a supporter of the "melting-pot" theory would never recognize any rational element behind the resistance of small nations to the expansion of big ones, nevertheless such conflicts multiply. To explain the underlying rationale, we may suggest that cultural diversity is one of the most important and powerful locomotives of the cultural development of the world community. Without ethnic minorities cultural diversity might simply disappear. This does not mean that peasants in remote villages fighting for their independence or self-determination are necessarily obsessed with the cultural heritage of humankind: but it does give a rational explanation to the feeling of justice and the desire to provide assistance that are experienced when the world community deals with ethnic problems.

Ethnic conflicts throughout the world may be divided into several groupings. We can begin with the most simple and "primitive" conflicts, where an ethnic minority wants to be recognized as such and to win the right to "cultural autonomy." This type of conflict exists in both developed and developing countries.

Another type occurs when an ethnic minority wants self-determination and independence. This also may happen both in developed and developing societies, although it is more typical of developing societies where the problems of self-determination have not yet been solved and society itself is in a state of rapid change.

The next type is the so-called "irredentist" movement, when an ethnic minority in one state wants to join its counterpart in another state and create a new nation (Basques in France and Spain, Ossetians in Russia and Georgia). Such movements may have as their goal national reunification under the auspices of a big nation which is either closer to them ethnically or which is regarded as capable of sponsoring such an endeavour.

What would be a totally new type of ethnic conflict characteristic of our times is the drive for unity of the so-called separated states, such as Germany, Laos and Viet Nam, and Korea.

It is important to have a typology of ethnic conflicts in order to understand the possible scale of their consequences for the social order in relevant countries and for the international system. Usually, conflicts of the primitive type do not produce large-scale consequences and they may be managed by governments. Depending upon the nature of the government and the conflict management approach chosen, this may either satisfy the world community or raise serious criticism on the part of those concerned over human rights and the rights of the minorities. Moving from more simple types of ethnic conflict towards more complex and sophisticated ones, the scale of consequences will be greater, as will the attention of the world community to the conflict. In the most sophisticated cases, ethnic conflicts become truly international, with all the corresponding consequences. What ethnic conflicts lose in their domestic dimension, they now gain on the international side.

This observation is a necessary preface to the analysis of ethnic conflict as an object of management. When confronted with the challenge of an ethnic conflict, any government will feel the attention of the outside world. No longer can ethnic problems be regarded simply as completely internal: the issues of self-determination and respect for the rights of minorities have already become part of international law. At the same time, an ethnic conflict is always a challenge to the authority of the state and a danger to its power, whether it is a democratic state or a totalitarian one. It would be naïve to expect that, because of the international dimension of ethnic conflict, a state will hesitate to use all the means at its disposal in order to minimize the damage it suffers. The real political problem facing the state in this case will be how to synchronize its domestic policy goals *vis-à-vis* ethnic conflict and its international obligations to avoid a situation in which, both domestically and internationally, ethnic conflict aggravates devolution of power.

Here, the type of conflict management and the mode of operation acquire crucial importance. If the culture of the given state is oriented towards brutal oppression of ethnic minorities, if it operates within the narrow limits of the "winning" approach, it will not only prefer forcible, imposed solutions of such conflicts but will also hold that if it does not demonstrate enough power and resolution, its foreign and domestic images will suffer. In this case the state will inevitably tend to use force and self-appointed conflict management, regarding any attempt on the part of the world community to criticize its approach as an attempt to "interfere in its domestic affairs," and will lock itself into a vicious circle of violence and failure: the less successful its efforts, the more it will be inclined to escalate violence. This may be seen in Saddam Hussein's policy towards the Kurds and the Shiite minority in Iraq.

In such situations, it is extremely difficult for the international community to do anything real and significant to help oppressed minorities. As the Kurdish uprising in early 1991 showed, even when foreign troops interfere to prevent a mass massacre on the part of the government forces, the result is still unsatisfactory and insignificant. One explanation may be that dealing with ethnic problems becomes a matter of survival for the government involved, and the minority experiences in its own destiny the consequences of the struggle for survival. The more the state is pressured, the lower are the hopes that it will change its attitude towards ethnic conflict. A similar process was under way in the former Soviet Union until it ceased to exist and turned into a loose commonwealth.

5 Ethnic conflicts in the former USSR: History and lessons

The emergence of a whole series of ethnic conflicts in the USSR in 1987–91 came both as a surprise and as something long expected by Soviet and foreign observers. On the one hand, it was no secret to those who knew Soviet history that there were dozens of ethnic minorities whose rights had been abused during the Communist regime; and it was only logical to expect these minorities to demand justice as soon as the situation in the country permitted. The period preceding 1985, when Mikhail Gorbachev came to power in the Kremlin, and the period immediately after that provided ample evidence of the struggles of the Crimean Tatars, the Armenians in Nagorno-Karabakh, the Meskhetian Turks in Uzbekistan, the Russian Germans, and many others. It became clear that all the minorities who had suffered serious dislocations during Stalin's rule would demand some historical satisfaction.

The ethnic situation was also unsettled for some minorities, like the Gagauz minority in Moldova, who had been deprived by the Communist regime of the possibility of autonomy and who now sought recognition of their right to self-determination. Ethnic issues also included relations between separate republics and ethnic minorities (in Russia, Georgia, Azerbaijan) dissatisfied with their dependent status inside those republics. Several "irredentist" movements appeared, in Georgia (Ossetians), Azerbaijan (Nagorno-Karabakh), Moldova (the Dniester Republic), as well as in the Baltic states (the Russian-speaking population), demanding union with their brothers and sisters in neighbouring states. All in all, it appeared that the ethnic problem was developing into a major source of devolution of power in the former Soviet Union, and, at the same time, a source of potential conflict.

On the other hand, there was a strong belief, shared not only by Gorbachev's government but by the public at large, that these cases of ethnic conflicts were basically mere exceptions: the major republics of the Union were more or less integrated socially and economically into an interdependent complex which could be preserved during a period of social change, helping to dampen the waves of instability produced by minor ethnic movements. This conclusion was based both upon the experience of World War II, when the Union had proved its integrity, and upon the determination of the centre to start a series of long-term profound changes linked with democratization, *perestroika*, openness, and other reforms, which would put the centre into the leading position among all other political forces, including leaders of republics.

The evident determination was to use the momentum of social change in order to navigate through the reefs of ethnic and nationalist moods. Here we may note how Gorbachev's *Concept of Perestroika*, published in 1987, was establishing a direct link between the speed of social change sponsored from above and the possibilities for quick and sound solutions to ethnic problems.[11]

The traditional Marxist-Leninist ideology assumed that national and ethnic issues are subordinate to the interests of class and large social groups, and are thus incapable of providing a powerful enough impulse to destroy the existing social order. The example of some developed nations (the USA first of all) was misused to "prove" that with the advent of economic progress minority issues will be solved easily, if not automatically. A devastating blow to these views came with the civil conflict in Yugoslavia. That country had been regarded as far more developed than the majority of the former Soviet republics; nevertheless, it suffered disintegration due to ethnic conflicts between Serbs and other nationalities. On the other hand, for some time a kind of euphoria persisted, both in the thinking of the Union leadership (until it was dissolved in December 1991) and in the Russian leadership. Judging by the Declaration of the Three Republics of 8 December 1991, which put an end to the existence of the USSR, the main emphasis was on economic rather than ethnic issues.[12]

This approach never worked; indeed it proved to be based on false assumptions. First, the speed of social change from above was much slower than expected, due to resistance on the part of hard-liners and the party *nomenklatura*. This produced the first open crisis in the Soviet leadership in 1987, when Boris Yeltsin revolted against Gorbachev's policy and was evicted from the ruling Politburo. Second, the nationalist movements in separate republics were gaining strength; their platforms appeared much more attractive for the large masses of people than that of the Communist Party. This produced another crisis, which was less spectacular than the so-called Yeltsin crisis but which nevertheless significantly narrowed Gorbachev's power base in the republics and turned the republics into a dominant force of development. Third, there was an attempt (at least, according to some reports) on the part of the central leadership to use, if not encourage, ethnic conflicts in the republics in order to strengthen the position of the centre.[13]

As these factors were unfolding, a specific policy regarding ethnic conflicts was formulated for the whole of the USSR. While the central government was counting on the "winning" approach and used force in Tbilisi (1989), Baku (1990), and Vilnius (1991) in order to put down nationalist uprisings, the republican governments, while resisting the policy of Moscow, were applying those same methods against their own ethnic minorities in Moldova, Georgia, Azerbaijan, Kyrgyzstan, Uzbekistan, and even in Lithuania against the Russian-speaking minority. Conflict management through force, directly or indirectly, and the inability to find other ways to keep those conflicts under control to prevent their escalation – this has become the norm.

Why has that situation developed? Here, we should stress that at the base of the whole pyramid of violence was the policy of the central government. It was not simply tradition and habit which formed the policy of Moscow, but also a strong commitment to keep on playing the role of the "supreme arbiter," which was considered necessary from both the domestic and the foreign policy perspectives. Domestically, it was considered necessary to use the situation of growing conflict between governments in the republics and ethnic minorities in order to increase the leverage of the centre and to dilute the power of the republics in the growing unrest of their minorities. This was especially important since Moscow found itself unable to start economic reform and was, thus, counting on circumventing economic hardships by stressing the gravity of ethnic problems. Internationally, the centre tried to continue to play a visible role in order to project an image of control over the spread of nuclear weapons in the new republics.

Thus, the ethnic problem, the importance of conflicts around the self-determination of the minorities, acquired unprecedented dimensions, threatening the existing order both in the republics and in the Union. In view of this, it was not unexpected that the leadership of the republics preferred to dismiss the central authority completely, exchanging it for some loose arrangement, rather than try to support Gorbachev and his policy. This was scarcely a free choice of alternatives, each with its pros and cons, but an enforced solution to save the public order in the republics. Of course, not all the republics were equally embroiled in ethnic problems, but for the majority it was clear that they could cope with the situation only if the interference of the central government could be removed once and for all. Thus came the events of December 1991, when the agreement on the Commonwealth was first signed by the three Slavic republics and then enlarged through addition of eight more by the end of that month.

The disintegration of the Soviet Union and the establishment of the Commonwealth of Independent States (CIS) have only partly helped to ease tensions between the republics. While this devolution of Soviet power has ended the confrontation between the centre and the republics, it has not brought a stable horizontal relationship. The worst evidence of this is seen in relations between Armenia and Azerbaijan and between Russia and Ukraine. The institutions of the CIS appear too weak to contain these conflicts and there seems a real possibility that they may escalate into a threat to East European or Transcaucasian order.

In view of the ethnic dimension of this development, the results of the devolution of the Soviet power have become even more disastrous. CIS attempts to moderate some of these conflicts have failed; nor have the attempts of some republican governments to control ethnic conflicts on their territories succeeded. In some cases, such as the Russian Federation, the government has tried to be more or less tolerant of various ethnic claims for independence (e.g. the Chechen or Tatar republics), though it is evident that the limits of its tolerance have been dwindling. In other republics the spectre of ethnic independence has created a critical situation.

Why has this happened? A whole group of the former Soviet republics have an artificial nature: Ukraine, Belarus, Kazakhstan, Uzbekistan, Tajikistan, Kyrgyzstan, and Turkmenistan. These nations either never had a state of their own, or were always parts of other states. During the Soviet period their statehood was artificially created as a subsidiary of the Party bureaucratic system, without any serious attempt to forge viable nations. Now that these republics have gained independence, their lack of historical experience in statehood and the absence of knowledge of how to deal with ethnic minorities make them rather aggressive and intolerant in their domestic policies and help to create further impasses in respect to ethnic minorities. The ethnic issue and the impossibility of finding sound solutions to it may lead to the further fragmentation of the geopolitical entity once called the Soviet Union.

Ethnic issues in the former USSR were not the only or even the main factor which destroyed the Union. Many other factors worked in the same direction. All the same, it is clear that the conflict management strategy which combined direct and forceful pressure from the centre on the republics with an indirect form of pressure through encouragement of some ethnic issues has produced a cumulative feedback which destroyed the Union. In order to avoid the impression that in this interplay of factors the politics of republics were justifiably directed against the Centre, it should be emphasized that the republics also followed the same line in their attitude toward ethnic conflicts. As a result, the whole structure of ethnic problems in the former USSR has become highly instrumental in devolution of the power of the state and in bringing it to the present state of affairs.

6 Conclusion: Learning lessons

The leaders of the republics are well aware that the inability to cope with ethnic problems – due either to the force of tradition or to the general state of the society, which cannot produce the sophisticated mechanisms of conflict management in use in developed nations – played a highly visible role in bringing an end to the Soviet Union. This does not mean, however, that they are inclined to make any significant changes in their methods and attitudes to this problem. In each of the sovereign republics, old traditions appear stronger than common sense and the knowledge of Western experience.

What then can we say about the lessons of the Union? The new independent states have started their existence amid two important processes: on one hand, there is the problem of overcoming the residues of Communist rule; on the other, nation-building under conditions of multi-ethnicity. It will be the balance between efforts in both directions that will determine their destinies. Not all of these republics are equally caught up in ethnic problems, although the heritage of both the Empire and Communist rule has left almost all of them with mixed populations. Neither are they all equally eager to continue democratic reforms, although they understand that without a certain democratization, in politics as well as in economics, they will not be able to survive as independent and integrated nations. On the other hand, all of them face the problem of having to learn modern and accepted methods of rule quickly; those who can be quick enough here will have greater chances for survival and a peaceful future.

It is evident that no model for managing ethnic conflicts exists that is fully suited to the new independent states. This can be seen from the failed efforts of Russia and Kazakhstan to play an intermediary role in the Armenian–Azerbaijani conflict. On the contrary, it seems that each of the republics will have to work out its own specific approaches and methods in order to keep its conflicts under control. International experience has demonstrated that using force as the main method is self-destructive. To hope for the United Nations or other international institutions to step in and take care of these conflicts is also unrealistic. Local governments will have to take the necessary steps to understand the depth and complexity of the issues they are facing. Finally, we should note that international experience also teaches us that handling ethnic conflicts is a long-term task which cannot be solved overnight.

Notes

1. T.C. Schelling, *Strategy of Conflict* (Cambridge, MA: Harvard University Press, 1959), p. 3.
2. Lao Tzu, *Te-Tao Ching: A New Tradition Based on the Recently Discovered Ma-Wang-Tui Texts* (New York: Ballantine Books, 1989).
3. *Bhagavadgita: Philosophical Texts* (Russian version; Ylm Publishing House, Ashkhabad, 1977).
4. See, for example, F.M. Deng and I.W. Zartman (eds.), *Conflict Resolution in Africa* (Washington DC: Brookings Institute, 1991).
5. In Russian, see N.N. Yakovlev, *Prestupivshije Gran* (Those who crossed the brink) (Moscow: Meghdunarodnye Otnoshenija, 1971), pp. 7–41.
6. T. Hoopes, *The Devil and J.F. Dulles* (Boston: Houghton, Mifflin, 1973).
7. An excellent overview of the major writings on conflict resolution was given in a recent work by a young scholar at the International Institute for Applied Systems Analysis (IIASA); see L. Wagner, *Processes for Impasse Resolution* (IIASA Working Paper, wp-91–43, December 1991).
8. Some Russian extremists respond to this claim that the conflict between Russians and Tatars started in the mid-1200s, when the Mongols invaded Russia and kept it under their rule for about 300 years. Both positions demonstrate that, in absence of a durable solution, conflicts may continue endlessly, with mixed results at different stages. See S.L. Tikhvinsky (ed.), *Tataro-Mongoly v Asii i Evrope* (Tatar-Mongols in Asia and Europe) (Moscow: Nauka 1977).
9. V.I. Lenin, *Gosudarstvo i revolutsiya* (State and Revolution), in *Complete Works* vol. 33 (Moscow: Politizdat, 1972) p. 43.
10. J.V. Stalin, *Voprosy Leninisma* (Problems of Leninism) (Moscow: Politizdat, 1941).
11. M.S. Gorbachev, *New Thinking for Our Country and for the Whole World* (Moscow: APN Publishers, 1987).
12. *Izvestija*, 9 December 1991.
13. R.I. Khasbulatov, Chairman of the Presidium of the Supreme Soviet of the Russian Federation, Interview with Soviet TV, 15 March 1992.

9

The dissolution of multi-ethnic states: The case of Yugoslavia

Silvo Devetak

In that day will I raise up the tabernacle of David that is fallen, and close up the breaches thereof; and I will raise up his ruins, and I will build it as in days of old; ...

And I will bring again the captivity of my people Israel, and they shall build the waste cities, and inhabit them; and they shall plant vineyards and drink the wine thereof; they shall also make gardens and eat the fruit of them.

And I will plant them upon their land, and they shall no more be plucked up out of their land which I have given them, saith the Lord my God.

(Amos 9:11–15)

Prologue

The consequences of the war in Yugoslavia which began in 1991 in Croatia and has now engulfed Bosnia and Herzegovina have been frightful: tens of thousands have been killed and at least three times that number wounded; millions will remain psychologically injured; more than seven hundred thousand people have become refugees; hundreds of thousands of homes have been ruined, families separated (a great number of whom were ethnically mixed), and industrial plants and infrastructure destroyed.

Seeing these atrocities and being aware that this is not yet the end of the destruction, one must ask a very logical question: Could the survival of the Yugoslav federation have avoided this cataclysm?

Before answering this question it is necessary to consider some facts. Economic, social, political, and other problems had been accumulating unresolved in Yugoslavia for decades, especially since the collapse of the economic reforms announced in the 1960s and the suppression of "liberal tendencies" at the beginning of the 1970s. The "results" of the "settlement" with liberalism in Yugoslavia could be compared with the "results" of two similar political-ideological phenomena in the communist world which were happening at approximately the same time: the cultural revolution in China and Brezhnev's rule in the Soviet Union. The dissolution of Yugoslavia had begun, in fact, in the seventies, after that liquidation of liberalism. The beginning of this process was marked by three factors of a general character.

First, the so-called "agreement economy" had been introduced, which meant, in fact, the abolition of market laws and legal obligations between economic entities.

Second, the decision-making process at the federal level regulated by the federal constitution of 1974 was ineffective. The major economic and political decisions regarding the "equality of nations and nationalities" had to be adopted by consensus of the republics and both autonomous provinces. It was very hard, if not impossible, to obtain, for instance, a consensus between the "developed" republics and provinces (Slovenia, Croatia, "inner" Serbia – without provinces, Vojvodina) and the "underdeveloped" ones (Macedonia, Montenegro, Bosnia and Herzegovina, Kosovo) on economic and political reforms and the restructuring of industry, reforms which have been in the last two decades a basic need for ensuring the stability and progress of the country.

Third, the political élites whom Marshal Tito had brought to power, at the levels both of the republics and the two autonomous provinces and of the federation, had neither adequate political wisdom nor the personal capacities necessary for managing the country.[1]

The one-party regime provided no opportunities for genuine corrections and adaptations of the political and economic system. The routine appointment of mediocre but contemptible "cadres" to political, economic, and other public posts further worsened the prospects for adequate governing of the country.

Inter-ethnic tensions, swept under the carpet by the political leadership of the country, have been another source of the ineffectiveness of the system. The situation was made even more complicated by political and legal systems which lacked effective methods and procedures for the democratic resolution of problems.[2] By the 1980s the country had become a pressure-cooker without a safety valve. The brutal reaction to the Albanian rebellion in 1981, and the escalation of Serbian and, later, all other nationalisms ignited the final explosion.

The answer to the question of whether the survival of the Yugoslav federation would have avoided the cataclysm in this country is therefore very simple: no, because the Yugoslav federation had few chances for survival. But another assertion is unfortunately very clear, too: most of the ethnic leaders chose the worst of all possible ways for dissolving the federation, and in so doing have driven several generations of the members of "their nations" into war, stagnation, misery, and humiliation.

How many successor states have emerged on the soil of former Yugoslavia, and what international status do they have at the beginning of 1995? Of the former six federal republics, Slovenia, Croatia, Bosnia and Herzegovina, and Macedonia have declared their independence. Serbia and Montenegro have prepared a draft project of their unification in new/old Yugoslavia. The leaders of the Albanian political and trade union organizations in Kosovo are persistently declaring the right of the Albanians to self-determination (and to unification with Albania on this basis) but so far no actions have been undertaken in this regard.

Slovenia, Croatia, and Bosnia and Herzegovina have been internationally recognized. The recognition of Macedonia has been delayed because of the objections of Greece, which is of the opinion that the use of the word "Macedonia" for the new state would imply territorial pretensions to that part of Greece with the same geographical name. Serbia and Montenegro claim to be the only successors of Yugoslavia and want thus enjoy the benefits of its legacy.

The situation concerning the territory of new states is thus complicated from the very outset. Approximately one-third of the territory of Croatia is under the control of the local Serbian population, strongly supported by the Yugoslav (federal) army. This is a territory where the UNPROFOR peace-keeping units are supposed to be deployed. In a part of "independent" Bosnia and Herzegovina, the Serbs have established the "Serbian Republic of Bosnia and Herzegovina." The Croats, on the other hand, are trying to gain de facto control over another "portion" of this state, western Herzegovina.[3]

The situation after the process of dissolution

Each of the successor states of the former Yugoslav federation has its own political, socio-economic, ethnic, and other circumstances. However, the following features could be a common denominator of the situation. (Slovenia has particular features which I shall mention when considering specific issues.)

1. There is terrible economic depression (in some cases even chaos). This is manifested, among other things, by a great diminution of industrial production, a fall in foreign trade and investments, and an enormous growth in unemployment. This situation is a logical continuation of the previous circumstances, which have rapidly worsened during the unmanageable process of Yugoslavia's dissolution which began in the seventies and continued apace in the eighties.

Generally speaking, the emerging states have similar economic, monetary, financial, and technological problems to the old Yugoslavia: an outdated industrial structure, low productivity, irrational and inefficient management of the economy and public affairs, foreign debt, unemployment, and declining standards of living. The social and economic situation in all the successor states has deteriorated tremendously in the last two years. The war in Croatia has worsened the social and economic situation in that country even more. Increasing misery and starvation of the population were the first "results" of the "democratic" changes in Bosnia and Herzegovina in 1991, when the three parties representing the three nations (Muslims, Serbs, and Croats) won the elections. With the beginning of the civil war in this republic the situation deteriorated rapidly overnight.

The main deficiency of all the regimes in power is their lack of global concepts of how to handle the economy, and of wisdom about how to develop the most-needed economic, technological, and other reforms or how to conduct the restructuring of industries, ownership, management of the economy, public services, and so forth.

2. One of the most sensitive results of a steady fall in the standard of living, the immense unemployment, uncontrolled price rises, and so on is the fostering of social tensions in the new emerging societies.[4] In these economic circumstances a tiny class of "haves" and a permanently increasing class of "have-nots" have been created in a short time. The gap between the two classes is larger every day. Such socio-political circumstances constitute a fertile ground for the spread of extremist ideas and activities.

Competition could be an effective impulse for development. But, according to many observations, the growing social differences are not always based on competition and law. Besides, in such circumstances the shortest way to enter the club of "haves" does not necessarily lead through the organization of new production but more often through "unproductive" activities, such as speculation of all kinds. This could work only in circumstances where capitalist economic methods are being introduced into the "socially-owned" economy, i.e., in a situation where nobody knows yet who owns the means of production.

3. The new nation states are being created as copies of the old state. Their common characteristics are thus the strengthening and growth of different kinds of administration and of the state apparatus of repression (national army, different branches of the regular and secret – civil and military – police forces, etc.). Looking at these developments, one could conclude that the primary goal of the "new ethnic élites" has been to replace the old "non-ethnic élites" in power, and not to reform the new societies and states in accordance with the democratic demands which were invoked in the endeavours to mobilize the masses against the old regimes.

It is hard to believe that the vanishing economies would be able to cover the increasing cost of these apparatus and services. On the other hand, less and less money is available for culture, science, research, health, or other social services. It is hardly necessary to explain what long-term consequences of such a division of the GNP might be expected.

4. Unreasonable ethnic nationalism and hatred of "the others" has become a cornerstone of the political mobilization of each group's own masses and of the creation of the new political regimes. After the atrocities of the Serbian–Croatian war, the ethnic animosity between these two nations has attained immeasurable dimensions. Since the beginning of the civil war in Bosnia and Herzegovina the same could be said for Serb–Muslim relations.

5. The isolation of the emerging states on the territory of former Yugoslavia at the beginning of 1992 was twofold. Some of the emerging states (Slovenia and Croatia) were included in the Conference on Security and Co-operation in Europe (CSCE) or were given the status of observers in European institutions such as the Council of Europe; but all of them, for the time being, have been left out of the process of European economic and financial integration.

Furthermore, there has been an immense fall in, or even interruption of, their political, economic, commercial, technological, scientific, and other bonds with foreign countries, especially Western Europe. The whole territory of former Yugoslavia is still treated as a war zone or at least as a zone of political turmoil. And it is well known that capital and economic activities in general avoid such risks.

Among the first consequences of the dramatic events in former Yugoslavia was a quick increase in the already existing trend towards developing the road, railway, and other communications from central and south Europe towards the Balkans via Hungary, Romania, Serbia, and Bulgaria, or via Italy and across the Otranto straits. However, the creation of new state borders between the former republics of Yugoslavia, with strict border and customs controls, and the adoption of many other measures of control of the new nation states over their territories, citizens, and the exchange of goods (and ideas), have contributed additionally to the reduction or interruption of European traffic through this territory. With the continuation of this trend, the physical isolation especially of Slovenia and Croatia will increase. Bosnia and Herzegovina has become a land-locked country, encircled by Croatia and Serbia, the two nation states which are potential claimants of "their ethnic parts" of its territory.

It will be extremely difficult, if not impossible, to redirect these new communication flows back to the previous routes. Nor are the successor states showing interest in this. For instance, in proposals for the construction of new international road connections, only those roads – if they should ever be constructed – that would "link" the successor states with "Europe" have been taken into consideration, and not the traditional communication routes that connected Central

Europe, via the territory of former Yugoslavia, with the Balkans and the Middle East.[5] On the other hand, all kinds of cooperation between the former republics of Yugoslavia have fallen drastically. In the case of Croatia and Serbia we can speak of the severance of all contacts. Restrictions on economic cooperation between the emerging states, bans on the export of various "strategic" goods (food, raw materials, etc.), transformation of the financial, commercial, and other bonds between them into inter-state (and as yet unregulated) relations – all these have further contributed to the disappearance of cooperation between the previous republics.

The new independent states of Slovenia, Croatia, Macedonia, Bosnia and Herzegovina, and of "united" Serbia and Montenegro, are strictly "defending" their "state interests." On the territory of former Yugoslavia, closed, politically controlled, and regulated markets have been created. The wars in Croatia and Bosnia and Herzegovina have destroyed chances for the beginning of genuine recovery for their economies and for the resolution of the most urgent social problems of the population.

Unresolved problems will remain

After the international recognition of the emerging states of former Yugoslavia, a great many very sensitive matters concerning future relations among them have remained unresolved. Each represents possible grounds for disputes, friction, even armed clashes. As an illustration, I will mention three of them:

1. The restoration of peace is a *sine qua non* for any political solution of the Yugoslav crisis. The UN peace-keeping forces (UNPROFOR) in Croatia – if the development of events provides the necessary conditions for their deployment at all – will have the mandate of ensuring respect for the cease-fire and of separating the two sides involved in the fighting. This is doubtless a precondition for any lasting peace. But the main issues concerning real pacification – the return of refugees and displaced persons to their homes, the rebuilding of ruined settlements, cultural monuments, industrial plants, etc. – will nevertheless remain open. The main political issue at stake remains how to ensure de facto control by the Croatian authorities over the whole territory of the new state. The problem has become politically even more sensitive, since Croatian propaganda has created in public opinion the impression that the deployment of UNPROFOR means the beginning of the "expulsion of the Serb invaders from the occupied territories of Croatia."[6]

Serbian ethnic nationalism and aggressiveness may be the main cause, but the Serbian–Croatian divergence is the main problem of the Yugoslav crisis. We are clear witnesses of the struggle between the two emerging nation states for the division of territories of former Yugoslavia along ethnic lines. The Serbian side is for the time being militarily stronger; but the new Republic of Croatia is very quickly building its own military force. The positions of the two sides regarding the territory of Croatia are defined: Croatia is defending its sovereignty over its national territory, which is now under the control of Serbian insurgents, while Serbia is claiming this territory as a zone of its interest on the basis of the local Serbian population's right to autonomy.

In this regard, Bosnia and Herzegovina is still an "open space." In spite of the recent international recognition of the independence of this former Yugoslav republic, its division along ethnic lines is the main goal of the Serbian and Croatian political strategy, the accomplishment of which depends on the present military actions. The first priority of both nationalisms is the de facto division of the republic, among other ways by the formation of "autonomous ethnic regions" which would, according to the authors of these policies, provide the legitimate basis for future territorial claims.[7] In other words, aware of the present international control over Bosnia and Herzegovina by the European Union (EU), the Serbian and Croatian ethnic nationalists are for the time being trying to ensure at least "their sphere of interest" in the country, as a starting point for also getting, later, "their portion" of "their own ethnic territory."[8]

Each nationalism takes into account the fact that Muslims constitute more than 40 per cent of the population only in order to create a favourable balance of power "against the other," and not as a basic political factor for the future stability of this part of former Yugoslavia.

In addition to the atrocities that are occurring in Bosnia and Herzegovina, the ruinous breakdown of Serbian–Muslim relations will probably also provoke "rescue actions" by Muslims in favour of their kith and kin, such as the Muslims from Sandjak in Serbia and the Yugoslav Albanians. Stopping the war in Bosnia and Herzegovina has become another urgent task for the international community.

2. The problem of the borders between the new states is the most vulnerable aspect of the relations between them. In normal circumstances the first step towards resolving this problem would have been recognition of the administrative borders between those former Yugoslav republics that have obtained their independence, and of the borders between them and the rest of the country (Serbia and Montenegro), as international borders under international law. This solution would have been in line with the (insufficient) rules of international law[9] and with the Helsinki Final Act of 1975.

Unfortunately, the question of borders has become a purely political matter. The division of territories of the former federal republic of Croatia was in fact the main reason for the bloody and destructive Serbian–Croatian war. Recent events have shown that Serbia, under the cloak of the continuity of the Yugoslav state, is claiming, at least, all the Croatian territories that are now under the control of the Yugoslav army and of the local and paramilitary Serbian forces.[10]

The division of Bosnia and Herzegovina between Croatia and Serbia along the lines of ethnic territories was reportedly the incentive for the talks between the leaders of the two republics/states after the elections in Croatia in 1990. Attempts to make this notion a reality remain, as I have explained above, the most sensitive and explosive problem involved in searching for adequate mechanisms for the peaceful resolution of the Yugoslav crisis. After the international recognition of Bosnia and Herzegovina as an independent state, the main task of the EU and the UN will therefore be to ensure peace in this new state and to protect its borders with the Republic of Croatia and with new/old Yugoslavia – or rather, with united Serbia and Montenegro.

Considering the traditional territorial pretensions of the Serbian nationalists towards Macedonia, it would be very naïve not to expect Serbian–Macedonian misunderstandings concerning their future relations.[11] Ambiguities over land and maritime borders exist even between Slovenia and Croatia, two states which have declared their friendly cooperation from the very beginning of the process of dissolution.[12] All the former Yugoslav republics except Slovenia have ethnically mixed populations.[13] In such circumstances it is not even possible in theory to draw inter-state borders along ethnic lines. It was in awareness of this fact that the Serbian nationalist strategists, during the war in Croatia, found another "method" for resolving this problem. By inflicting unprecedented atrocities on civilians, they frightened the remaining population of "other ethnic origin" into fleeing from their homes, thus transforming the area of "operations" into "ethnically clean" territories. Subsequently, the Croatian extremists have adopted the same methods for "cleansing" their territories of the Serbian population.

According to these strategies, the second step should be the settlement of these areas with the people of "their ethnic origin." The result of the implementation of this "strategy" in Croatia were hundreds of thousands of refugees, displaced, and missing persons not only of Croatian but also of Serbian, Hungarian, and other ethnic origins. These "methods" were known, for instance, from historical events on the Indian subcontinent and in Palestine.

The use of these methods for creating "clean ethnic borders" in ethnically completely mixed Bosnia and Herzegovina, as is obviously already happening, has as its first consequences a horrendous number of people killed and wounded, at least a million displaced persons, and a human tragedy on the continent that has declared the last decade of the century as the period of its decisive economic and political unification.

There is a real possibility of the renewal of another "historical border" on this part of Europe. On the territory where the UNPRO-FOR units should be deployed, there existed during the Austro-Hungarian empire a so-called military zone (*militärgrenze, Vojna krajina*) where the settlers (many of them of Serbian origin) had a duty to defend the empire (and Europe) against the Turkish invaders. If it lasts for a long period, the deployment of the UNPROFOR units will renew this "historical border," separating nations, cultures, and religious communities. This would be a catastrophe not only for peoples living in this area but for Europe as a whole.

3. The problem of succession is another Pandora's box in the Yugoslav crisis. First, the successor states have no sincere political will to regulate this matter. Second, the dissolution of Yugoslavia has not been yet completed; Serbia, together with Montenegro, for example, considers itself to be the sole successor to Yugoslavia. Third, a great many matters concerning the succession of the state are impossible to regulate on the basis of the inadequate rules of the various Vienna conventions – which, moreover, are not yet in force for the Yugoslav area.[14] The regulation of the succession calls for the cooperation of the states concerned. But as things now stand, some of the successor states have not expressed clear ideas on how to resolve this problem (except the division of debts and embassies!), and the others (Serbia and Montenegro) do not have the political will to do it. As completely different stands can be expected from the Yugoslav successor states concerning this matter also, there seems no possibility of settling it even partially without international assistance, first of all from the European Union.

The regulation of this matter would represent the definitive dissolution of Yugoslavia and would make easier the international affirmation of the successor states (membership of the UN and its specialized agencies and the conclusion of international agreements). Last but not least, in normal circumstances it could be expected that the successor states would establish, together with the agreement on dissolution, a basis for future international cooperation among themselves.

What are the prospects?

Before considering whether cooperation or integration is possible between states after so violent a split, it is necessary to consider some pertinent questions concerning the organization of future life in the successor states, peace and stability in the region, and the inclusion of this part of Europe in the process of European cooperation and integration. In considering these issues it would be wise also to take into account the following views and assertions:

1. The end of hostilities in Croatia and in Bosnia and Herzegovina can be only the first step towards the real pacification of the Serbian–Croatian confrontations; it will not resolve the basic political problems that have brought the Yugoslav federation into this cataclysm. As I have already suggested, the deployment of UNPROFOR forces in Croatia and probably in Bosnia and Herzegovina would be the only way to oblige the parties involved to stop fighting. If, on the other hand, political solutions concerning the occupied territories of Croatia are not achieved and respect for the borders and territorial integrity of Bosnia and Herzegovina is not assured, the explosion of a new war, this time a total war, will be a real danger. I believe Serbian and Croatian – especially the former – territorial pretensions towards Bosnia and Herzegovina, can checked only by direct political and military intervention on the part of the EU and the UN (UNPROFOR, NATO, the WEU?), aimed at introducing some kind of provisional international protectorate over the country.[15]

It is most likely that particular European states will become more and more involved in the confrontations between the successor states of Yugoslavia, either by giving political support (to their allies or client states) or by supplying them with military equipment.

Ensuring respect for the inviolability of the "external" borders of the successor states on the soil of former Yugoslavia, especially by their neighbours, will be a great challenge for European and world policy. The destruction of the first Yugoslavia at the beginning of World War II, and the division of its territory between Germany (which annexed Austria), Italy, Hungary, Bulgaria, and "Greater Albania," are still present in the historical memory of the people. Europe is thus, in my opinion, confronted with one of the greatest dangers for peace since World War II. It is to be hoped that the city of Sarajevo will not be mentioned in history as a place where two human disasters have been ignited in one century.

2. The primary challenge for all the new governments will be to show their ability to reform their economies and resolve without delay the large number of social, economic, political, and other problems which represent a nightmare for the great majority of the population of all the successor states. Recent events have shown that ethnic nationalism, ideology, and the insignia of statehood – to mention only few of the political tools of the new élite – are not a sufficient basis for achieving economic and social progress for the emerging societies.

Owing to the level of its economic development and the proximity of Western markets, Slovenia probably has the best chances for recovery and for achieving relatively sound progress in the near future. This could occur if a wise political regime were to come to power with the next elections and if it were able to create the basic political, economic, and other conditions required for the steady development of the country.[16]

Economic revival also depends on the political stability in the area as a whole. The prospects for achieving stable political solutions do not encourage optimism. The EU Conference on Yugoslavia, for instance, has not yet resolved any of the important issues on its agenda. Unless things change in the near future, there will be few chances for larger foreign economic and financial involvement, especially as regards investments, in this geographical area, and minimal chances for the renewal of the traditional European tourist flows in these directions as well.

3. It is hard to imagine that progress can be achieved without a genuine democratization of the emerging societies. Despite the formal changes of regime, the political methods developed by the communist rulers have remained the favourite tools of the new rulers of the successor states, partly because most of them were important figures during different phases of the former regimes.

Here we must recall how democracy has been widely misused to spread ethnic nationalism, racism, hate, and destruction of all that is different from "us". Mass media have become the most efficient tool for achieving this goal. In some of the emerging post-Yugoslavia nation states, very sophisticated political propaganda has completely overshadowed democracy. However, the nationalist wave that brought the new élite to power is losing the magical attractions it once had when the people, regardless of their ethnic origin, could not see optimistic prospects for their lives. Nevertheless, nationalism is still the main element of the programmes of the political parties in most of the successors of Yugoslavia. The structure of membership of the political parties in Bosnia and Herzegovina, for instance, fully corresponds to the ethnic and religious composition of the population.

The growth of extremist behaviour of a fascist nature, both in Croatia and Serbia and with less significant manifestations in other successor states, is another noxious nuisance. The uncertainties surrounding the fate of the occupied territories of Croatia will open even wider the door for the radicalization of the Croatian political and military bodies, where extremist groups of belligerent orientation already exist. The effect, both in Serbia and Croatia, will be unfettered pretensions to the division of Bosnia and Herzegovina on an ethnic basis. In Serbia and Croatia, distinct signs of authoritarian behaviour on the part of the "national leaders" could be identified. The presidents of the two countries have concentrated in their hands a huge amount of political power which hinders fulfilment of the competencies of parliaments and governments and diminishes the chances for these states and societies to take up other democratic options subsequently.

Looking at the situation from this point of view, one could conclude that the more decisive changes concerning the development of the successors of Yugoslavia will be achieved only if a genuine democratic reconstruction of these societies is undertaken. This is one of the preconditions for the urgently needed recovery of the emerging societies and states. Unfortunately, the possible development of

171

other, non-democratic solutions in this area of Europe cannot be excluded.

Thoroughgoing and large-scale integration of the successor states into the European structures would doubtless contribute to their democratization. But the main issues concerning democracy must be first of all resolved at home.

4. Improving inter-ethnic relations after the cataclysm that has stricken the people of former Yugoslavia will be the main task for future generations in their endeavours to resume normal life, cooperation, and political stability and peace in this part of Europe. The relations between Serbs and Croats will also be a crucial problem, and the future revitalization of former Yugoslavia and its inclusion in the processes of European integration will depend on the regulation of those relations. Further political and military intervention by the UN and the EU will probably be the only way to stop these two nation states from fighting for the redistribution of the territory of former Yugoslavia, in particular Bosnia and Herzegovina, along ethnic principles.

Real pacification, however, can be achieved only on the basis of the restoration of the now-broken confidence between the two ethnic groups. Looking at the demographic structure of Croatia, Serbia, Montenegro, and especially Bosnia and Herzegovina leads one to the conclusion that dividing them politically by means of ethnically "purified" frontiers between nation states is unrealizable even in theory. As in the past, they will also have to live together in the future. Any attempt at other solutions is sure to lead to new wars, even bloodier than the present.

5. Cooperation among the new states is a *sine qua non* for the formation of any system of security in the area, for healing the terrible consequences of war, for development, and for the region's future integration into European structures. In 70 years of common life many bonds have been established between the peoples of Yugoslavia, and many common economic and other interests developed. However this fact should not be overestimated. For instance, because of the unskilful governance of the country and polycentric ethnic tendencies, the integration of markets, technical systems, and other entities was never achieved. The result of the recent events, as I have said, is the interruption of cooperation between the former republics, including the functioning of transport and communication facilities, financial traffic, and so on. It is self-evident that such a state of affairs could not be the basis either for the renewal of life in this European area nor for its integration with the rest of Europe.

All the emerging states have declared their "European orientation." By this they mean, first of all, membership of the EU and other supranational European organizations. What is less certain is whether the people are fully aware that the first step towards the EU, for instance, must be made at home, by reforming the economy so as to enable it to cope with the standards adopted by the EU. The same applies to the need to develop among the successor states a level of cooperation at least as high as that existing among the other countries of Europe.

No serious analysis or consideration of this problem is known to the public. We have the impression that more or less all governments are of the opinion that cooperation between the successors of Yugoslavia is not important for their development or future incorporation in the EU and other European and international organizations and institutions, especially those dealing with economic and financial matters, such as the World Bank and the International Monetary Fund. I am of the opinion, on the contrary, that developing mutual cooperation between the emerging successor states would make it easier to resolve accumulated domestic problems and to work towards integration in international institutions as well.

It is very risky to speculate as to which fields will be most suitable for developing cooperation among Yugoslavia's successors, based on mutual interests. But even a general consideration of this issue reveals the need to try to develop such a cooperation in at least the following areas:

(*a*) Intercultural exchange and cooperation in the spirit of the various conventions of the Council of Europe.

(*b*) Economic cooperation concerning the functioning of infrastructure and communication facilities; assurance of minimal conditions for unhampered financial flows, open markets, investment opportunities, and exchange of goods; cooperation in the production and distribution of energy, food, and other goods. However, apparently nobody in former Yugoslavia is taking seriously the proposals put forward in this regard by the Hague Conference on Yugoslavia or by the president of the Conference, Lord Carrington.[17]

(*c*) Free exchange of information;[18] a ban of any kind of political propaganda aimed at incitement to racism, racial discrimination, or hate, or making any distinction between people because of their ethnic origin or religious belief.

(*d*) Free movement of people in the territories of the successor states of Yugoslavia and the elimination of any discrimination concerning the conditions for obtaining passports and other relevant documents.

(*e*) International guarantees of basic human rights and freedoms for all citizens of the successors of Yugoslavia, including a ban on any kind of discrimination among former Yugoslav citizens because of their ethnic origin.

(*f*) Guarantees of individual and collective rights for ethnic minorities;[19] this should be regulated preferably by international regional treaty or treaties signed also by the neighbouring states of former Yugoslavia. The agreement should regulate the rights of minorities living in successor states and in these neighbouring states. The efforts of the EU Conference on Yugoslavia in this regard have not yet been successful.[20]

(*g*) Cooperation concerning succession. In dealing with this issue it is recommended that future common interests, not only the division of the (miserable) heritage of the Yugoslav federation, be addressed.

Conclusion

The resolution of the complicated problems connected with the dissolution of Yugoslavia, and the development of the emerging successor societies and nation states, will take a long time. The idea that quick changes for the better are possible is an illusion, owing more to propaganda on the part of some of the new regimes than to real opportunities.[21]

The United Nations will have, together with the EU, a great and decisive responsibility in this regard. As we have already said, it would be a historical error if the UNPROFOR units were to establish some sort of new military buffer zone. For centuries, such a zone not only protected Europe from Turkish invasions but separated its peoples and cultures as well. From this point of view a "Cyprus-like green line," separating peoples on the basis of their ethnicity and religion, like the lines drawn in 1054 owing to the schism between "Eastern" and "Western" Christianity, would also be unacceptable.

In conclusion, I should like to reaffirm my conviction that cooperation between the successor states of Yugoslavia could be an important agent in their progress and in the region's political stability as well.

In view of the atrocities which the peoples involved in them have inflicted on each other and the hatred and vindictiveness overshadowing their relations, many readers may feel that the notion of such cooperation, in such circumstances, is a groundless illusion. They could be right. Nonetheless, I should like to remind them of two encouraging historical examples. During the American Civil War, Abraham Lincoln made a speech in which he referred sympathetically to the Southern rebels. An elderly lady, a staunch Unionist, upbraided him for speaking kindly of his enemies when he ought to be thinking of destroying them. His reply was classic: "Why, madam," Lincoln answered, "do I not destroy my enemies when I make them my friends?"[22]

The other encouraging example is the development of cooperation between France and Germany immediately after the Second World War. The godfathers of this concept, which was to become a basis for the unification of Europe, were planning it at the time when German V-1 and V-2 rockets were destroying London around them.

Why should this notion not become a challenge also for the peoples of the successor states of Yugoslavia? Why should they not try to destroy their enemies, as Abraham Lincoln did long ago, by making them their partners in problem-solving negotiation?

Notes

1. For a description of the political and socio-economic circumstances in Yugoslavia from the ethnic point of view, see Silvo Devetak, *The Equality of Nations and Nationalism in Yugoslavia, Successes and Dilemmas* (Vienna: W. Braumüller, 1988), pp. 99–132.
2. Op. cit., pp. 3–5.
3. The heartbreaking Croatian propaganda denominates this part of the independent state of Bosnia and Herzegovina as the "historic home" of the Croats. At the beginning of the democratic changes in Croatia the most militant members of the Croatian police and army were recruited from among the Croats of western Herzegovina. Persons coming from this region were disproportionately represented in the government of Croatia. During World War II this region was reportedly the stronghold of the pro-Nazi Croatian state.
4. In illustration: Of 616,000 of the population of Montenegro in April 1992, only 141,000 persons were working. Their average income was 10,000 Yugoslav dinars per month (at that time around 50–60 DM). See N.N., "Obraz na čitulji" (The face on the obituary), *Nedjelja* (Sarajevo) 111 (5 April 1992), p. 13. Similar social situations were found in Macedonia, Bosnia and Herzegovina, and Kosovo. In Slovenia, the "most developed republic" of the former Yugoslavia, considered to be a "welfare state," unemployment in a recent 18-month period rose from 0.8–1.00 per cent to 12–15 per cent, and seemed set to continue increasing steadily.
5. Slovenia is planning reconstructed or new road connections, due to available financial

resources, with Italy, Austria, and Hungary. The government of Croatia is, for instance, discussing the possibilities of constructing roads connecting Budapest with the Adriatic port of Rijeka, Zagreb with Graz, and Rijeka via Istria with Trieste. In Serbia, plans are under way for communication facilities towards Hungary in the north-east and towards Montenegro and Greece in the south-west and south-east.

6. The so-called plan of Cyrus Vance, special envoy of the Secretary-General of the United Nations (see UN Security Council S/23280 of 11 December 1991). For the stance of the Croatian government on this plan, see "Trideset dana za razvojačenje i odlazak stranih postrojbi" (Thirty days for demilitarization and withdrawal of foreign units), *Vjesnik* (Zagreb), 22 February 1992, p. 2. The title of the declaration reveals in itself the government's view of this issue.

7. To understand the problems connected with the demographic composition of this country, consult also Zlata Grebo, *Population of Bosnia and Herzegovina in the 80's*, Survey 11 (Sarajevo, December 1986), pp. 1273–4, and Dorde Pejanović, *Population of Bosnia and Herzegovina*, book 12 (Serbian Academy of Sciences, Belgrade, 1955), table 2.

8. The Croatian leader Tudjman wants, according to Mr Geršak, after the military defeat of Croatia and the wrong political assessments he made in the past, to rescue his position by occupying the region of Posavina (along the river Sava, from the city of Županja to Bosanski Brod in Bosnia and Herzegovina), western Herzegovina, and the places where Croats live around the cities of Bugojno, Travnik, and Prozor. See A. Geršak, "Bosanska ravnoteža straha" (The Bosnian equilibrium of fear), *Nedjelja* 111 (5 April 1992), p. 9.

9. See *Convention de Vienne sur la succession d'États en matière de traités*, 23 août 1978, Nations Unies, *Annuaire juridique 1978*, p. 130; and *Convention on State Succession in Respect of State Property, Archives and Debts*, 8 August 1983, UN Doc. A.CONF.117/14.

10. This intention could be proved also by the fact that the remnants of the Federal Parliament have adopted a law according to which "federal" legislation will be in force in these territories of Croatia. The director of the "federal" customs agency has announced the building of 18 new checkpoints "on the border with Croatia" in the same area.

11. The establishment of the independent state of Macedonia has also raised other questions in relation to Serbia and Macedonia. The Serbian Orthodox Church did not consider legitimate the establishment of the Macedonian Orthodox Church after World War II. In view of the possibility of the formation of an independent state of Macedonia and of the related Orthodox Church, the Serbian Church has put forward a request in which it claims ownership of "immoveable" and "moveable" property in Macedonia (20 churches and monasteries, among them the eleventh-century church of Saint Sofia in Ohrid). They have asked UNESCO's protection for the most valuable cultural documents. See "Bratku država – Srbima crkve" (The state to the brother, the churches to the Serbs) *Borba* (Belgrade), 9 April 1992, p. 9 (non-signed).

12. The Minister of the Interior of the Republic of Slovenia has spoken of 17 "unregulated points" on the Slovenia–Croatia border. The delimitation between the two states on the Adriatic Sea was opened for discussion, including the problem of access from the Slovenian harbour of Koper/Capodistria to the open sea.

13. See Appendix, p. 178.

14. See above, n. 9.

15. See Zoran Pajić, "Apartheid," *Nedjelja* 111 (5 April 1992), p. 5; also "Bosanska ravnoteža straha," op. cit., p. 9.

16. There is considerable evidence that the present government is not competent to rule the economy or other public affairs of the country. On the basis of the new constitution of 1992, elections should have been organized six months after its adoption.

17. See *Treaty Provisions for the Convention*, corrected version of 3 November 1991, Den Haag, and previous proposals made by Lord Carrington.

18. For example, Slavko Perovic, president of the Liberal Alliance of Montenegro, said in April 1992 that in that republic, 35 newspapers from Belgrade and two or three from Sarajevo are

sold, but none from Croatia, Slovenia, or Macedonia. A similar situation with regard to the Serbian press exists in Croatia. In Slovenia, however, all the newspapers are available without any restrictions.

19. As an illustration of how the new states were regulating these issues, see, among others:

Serbia: *Ustav Republike Srbije* (The Constitution of the Republic of Serbia), Službeni glasnik RS, 1/90 (art. 6, 8, 13, 41); *Zakon o službenoj upotrebi jezika i pisama* (Law on the official use of languages and alphabets), SG RS 45/91; *Zakon o osnovnom obrazovanju* (Law on primary education), SG RS 5/90 (čl. 2, 15); *Zakon o radioteleviziji* (Law on radio and television), SG RS 5/90 (art. 20, paras. 2 and 3); *Deklaracija o neotudjivom pravu srbskog naroda na samoopredeljenje* (Law on the inalienable right of the Serbian nation to self-determination), SG RS 79/91; *Zakon o prestanku rada Predsedništva Socijalističke autonomne pokraijine Kosovo* (Law on the termination of work of the Presidency of the Socialist Autonomous Region of Kosovo), SG RS 15/91.

Croatia: *Ustav Republike Hrvatske* (Constitution of the Republic of Croatia), Narodne novine 56/90 (art. 3, 12, 14, 15); *Ustavni zakon o ljudskim pravima i slobodama i o pravima etničkih i nacionalnih zajednica ili manjinama u Republici Hrvatskoj* (Constitutional Law on human rights and liberties and on the rights of ethnic and national communities or minorities in the Republic of Croatia), NN SL RH, 65/91; *Uredba o uredu za nacionalne manjine* (Decree on the office for national minorities), NN SL RH, 52/90; *Zakon o osnovnom školstvu* (Law on primary schools), NN SL RH, 59/90; *Zakon o Hervatskoj radio-televiziji* (Law on Croatian radio and television), NN SL RH, 28/9035/91 (art. 7, 8, 9, 13).

Macedonia: *Ustav na Republika Makedonija, Služben vestnik na*, RM 52/91 (art. 7, 8, 19, 48).

20. See, for instance, the opinion of the Arbitration Commission of 11 January 1992 concerning the international recognition of the Republic of Croatia, *Conference on Yugoslavia paper*, Den Haag, 11 January 1992.

21. Typical examples have been the items on Croatian television showing the year 1990 as the year of democratic elections, 1991 as a year of war, and 1992 as a year of unification of Croatia with Europe.

22. W. Ury, *Getting Past No: Negotiating with Difficult People* (Bantam Books, New York/Toronto/London/Sydney, 1991), p. 146.

Appendix

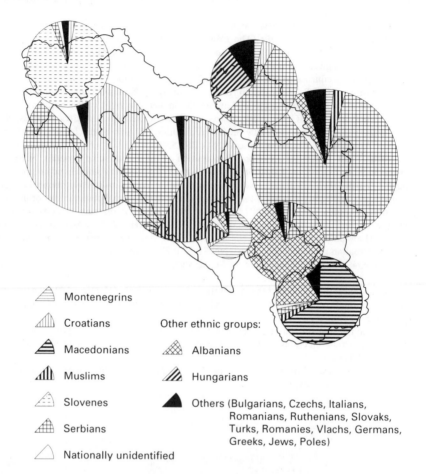

Montenegrins

Croatians

Macedonians

Muslims

Slovenes

Serbians

Nationally unidentified

Other ethnic groups:

Albanians

Hungarians

Others (Bulgarians, Czechs, Italians, Romanians, Ruthenians, Slovaks, Turks, Romanies, Vlachs, Germans, Greeks, Jews, Poles)

Ethnic composition of the Yugoslav population according to census, 1981. Source: Silvo Devetak, *The Equality of Nations and Nationalities in Yugoslavia, Successes and Dilemmas* (Vienna: W. Braumüller, 1988), p. 3.

10

Ethnic conflict, federalism, and democracy in India

S.D. Muni

India's ethnic spectrum

India has a highly complex and colourful social mosaic. Yet, although characterized by a vast spread of cultural diversity and heterogeneity, this mosaic is not chaotic. It has a clearly discernible pattern, wherein socio-cultural diversity draws its strength and sustenance from India's composite culture and civilizational thrust. This culture has evolved over centuries, through a process of assimilation and amalgamation of the diverse cultural influxes coming with the hordes of invaders – the Aryans, the Sakas, the Huns, the Pathans, the Moghuls, and the Europeans. Thus, the evolved composite culture of India cannot be compared either with the melting-pot of American society or with the multinational state exemplified by the now-defunct Soviet Union. India's socio-cultural mosaic is the true picture of "unity in diversity," like a bouquet of flowers or vegetables in a salad bowl, where every component, while retaining its specific identity, is a part of a larger whole.[1]

Upon this cultural diversity, within the ambit of civilizational unity, is based the reality of the multi-ethnic society of India. Several cul-

179

tural markers – language, race, tribe, caste, religion, and region – serve as identity axes for ethnic groups and their mobilization. In most of the ethnic groups, more than one of these cultural markers are pertinent for identification. In other words, India's ethno-communities have multilayered and multidimensional identities that impinge on each other in a non-stratified and dynamic manner. The identity composition of ethno-communities has been further complicated by the imposition of class distinctions, not only between one and another ethno-community, but also within each.[2] Multilayered, non-stratified identity composition has enabled ethnic groups to assert and reshuffle their cultural markers to advance their perceived objectives.

Two other commonly accepted characteristics of the spectrum of ethnic diversity in India deserve attention. One is that there is no subordinate–dominant pattern between the ethnic groups.[3] Thus, the patterns of conflicts and contradictions between ethno-communities vary along scales of time and place. Secondly, the ethnic groups do not have territories marked out for them because the cultural markers identifying such groups do not coincide with territorial boundaries.[4] Accordingly, people belonging to specific religions, tribes, castes, races, and languages are found scattered in various territorial regions. We shall see later that not even the reorganization of states in India on linguistic lines has been able to overcome this aspect.

Potential for conflicts and their protraction

Any diversity and heterogeneity is not conflict-producing *per se*, although it may carry a potential for conflict. India has witnessed ethnic conflicts in the process of its historical evolution, and the leadership of independent India was conscious that while India presents the picture of "unity and diversity," the possibility of conflict between the "unity" and the "diversity" could not be ruled out. Independent India's first prime minister, Jawaharlal Nehru, said:

While on the one hand, we the people of India are bound together by strong bonds of culture, common objectives, friendship and affection, on the other hand, unfortunately, there are inherent in India, separatist and disruptive tendencies ... [which made India suffer in the past. In preserving its unity, India needed to] ... fight communalism, provincialism, separatism, statism and casteism.[5]

On another occasion, he admitted that:

When we talk loudly of our nationalism, each person's idea of nationalism is his own brand of nationalism. It may be Assamese nationalism, it may be

Bengali, it may be Gujrati, Uttar Pradesh, Punjabi or Madrasi. Each one has his own particular brand in mind. He may use the word nationalism of India but in his mind, he is thinking of that nationalism in terms of his own brand of it. When two brands of nationalism come into conflict, there is trouble.[6]

Even when such apprehensions have been expressed and real conflicts have been experienced, it is theoretically erroneous to assume, as has been done by many scholars and analysts, that transformation of a peacefully coexisting, collaborating and competing diversity into a conflictual one is inevitable and/or automatic. Social reality in India and elsewhere clearly reveals, on closer scrutiny, that the precipitation of ethnic conflict from a situation of ethnic diversity and heterogeneity is a rather complex process. Through this process, the boundaries of a given ethnic group are activated, resulting in the awareness and politicization of ethnic identities. Further, political mobilization for given goals leads to the building up of an ethnic movement which subsequently may or may not be transformed from one stage to another.

Underlining this aspect, Tambiah states:

Although the actors themselves ... speak as if ethnic boundaries are clearcut and defined for all time; and think of ethnic collectivities as self-reproducing bounded groups, it is also clear that from a dynamic and procedural perspective, there are many precedents of 'passing' and the change of identity, for incorporation and assimilation of new members and for changing the scales and criteria of collective identity.[7]

In the process of the "passing" of ethnic identities and politicization of ethnic groups, a number of "secular" or "non-ethnic" factors play a critical role. These include the state, pace, and pattern of economic development, political élites and forces, and outside subversion. Without these factors and the process of transformations in the ethnic groups, diversity would not assume conflictual dimensions. Emphasizing the role of political vested interests in precipitating ethnic conflicts, Gupta observes:

The manifestation of ethnicity in Indian politics is not so much an outcome of popular grassroots passions as it is a creation of vested political interests. The reason for stressing this is because it is often uncritically accepted that politicians at the secular centre are holding back the popular surge of communalism, for ethnicised politics is a natural inclination of the Indian people. On the other hand, I argue here that communal ideologies are hatched up at the perennially hot house top, then broadcast below, and only sometimes do they take root. On many other occasions, they languish as amorphous judgements, without concrete action prescriptions.[8]

Owing to the varying parameters of the process of identity trans-formations and the roles of external (non-ethnic) factors, ethnic con-flicts and politics in India have "waxed and waned."[9] Even some of the raging ethnic conflicts in India have shown inconsistencies in their ideological manifestations and intensity. The conflict in the Punjab, for instance, had a dominant linguistic thrust during the mid-1960s. In the late 1970s and early 1980s it was rekindled by the rivalry between competing Sikh sects, the Nirankaris and the Akalis. To this was added intra-group political rivalries amongst the Sikhs in the Punjab. Subsequently, it assumed both religious and economic dimensions in the form of the Anandpur Sahib Resolution. At present, it is fast acquiring a Sikh fundamentalist character, with growing emphasis on the assertion of Sikh religious and cultural symbols to legitimize militancy and violence. Elements of the Punjab situation are also reflected in the Kashmir conflict, where the initial movement of the state's political and economic neglect has now clearly acquired over-tones of Islamic religious assertion, to the extent of becoming funda-mentalist. Accordingly, the earlier concept of Kashmir identity, or *Kashmiriat*, has been replaced by communal confrontation, wherein the Muslim militants have pushed Hindu Kashmiris out of the valley.

India also bears witness to the fact that the precipitation and intensification of ethnic conflicts by cultural diversity is not a uni-linear or irreversible process. Ethnic conflicts have been resolved and reduced, but also re-created. The conflict arising out of the demand for the Tamil language and land during the early 1960s was resolved, although potential tension between Tamil and the declared (but not imposed) national language, Hindi, still exists. In the context of the Punjab conflict, the Rajiv–Longowal accord of 1985 was a major move to contain the conflict, although it proved futile. The initial thrust of ethnic conflict in Assam, which was directed against the influx of foreigners, experienced some respite in the mid-1980s, although now it has re-emerged in violent form under the leadership of the Bodos and ULFA (United Liberation Front of Assam) groups. Similarly, some of the tribal insurgencies in the North-East have also been politically contained.

These varying patterns of conflict formation and containment (including resolution) are likely to persist in the future. For instance, a communal and fundamentalist conflict such as the clash between a temple (Hindu) and a mosque (Muslim) in Ayodhya seems to have lost its militancy and violent thrust after climaxing in 1990–91. At the same time there are signs of new conflict formations among some of the hitherto neglected tribes. The movements of Tribals in the Jharkand region (Bihar) and of Nepalis in Darjeeling and Sikkim over the language issue, have become sufficiently politicized and militant to create flashpoints.

Simultaneous conflict formation and conflict containment

The inconsistent and reversible processes of ethnic conflicts can be understood in the context of India's developmental dynamics, which have been releasing simultaneously the impulses of both conflict formation and containment. Both the alienation and integration of ethnic groups have been going on side by side, a process which Arun Bose describes as "Disintegration and Reintegration."[10]

Looking at the politics of ethnicity in South Asia with reference to developmental dynamics, either of the two trends can be emphasized. On the one hand, Asaf Husain presupposed that "successful national integration would cut across structures," while on the other hand, Paul Brass highlighted a "process of nationality formation rather than state-building."[11] The reality is that both these views are tenable since one "does not preclude the other."[12] It is this dual character of social development which prompts David Washbrook to say that "the politics of ethnicity have been remarkably ineffective in directing the course of modern Indian history,"[13] although many may seriously question this categorical assertion.

The fact that the sharpening of ethnic boundaries and conflicts in India has been on the rise cannot be disputed. Studies have shown an increase in communal riots, and the rise in the number of persons killed in these riots has become alarming since 1985, as can be seen from official data:[14]

Year	Communal incidents	Persons killed	Persons injured
1955	75	24	475
1965	173	34	758
1975	205	33	890
1985	525	328	3,665

In 1985, rural areas which thus far had remained unaffected also accounted for 46 per cent of communal incidents. The momentum in communal violence has kept up in recent years. In 1989 there were 18 major riots, in which 1,174 persons were killed. The number of persons killed in 1986 was 418; 383 were killed in 1987, 223 in 1988, and 693 in 1990.[15] One of the major factors behind the deterioration in the communal situation is the rise of Hindu fundamentalism and its corresponding majoritarian ethnic nationalism based on *Hindutva*. The temple–mosque conflict in Ayodhya was a concrete manifestation of this.[16] Political vested interests have obviously played a decisive role in this development, which if allowed to go on unabated will worsen the situation and endanger India's unity and integrity.[17]

As for the persistent and festering ethnic conflicts in the Punjab, Kashmir, and Assam, we have already noted that they have intensified and the extent of violence has grown. Even the character of these insurgencies, in terms of their objectives, ideologies, leadership, and methods, is becoming more strident and uncompromising. The growing violent activities of Sikh militants in the Terai region of Uttar Pradesh have become a matter of serious concern. In addition to this, other potential ethnic conflicts such as in Jharkand and the Nepali/ Gurkha communities are reportedly gathering political momentum.[18] In the north-eastern tribal areas, the Naga National Council (NNC) has decided to take up arms and coordinate its activities with the National Socialist Council of Nagaland (NSCN). The tribal situation in Manipur, Tripura, and Mizoran is also moving fast towards the boil.[19]

No less significant than this process of disintegration and conflict have been the forces of integration and mutual identification of diverse ethnic and cultural streams. We have noted earlier that the basis of the integrative process is India's composite culture, expressed in the form of secular national identity. Indian secularism did not evolve on the pattern of European secularism, which strove to detach the spiritual from the temporal. In India, all religions were accepted on an equal footing. The state gave equal rights to all religious and ethnic groups so that they could protect and promote their educational and cultural interests, by virtue of the Indian Constitution (arts. 26–30). (An exception was made for scheduled castes and tribes, which were brought under the umbrella of "protective discrimination," according to Part X, arts. 30, 46, 244, 244A, and 335 of the Indian Constitution.) This secular identity was not an imposition by the state on society but a recognition of a deep-rooted social reality – that erosion of this identity would mean the disintegration of India along sectarian lines. Hence, firm constitutional provisions were made to preserve secular identity. In a way, they were necessary, owing to the trauma of India's partition.

To have a better appreciation of the dual process of integration and alienation of ethnic and national groups/identities – that is, the simultaneous occurrence of ethnic conflict formation and containment, we must look more closely at India's developmental dynamics, federalism, and democracy.

Dynamics of development

The significance of linkages between the dynamics of development and ethnic conflicts has been widely recognized. Reetz, in discussing the ethnic dilemma in Pakistan, observes that:

ethnic and national group formation ... could be separated from modern socio-economic development trends of emerging capitalism. The growth of market relations at regional and national levels was the driving force behind the increasing articulation of both separate ethnic and common national interests.[20]

This is equally relevant to the Indian situation, where the national and regional market developed much faster and more strongly than anywhere else in South Asia. The development of this market, backed by the growth of industry and commerce, brought diverse regional and ethnic interests together to interact, collaborate, and compete. As a result, regional and ethnic interests have developed stakes in expanding and strengthening the national market and linking it with the network of regional interests. Capital, technology, industry and commerce, and labour have moved from one region to another, cutting across and subordinating ethnic diversities. Diverse interest groups have come into being; industrialists, traders, transporters, and workers (trade unions). In the mixed economy of India, the process of development planning for target groups and regions has greatly helped various neglected and marginalized sections of society to join the national mainstream. Allocation of plan resources by the centre to the states has also bound them in a nexus of mutual bargaining and collaboration, notwithstanding the displeasure of the states over the amounts of resources transferred.

But these integrative pulls have not been without disintegrative implications. One of the common causes of the politicization of ethnicity and the formation of ethnic conflict is said to be the relative and perceived sense of economic deprivation by a given ethnic group. Tambiah, looking at national and international factors behind the cause of economic deprivation, says:

The present plethora of ethnic conflicts ... coincides with an increasing sense of shrinking economic horizons and political battlement. Many things have gone awry with economic development: the declining terms of trade dictated by the industrialised West; internal bottlenecks; agricultural under-employment and migration to cities; increasing disparities of income among the expectant participants in the literacy explosion; the visible pauperisa-tion of the urban underclass...[21]

All this has happened in the course of India's economic develop-ment. The most illustrative aspect of this development is the lopsided and uneven growth of the national market, prosperity, and income distribution, and the sensitization of underprivileged groups to their disadvantageous placement in the national division of labour. In some cases, bouts of prosperity have resulted in inflating expect-ations, which national resource generation and distribution mecha-nism have not been able to fulfil. In others, the slow pace of building prosperity has given rise to the sense of relative deprivation. Equally pertinent here is to note that corruption and family or "ethnic nepo-tism"[22] have given impetus to alienation and conflict formation.

It is illustrative in this respect that economic maldevelopment has fuelled diverse ethnic insurgencies in India. Some recent studies on communal conflicts in North India show that the prosperity of Muslim artisans has given them confidence to free themselves from exploita-tion by Hindu traders and moneylenders, helping precipitate such conflicts. In the Punjab, it has been a problem of prosperity combined with unequal distribution of wealth resulting from the green revolu-tion boom. The rich Punjabi farmers, in search of investing their sur-pluses for better returns, found it compelling to capture state power. Further marginalization of small and landless peasants forced them into militancy for bare survival.[23]

By contrast, the situation in Kashmir, Assam, and the North-East has been one of economic neglect and discrimination in the percep-tion of the affected masses. Even when national funds were allocated, they did not reach the targeted groups, because of the corruption of bureaucrats, politicians, and other mediators. In the absence of any serious attempt to correct these economic distortions, it may not be realistic to expect resolution of these raging ethnic conflicts.

Federalism

In the debate on India's national integration and ethnic tensions, the nature and functioning of the federal power structure occupies an important place. The foundations of federalism were laid down on the grounds of concern for the unity and integrity of a culturally diverse nation. In view of historical experiences of disruptive and disintegrative sectarian forces and the political context of partition prevailing at the time of independence, the founding fathers of the Indian Constitution wanted to strengthen the Union against possible disintegrative pressures. Introducing the draft Constitution in the Constituent Assembly, Dr Ambedkar said:

though India was to be a federation, the federation was not the result of an agreement by the states to join in a federation. Not being a result of an agreement, no state has the right to secede from it. Though the country and the people may be divided into different states for convenience of administration, the country is one integral whole, its people a single people living under a single *imperium* derived from a single source ... The Drafting Committee thought it was better to make [this] clear at the outset rather than leave it to speculation ...[24]

Thus the perceived basis of structuring the federation was "administrative convenience." Unlike the American and the (erstwhile) Soviet constitutions, the states had no inherent, not even notional, right to secede from the Union or demand self-determination. In fact the Union in India was empowered to frustrate any such separatist or secessionist pressures if and when they arose.

With administrative convenience the avowed guiding principle for designing the federation, not much weight was given to the need for reflecting India's cultural design. No specific provisions for religious or cultural minorities were incorporated, except that they were given equal rights. The principle of "preventive discrimination," applied in the case of scheduled castes and scheduled tribes, was designed more to undo their social and economic backwardness than to help them preserve and promote their cultural distinctiveness.

The Constitution's initial provisions and subsequent amendments provided for self-government under special administrative provisions for Jammu and Kashmir (Schedule IV, article 370) and to the tribal areas of North-East (Nagas, Mizos, Manipuri, Tripura, under articles 371 and 371A–I), but the Constituent Assembly refused to endorse proposals for constituting states on a linguistic basis. Nehru even

187

went to the extent of threatening his resignation if that was to be done, as he apprehended that such a provision would endanger India's unity and integrity.[25]

Nehru was soon to revise his position on this vital issue under the force of circumstances when, in 1953, the linguistic basis of reorganizing states was accepted and Telugu-speaking Andhra emerged as the first such state. The Commission Constituted to Reorganise States in the Indian Federation nonetheless continued to emphasize that "it is the Union of India that is the basis of our nationality."[26] Explaining the criterion of language as the basis for constituting a state, it said:

Linguistic homogeneity provides the only rational basis for reconstituting the state, for it reflects the social and cultural pattern of living obtaining in well defined regions of the country.

The congress leadership, including Nehru, which had earlier opposed the idea, conceded, saying that, being democrats, they had to respect people's wishes.

The process of linguistic reorganization of states initiated in 1953 has been carried forward under the recommendations of the States Reorganisation Commission since 1956 and was broadly completed by the end of the 1960s.[27] This was a major development toward incorporating cultural identities into political and administrative units. The federal devolution of power strengthened this expression of cultural diversity.

The devolution of powers between the Union (or the centre) and the states was laid down in separate lists prepared for this purpose. Accordingly, the list of the states' "exclusive" powers includes: public order; police; education; local government; roads and transport; agriculture; land and land revenue; forests; fisheries; industry and trade (limited); state Public Service Commissions; and Courts (except the Supreme Court). The states can also make laws along with the centre (provided the two do not clash), on subjects included in a "Concurrent List." These subjects include: criminal laws and their administration; economic and social planning; commercial and industrial monopolies; shipping and navigation on the inland waterways; drugs; ports (limited); courts and civil procedures. The arrangement for distribution of powers between the Union and the states has remained generally stable.[28]

One of the controversial aspects of centre–state relations has been the allocation of economic resources by the Union to the states. Such allocation is carried out by the Planning Commission in the area of developmental expenditure and has led to complaint by the states that the resources provided are inadequate. The states also have their own power to raise revenues. The "Gadgil Plan," regarding financial relations between the Union and the states, was not acceptable to the Sarkaria Commission, which was appointed to review the whole gamut of centre–state relations in view of the state's growing unhappiness in this regard. The Commission reported in 1988, but successive Finance Commissions have gradually enlarged the scope of devolution of taxes to the states. (These later Commissions were appointed under articles 280–1 of the Constitution to decide the distribution of taxes between the Union and the states as well as grants-in-aid to the states out of the Consolidated Fund of India.) The Eighth Finance Commission raised the level of such tax revenues in favour of the states from 55 to 85 per cent.[29]

Such an elaborate structure of power devolution has combined with the linguistic basis of federal unity to facilitate the management of cultural diversity in India and help mitigate pulls toward separatism and disintegration. Centre–state relations, whether based on ethnicity or otherwise, have not been peaceful or tension-free, but the competition has tended to focus on securing resources and greater power. States of diverse languages and cultures have often joined together to enhance their bargaining power. In some cases the Indian federal structure even provides for such bargaining through bodies such as the Inter-State and National Development Councils. Examples of bargaining coalitions include that of four Southern Chief Ministers joining in 1983 to negotiate with the centre. Similarly, in 1987 a conclave of nine opposition parties held near Delhi under the leadership of the Andhra Telugu Desham leader, N.T. Rama Rao, demanded the restoration of "co-operative federalism enshrined in the Constitution."[30]

In 1992, the Sikkim Chief Minister and his regional party, the Sikkim Sangram Parishad, asked for membership in the North-East Council (of North-East States and Tribal Areas) for this same purpose.[31] Some scholars have described the federal system in India as one of "coalition and administration," or one with a "high degree of collaborative partnership."[32] In addition, both at the central and state levels, a consciously followed approach to preserve and promote the cultural specificities of diverse groups has helped such groups identify with the national mainstream.[33] All this has contributed to the secularization of ethnicity and has thus helped strengthen integrative forces.

It is interesting to note that most of the ethnic conflicts are between one given ethnic group and the Union of India, as if there were no ethnic contradictions and incompatibilities between individual groups. As noted earlier, the issues involved in such conflicts are invariably mixed with questions of sharing economic resources and decision-making power.

The functioning of federalism has nevertheless also had undesirable implications for the ethnic scene in India. The linguistic reorganization of the states gave impetus to various groups of specific cultural markers and ethnic identities to seek political expression and legitimacy. This was because ethnic identity was provided a territory under the scheme of reorganization. The importance of ethnic territory in ethnic conflict is very crucial, as can be gathered from recent developments in the Punjab and Kashmir and earlier events in Assam. In the Punjab and Kashmir conflicts, along with the transformation of identities and issues, the territorial base of ethnicity is being perfected by driving out Punjabi-speaking Hindus from the Punjab and Kashmiri-speaking Hindus from Kashmir. The potential for conflict formation along ethnic identity lines has thus been encouraged.

This potential has been further sharpened because linguistic reorganization in a vast and diverse country like India cannot be perfectly precise. On the periphery of the newly formed linguistic states, unassimilated linguistic minorities continued to exist. Then many other linguistic groups continued to remain in the larger Hindi-speaking states without being accommodated in the new political arrangement. The dissatisfactions of some of the unrecognized minority linguistic groups also continue to simmer. Such problems exist with regard to the Konkan region of Maharasthra/Goa, Nepali-speaking groups of Darjeeling, Sikkim, and Assam, and Maithili and Avadhi language groups in Bihar.

The possibility of political movements and conflict formation arising out of these problems cannot be ruled out. There are already several political parties which are ethnicity-based, and they will very willingly build their strength by exploiting the linguistic frustrations of their constituencies. The Sarkaria Commission (1988) clearly hinted at weaknesses of the linguistic reorganization of states in this respect when it said:

Very often, the sub-national sentiment which is initially based on linguistic, religious or ethnic groupings, gains strength with a blend of economic issues, such as those relating to ... economic backwardness. One of the most significant developments has been the rise of linguistic chauvinism, rearrangement of the boundaries of the States on linguistic basis ... resulting in fissiparous tendencies.[34]

In a very significant way, federalism has fuelled ethnic conflict through the use of the Union's special provisions over the states. The use of article 356, which provides for imposition of presidential rule in a state in the "event of the failure of constitutional machinery," has been the subject of considerable controversy and debate in this regard. Political use of this provision has been extensive, particularly by the Congress-ruled centre. It can be employed to dismiss the state government of an opposition party or to manipulate political advantages for a ruling party or a particularly favoured political leader. In such manipulative machinations, the centre-appointed governor has played a decisive role, bringing the status and integrity of the governorship into considerable disrepute. The victimized party and leaders have sought to project this abuse of power as an instance of suppression of the political rights of the dominant ethnic group in the given state.

This has been an important factor behind the alienation of the Punjab, Kashmir, and Assam.[35] Nagaland, where presidential rule was imposed in April 1992, is a recent example of the alleged misuse of article 356. In reaction, Nagaland's Chief Minister Vamuzo, who was ousted, said:

The 'imperial character' of the Delhi government has manifested itself in its most perverted and brutal forms in the north-eastern states. The latest act of perfidy by the Congress government has come at a time when, with the knowledge and approval of Delhi, I was engaged in an effort to persuade the underground insurgents in Nagaland to give up arms and join the political process. Obviously, such efforts were not to the liking of certain sections of the political leadership in the state who have a vested interest in a violent underground movement ...

Let me, however, sound a note of warning. The entire North-East is in a state of turmoil. Frustration because of unemployment is driving the educated youth of this region to desperation. The sense of alienation due to the overbearing presence of the army is being compounded by the lack of opportunity. And the denial to the people of their right to govern themselves in accordance with the

191

Constitution is creating situations that will ultimately convince the people of the entire North-East, from Arunachal to Mizoram, that they have no hope of a life of peace and dignity under the present dispensation.[36]

While the abuse of some constitutional provisions by the centre against the states has tended to alienate the states-based ethnic leadership, the creation and use of other specific provisions at the local level by the army, state governments, or police have resulted in distancing the common people from the Union. (Such provisions include the Disturbed Areas Act, the Armed Forces Special Powers Act of 1958 for the Eastern region and of 1983 for Punjab and Chandigarh, and the act relating to "Terrorist Affected Disturbed Areas.") As a consequence of their application, the social bases of ethnic conflicts have widened and deepened. The Sarkaria Commission blamed those in charge of the centre for this misuse and centralization of power in the Union, saying:

Those in power at the centre, have been obliged to use diverse strategies and tactics which were not always sound from [a] long-term [point of view] to maintain their control over state level forces. Many a time, the actions of the centre, its discriminatory approach towards some states, its lack of understanding of local problems, its abject insensitiveness (*sic*) and the blatant misuse of authority *vis-a-vis* the states, have all distanced it from the people. This in turn has, it is believed, reversed the process of national integration ...[37]

Based on federal experience in India, it may not be out of place to assume that the structure of federalism and its inherent resilience can cope with the pressures of ethnicity and conflicts. It can even help resolve, or at least contain, some of these pressures, if the imperatives of federal devolution of power and obligations of mutual accommodation and adjustments are observed sincerely. The diffusion of Tamil militancy and separatism during the 1960s and instances of moderation of tribal insurgencies in the North-East and Assam during the 1980s may be recalled in this regard. Against this, politically motivated distortions and manipulation of federal powers and institutions can worsen ethnic conflicts.

Punjab and Kashmir are painful illustrations of this. In the case of Punjab, if the political expediency of appeasing Haryana had not hamstrung the centre (irrespective of the party in power), the Rajiv–Longowal Agreement of 1985 would have been implemented to ease the conflict there, if not completely resolve it. The statement of the dismissed Nagaland Chief Minister Vamuzo cited earlier is also relevant here.

In an important way, federal relations have been vitiated by the breakdown of the Congress Party's dominance of the centre and the states since the 1960s and the emergence of political incompatibility and competition between the party ruling at the centre and in the various states. As these incompatibilities have grown, demands for redefining and restructuring these relations have been most pronounced, because the forum consisting of a single party in power everywhere could not be utilized to sort out federal tensions.

Reacting to distortions in federal relations and the abuse of powers devolved under the constitutional arrangement, some scholars have called for restructuring Indian federalism.[38] That may be neither practical nor offer a real panacea, because the structure so redefined may also be misused or manipulated for political purposes. The remedy lies in the evolution and strict observance of healthy guidelines and norms in the operational aspects of federalism, which have to become a reliable instrument for containing, moderating, and resolving ethnic conflicts.

Democratic politics

Dual impulses of ethnic integration and disintegration have been released by the democratic politics of India. Democracy as an ideology and system of governance centres around the individual; hence, it underplays the ethnic specificity and group feeling of individuals. It also prescribes and permits the pursuance of multiple interests by individuals, who accordingly associate in interest groups that cut across ethnic identities.[39]

Indian experience confirms this theoretical assumption. Adult franchise and Panchayati Raj institutions in India have brought people together to communicate and interact. This has given them a sense of sharing and access to decision-making power, however ineffective and fragile this access may be. Communication and consciousness of individual rights have bound them together in non-ethnic ties and prevented the state from acquiring a specific ethnic character or bias. Seth, in discussing the problems of ethnic movements and the role of the state in pluralistic societies, holds that:

The forces generated by democratic politics prevent the state from choosing a single cultural identity, even majoritarian, [as] the basis of nationhood.

193

Thus, the project of nation-building in a democratic polity becomes insepa-rable from building a civil society ...[40]

Such "civil societies" do not host ethnic conflicts or movements in any negative sense of the term. Democracy is helpful in averting ethnic precipitation in other ways, too. Freedom of expression and powerful, sensitive national media not only promote a broader national consensus but also alert and forewarn the state and society when ethnic distortions and conflict formations become imminent.

There is, however, another side to democratic politics in India. Though democratic ideology focuses on the individual, political mobilization (electoral and otherwise) in a highly stratified, diverse, and clustered society like India, it has also taken place on a group basis. Accordingly, caste blocs have acted as basic and lasting "vote banks" in democratic elections.[41] To some extent, the British legacy can be blamed for the communalization of Indian politics, because concepts like "communal representation" were introduced during the British period. But then, in independent India the reservation of elected seats and constituencies for specific caste groups (Schedule Castes and Tribes), though based on strong commitment to social justice and change, has been a persistent endorsement of politics based on social divisions. Political polarization on the Mandal Com-mission implementation and reservations for the Other Backward Castes (OBCs) were an outcome of this legacy. The political tallying of lower castes and ethnic loyalties has tended to encourage the upper castes and Hindu backlash emerging in the form of *Hindutva* politics.

The root cause of the growing recourse to caste and ethnic mobi-lization in India's democratic politics has been the erosion of ideology and viable socio-economic programmes around which electoral and political mobilization ought to take place. This erosion became prominent in the mid-1960s, when even the Congress Party started feeling insecure about its capacity to maintain its dominance. Mobi-lization along communal, caste, religious, regional, and tribal lines sought to fill in the ideological vacuum. There followed a rise, both in number and political clout, of ethnic and region-based parties.[42]

The imperatives of federalism in India, particularly with linguistic states as a vital political category, have encouraged and strengthened regional parties.[43] This has given impetus to the activation of ethnic identities and has contributed to the process of conflict formation along ethnic lines. There has also been a positive aspect, in the sense that no ethnic or regional party is capable of assuming power at the centre on its own. Parties have therefore endeavoured to form alliances and coalitions with national parties to evolve alternative and competing structures of power. Experiments like the Samyukt Vidhayak Dal of the 1960s, the Janata Party of the 1970s, and the National Front since the 1980s are examples. These experiments have tended to broaden and facilitate national consensus rather than hinder it.

The more dangerous aspect of India's emerging democratic politics has been political parties' ruthless and cynical use of communal and ethnic contradictions for short-term, narrow political gains. Monsters of ethnic separatism and conflict were created or encouraged out of such expediency. A typical example was the building up of San Bhindrawale by the Congress (particularly Mrs Indira Gandhi and her Sikh associates like Zail Singh and Buta Singh) to contain Akali challenges in the Punjab.[44] The encouragement of Subhas Ghiesing of the Gurkha National Liberation Front in Darjeeling to weaken the CPM's hold over West Bengal falls into the same category.[45] While Bhindrawale's shadow looms large on the Punjab ethnic conflict, Ghiesing threatens to provoke a Nepali ethnic explosion.

It is not only the Congress Party which has indulged in opportunistic political endeavours at the cost of national unity and ethnic peace. Unfortunately, other parties have not lagged behind. The Janata Dal's projection of the Mandal issue and the BHP's exploitation of the Ayodhya temple–mosque controversy may be recalled in this respect.

Conclusion

It is clear from the foregoing discussion that both integrative and disruptive forces have been simultaneously released by developmental and political dynamics in India. It is the changing balance between these two mutually incompatible forces that defines the characteristics of the ethnic scene in the country. Looking at the prevailing situation, one cannot avoid the impression that over the past few years ethnic conflicts and disorders in India have gained in ascendancy and ugliness.

However, the battle of preserving and promoting "unity in diversity" in India is far from being lost. It can be won not because of the coercive power of the Indian state, but because of the inherent strength and resilience of Indian society. Notwithstanding the raging ethnic conflicts in the Punjab, Kashmir, Assam, and the North-East region, the ethnic situation in India is still not unmanageable, keeping in view India's vastness and diversity and the challenge of externally inspired subversion (which we have not discussed in this paper).

It must be recognized that the Indian masses, not the power élites, are strongly rooted in their composite culture and secular commitments, evolved over centuries of cultural synthesis. This composite culture's vitality and resilience have not been lost even in the face of distortions brought about by India's power élites, its developmental dynamics, federal polity, or democratic politics. No wonder, then, that the Akalis in the Punjab have to accept the reality of their internal ethnic contradictions and fluctuating electoral fortunes. Similarly, the BJP has to realize that there are severe limits on the "profitability" of communalizing politics – otherwise they could continue to spit fire on the Ayodhya issue. Even the intensity of the Mandal issue, so closely linked to the ideas of social justice and egalitarianism enshrined in the Indian Constitution, has had to fade out politically.

For the future, one thing is clear: if India is to resolve its ethnic conflicts and work for a harmonious balance in its ethnic and cultural fibre, political opportunism and expediency cannot be allowed to go uncurbed. To permit this would distort the logic of development and the thrust of federal and democratic institutions. The problem is not with the institutions and the common people in India, but with a leadership that surrenders values and larger gains for short-term, selfish advantages.

Notes

1. Rashiduddin Khan, *Federal India: A Design for Change* (New Delhi: Vikas, 1992).
2. Marguerite Ross Barnett, *The Politics of Cultural Nationalism in South India* (Princeton: Princeton University Press, 1976).
3. Samina Ahmed, "The Politics of Ethnicity in India," *Regional Studies* (Islamabad) IX, no. 4, (Autumn 1991): 22–50.
4. Arun Bose, "India and Indians: Disintegration and Reintegration," *Contributions to Indian Sociology* 25, no. 1 (Jan.–Jun. 1991); David Washbrook, "Ethnicity in Contemporary Indian Politics," in Hamza Alavi and John Harris (eds), *South Asia: Sociology of "Developing Societies"* (London: Macmillan, 1989), pp. 174–86.
5. India, Ministry of Information and Broadcasting, *Jawaharlal Nehru's Speeches September 1953 – August 1957*, vol. 3 (Delhi, 1950), pp. 36–7.
6. Op. cit., vol. 4 (September 1957 – April 1953), pp. 7–20.
7. Stanley J. Tambiah, "Ethnic Conflicts in the World Today," *American Ethnologist* 16 (1989): 335–49.
8. Dipankar Gupta, "Communalism and Fundamentalism: Some Notes on the Nature of

Ethnic Politics in India," *Economic and Political Weekly*, Annual Number (March 1991): 573.

9. Op. cit., p. 579.

10. Bose, op. cit.

11. Asaf Hussain, "Ethnicity, National Identity and Praetorianism: The Case of Pakistan," *Asian Survey* XVI, no. 10 (1976): 925; Paul R. Brass, *Language, Religion and Politics in Northern India* (London/New York: Cambridge University Press, 1974), pp. 14–20, cited in D. Reetz, "National Consolidation or Fragmentation in Pakistan: The Dilemma of General Zia ul-Haq (1977–1988)," in Diethelm Weidemann (ed.), *Nationalism, Ethnicity and Political Development in South Asia*, (New Delhi: Manohar Publications, 1991), p. 126.

12. Weidemann, op. cit.

13. Washbrook, op. cit.

14. P.R. Rajgopal, *Communal Violence in India* (New Delhi: Uppal, 1991); Jaytilak Guha Roy, "Politics, Religion and Violence in India," *Indian Journal of Political Science* 52, no. 4 (Oct.–Dec. 1991): 439–47; S.K. Ghosh, "The Changing Faces of Communal Riots," *The Hindustan Times* (New Delhi), Sunday Magazine section, 31 May, 1992.

15. Ibid. Also Dennis Austine and Anirudha Gupta, "Politics of Violence in India and South Asia: Is Democracy an Endangered Species?", *Conflict Studies* 233 (July–Aug. 1990); Asghar Ali Engineer (ed.), *Communal Riots in Post Independence India*, (Delhi: Sangam Publications, 1984); Asghar Ali Engineer and Moin Shakir (eds), *Communalism in India* (Delhi: Ajanta Publications, 1985); Veena Das (ed.), *Mirrors of Violence: Communities, Riots, Survivors in South Asia* (Delhi: Oxford University Press, 1990), pp. 1–34.

16. Yogendra K. Malik and Dhirendra K. Vajpeyi, "Rise of Hindu Militancy: India's Secular Democracy at Risk," *Asian Survey* 29, no. 3 (March 1989): 308–25; Premshankar Jha, "Fascist Upsurge Against Secular Democracy," *Mainstream* 29, no. 6 (1 December 1990): 7–8, 35; *Ayodhya Movement in Manthan* (special issue), May–June 1991.

17. Gupta, op. cit.; D.L. Seth, "Movements, Intellectuals and the State," *Economic and Political Weekly* 27, no. 8 (22 February 1992): 425–30.

18. On the Jharkhand Movement, see A.L. Raj, "Ideology and Hegemony in Jharkhand," *Economic and Political Weekly* 27, no. 5 (1 February 1992): 200–3; Upjit Singh Rekhi, *Jharkhand Movement in Bihar*, New Delhi: Nunes Publications, 1988.

19. See editorial on the subject in *The Hindustan Times* (New Delhi), 1 June 1992.

20. D. Reetz, in Weidemann (ed.), op. cit., p. 126.

21. Tambiah, op. cit., p. 347.

22. For the concept of "ethnic nepotism" see Tatu Vanhanen, "Politics of Ethnic Nepotism in India," in Weidemann (ed.), op. cit., pp. 69–92.

23. Pramod Kumar; Manmohan Sharma, Atul Sood, and Ashwin Handa, *Punjab Crisis: Context and Trends* (Chandigarh: Centre for Research in Rural and Industrial Development, 1984); Lloyd I. and Susan H. Rudolph, *In Pursuit of Lakshmi: The Political Economy of the Indian State* (Chicago/London: University of Chicago Press, 1987); Patwant Singh and Harji Malik (eds), *Punjab: The Fatal Miscalculations* (New Delhi: Patwant Singh 1985); Sucha Singh Gill and K.C., Singhal, "Punjab Problem: A Genesis of Present Crisis," *Economic and Political Weekly* 19 (7 April 1984).

24. India, *Constituent Assembly Debates*, vol. 7, p. 43.

25. As cited in Sandeep Shastri, "Indian Federalism and National Integration," *Indian Journal of Political Science* 51, no. 2 (April–June 1990): 172–85.

26. States Reorganisation Commission's Report, as cited in Sandeep Shastri, op. cit.

27. For a brief description of the reorganization of states in India, see P.C. Mathur, *Social Bases of Indian Politics* (Jaipur: Aalekh Publishers, 1984), chap. 9, pp. 135–91.

28. These lists, along with the "Union list," where only the Union Parliament has exclusive rights to make laws, are included in the Seventh Schedule of the Indian Constitution. A detailed definition of the devolution of power and the conduct of relations between the centre and the States is given in Part XI (arts. 245–263) of the Constitution.

29. Paul R. Brass, "Pluralism, Regionalism and Decentralising Tendencies in Contemporary Indian Politics," in A.J. Wilson and D. Dalton (eds.), *The States of South Asia* (New Delhi: Vikas Publishing House, 1982); K. Rangachari, "Centre–State Dialogue: Focus on Finance Commission," in *Statesman* (New Delhi), 24 September 1987.
30. *Times of India* (New Delhi), 24 September 1987.
31. This demand of Sikkim is based upon the fact that, as articulated in the ruling Sikkim Sangram Parishad Party's May 1992 convention, Sikkim shared difficult mountainous terrain, poor resources, and mass poverty with the North-East states. The idea is therefore to enhance Sikkim's bargaining position *vis-à-vis* the centre.
32. Satish K. Sharma, "Social Mobility and Growing Resistance: A Study of Social Development and Ethnic Conflicts in India," *Social Action* 41, no. 1 (Jan.–Mar. 1991): 64–77.
33. For a discussion of this issue, see Richard Sisson, *Politics and Culture in India*, Ann Arbor, MI: University of Michigan Press, 1988; Iqbal Narain, "Cultural Pluralism, National Integration and Democracy in India," *Asian Survey* 19, no. 2 (February 1979): 165–77. India's State Ministers of Culture debated a new cultural policy for India: see *The Hindu* (New Delhi), 25 and 27 May 1992.
34. Government of India, *Report on the Centre–State Relations in India* (Sarkaria Commission) (New Delhi: 1988).
35. Dipankar Gupta, "The Communalizing of Punjab, 1980–85," *Economic and Political Weekly* 20, no. 28 (13 July 1985): 1185–90; Bhagwan G. Dua, "Federalism or Patrimonialism: The Unmaking of Chief Ministers in India," *Asian Survey* 25, no. 8 (August 1985): 793–804; Jagmohan, *My Frozen Turbulence in Kashmir* (New Delhi: Allied Publishers, 1991).
36. Nagaland People's Council, *Subversion of the Constitution of India in Nagaland* (New Delhi: 1992), pp. 1–2.
37. As cited in Shastri, op. cit.
38. Khan, op. cit.
39. Cynthia H. Enole, *Ethnic Conflict and Political Development* (New York: University Press of America, 1986), pp. 59–60.
40. D.L. Seth, "Movements, Intellectuals and the State," *Economic and Political Weekly* 27, no. 8 (22 February 1992): 425–30.
41. Ratna Naidu, *The Commercial Edge of Plural Societies: India and Malaysia*, (New Delhi: Vikas, 1980).
42. Vanhanan, op. cit. (see Table 1 for identification of ethnicity and region based parties).
43. Sudha Pai, "Regional Parties and the Emerging Pattern of Politics in India," in *Indian Journal of Political Science* 51, no. 3 (Jul.–Sep. 1990): 393–415.
44. Gupta, op. cit., n. 35; Mark Tully and Satish Jacob, *Amritsar: Mrs. Gandhi's Last Battle* (London: Jonathan Cape, 1985).
45. *Sunday* (weekly magazine, Calcutta) vol. 15, 14–20 February 1988.

11

An intractable conflict?
Northern Ireland: A need
for pragmatism

John Darby

Introduction

The conflict in Northern Ireland is often seen as intractable, mainly because of the persistence of violence in conducting it and the failure of Catholics and Protestants to reach political accord. Both indicators must be qualified. The violence, though persistent, operates under a number of military and social constraints which have prevented it from spiralling out of control.

Although no political accommodation has yet been reached, progress has been made on other elements – social reforms, respect for cultural diversity, discrimination, and socio-economic inequities – of this multi-faceted problem. It is clear that the problem will remain until it is tackled across a broad front.

One of the numerous apocryphal stories arising from Northern Ireland's violence concerns an event which allegedly took place in 1969. That was the first year of serious widespread violence in the current outbreak of what we euphemistically call the "Troubles." The British army had just arrived to separate the warring factions and was still regarded with benevolence by the Catholic community. Some soldiers based in Derry, therefore, were surprised to find themselves the targets of stone-throwing children. Grabbing an eight-year-old boy, one of the soldiers asked him for an explanation. "Listen," said the child. "You English bastards have been pushing us around for 800 years and we're taking no more of it."

Two points about the anecdote are illuminative. First, it seems to confirm the widely held view that the conflict in Ireland has remained essentially unchanged since the English invasion in the twelfth century, that it is essentially a colonial struggle, and that it cannot be solved. The second point is that the child knew, with some precision, that the English had first invaded Ireland in 1170. Dates, slogans, and apocryphal stories are important in Ireland. They provide the furniture for debate and disagreement. The following observation was made in 1976:

Sellar and Yeatman, in their comic history of Britain, *1066 and All That*, decided to include only two dates in the book, because all others were 'not memorable'. They would have had much greater difficulty writing an equivalent volume on Irish history. 1170, 1641, 1690, 1798, 1912, 1916, 1921, 1969 – all these dates are fixed like beacons in the folklore and mythology of Irishmen. They trip off the tongue during ordinary conversation like the latest football scores in other environments, and are recorded for posterity on gable walls all over Northern Ireland. (Darby, 1976: 1)

The intervening 15 years of violence – on top of the seven already experienced by 1976 – have changed public perceptions of history, shifted the furniture around. A succession of historians has radically challenged the nationalist interpretation upon which Irish historiography was based for almost a century; that is, the view that all Irish history exists only to justify the struggle for unification.

I teach a course on the Irish conflict in the University of Ulster. The students, most of them from Northern Ireland, enter readily into class discussions. The same issues are not discussed afterwards over cups of coffee or pints of beer. It is certainly not that they are uninterested – the course, which is optional, is currently being taken by all final-year undergraduates. It is that they have become heartily sick and deeply wary of discussing the Troubles outside the formal setting of a university lecture theatre. Could it be that they share the gloomy analysis that nothing has changed, or can be changed?

If so they would cite in support two of the most over-used quotations about the Irish problem. The first is from Winston Churchill, describing the end of the first world war:

Then came the Great War. Every institution, almost, in the world was strained. Great empires have been overturned. The whole map of Europe has been changed ... The modes of thought of men, the whole outlook on affairs, the grouping of parties, all have encountered violent and tremendous changes in the deluge of the world. But as the deluge subsides and the waters fall short, we see the dreary steeples of Fermanagh and Tyrone emerging once again. The integrity of their quarrel is one of the few institutions that has been unaltered in the cataclysm which has swept the world. (Churchill, 1934)

More recently, Richard Rose offered this devastating conclusion:

Many talk about a solution to Ulster's political problem but few are prepared to say what the problem is. The reason is simple. The problem is that there is no solution. (Rose, 1976: 139)

An intractable conflict?

How is such a proposition to be examined? What evidence might inform the proposition that the conflict is intractable? Two main arguments might be presented. First is its persistent tendency towards violence; second is the failure to find political structures acceptable to both Catholics and Protestants.

1   The persistence of violence

Persistent it certainly is. The seventeenth-century Plantation of Ulster, when large numbers of Protestant settlers were attracted from Britain to the province by generous grants of land confiscated from the native Catholic Irish, provided its demographic base. Scarcely a decade since then has not been marked by political violence. Between 1835 and 1969 there were nine periods of serious rioting in Belfast alone and many other years where disturbances have been recorded (Boyd, 1969; Townshend, 1983). The current period of violence is the longest and most sustained of all. It has been uninterrupted, except for variations in form and intensity, for more than twenty years.

This persistent antagonism has not been between hostile neighbouring countries, but between two internal groups occupying what Stewart called the same "narrow ground" (Stewart, 1977). The distinction between ethnic conflicts and international wars needs to be emphasized. In most ethnic conflicts the combatants permanently inhabit the same battlefield. Even during periods of tranquillity their lives are often intermeshed with those of their enemies. It is not possible to terminate hostilities by withdrawal behind national frontiers. As a consequence, ethnic conflict is often characterized by internecine viciousness rather than by the more impassive slaughter of international wars.

In such circumstances violence, unless arrested at an early stage, tends to develop along predictable lines: disagreements harden into disputes; the violence expands to involve a greater number of activists disputing a greater number of issues; the combatants become more efficiently organized under more implacable leaders; the restraints on decent behaviour are eroded. Conflict is, after all, a "joint interaction" (Shibutani and Kwan, 1971: 135) and tends to spiral from reciprocal tit-for-tat attacks. As Coleman (1971: 256) put it, "the harmful and dangerous elements drive out those which keep the conflict within bounds," creating a Gresham's law of conflict.

The last twenty years, it might be argued, confirm this. More than 3,000 people have died as a result of political violence, and much greater numbers have been injured.

2 The failure to reach political accord

The inability of the protagonists to reach an agreed political accord is often cited as evidence of intractability. In 1972, following growing civil disorder and violence, the Northern Ireland Parliament and Government at Stormont were prorogued. They were replaced by Direct Rule from Westminster. The Stormont regime had lasted since 1921, in 51 years of majority rule, which had been characterized by minority exclusion from power and abuses of electoral, judicial, and policing functions. During its existence, only one measure proposed by the opposition had passed into law – the Wild Bird Act of 1932, a measure which not even the most ingenious argument could classify as sectarian.

Since then there have been six attempts to restore self-government to Northern Ireland. All have failed.

- **1973–4:** The Power-sharing Executive, which lasted for three months, remains Northern Ireland's only experience of a government shared by Catholics and Protestants. It attempted to construct a devolved system based on power-sharing between Protestants and Catholics, and on a Council of Ireland to regulate affairs between the two parts of Ireland. It was opposed by the Democratic Unionist Party (DUP) and most of the Ulster Unionist Party (UUP), but eventually was brought down through a Protestant workers' strike in May 1974.

- **1975–6:** A Constitutional Convention was convened to enable elected representatives from Northern Ireland to propose their own solution. Not surprisingly the majority Unionist parties proposed a return to majority rule, modified by a committee system with some minority rights inbuilt. It was rejected by both the British government and by the minority Social Democratic and Labour Party (SDLP).
- **1977–8 and 1980:** Two attempts to set up devolved institutions were initiated by two Northern Ireland secretaries of state, Roy Mason and Humphrey Atkins. Neither got to first base. They were opposed, for different reasons, by the SDLP and the UUP, but both simply petered out. As a measure of the cultural gap between the two sides, two bars were set up in Stormont during the Atkins talks of 1980, one serving only non-alcoholic beverages. Students of national stereotyping may guess which bar was designed for which political parties.
- **1982–4:** Rolling Devolution, introduced by James Prior, was perhaps the most ingenious proposal, again involving an elected assembly and a committee system. This envisaged a gradual return to power by elected representatives, but only if the proposed powers had "widespread acceptance," defined as 70 per cent agreement. In other words, the amount of power allowed to local political parties depended on their ability to agree, and would roll along at the speed of progress determined by them. It was boycotted by the SDLP because it did not guarantee power sharing.
- **1991:** The Brooke Initiative, which sought to introduce phased talks, involving the Northern Irish parties first and the Dublin government at a later stage. This initiative followed the introduction of the Anglo-Irish Agreement in 1985, an agreement signed by the governments of the United Kingdom and the Irish Republic, but which did not involve local politicians and has been bitterly opposed by Unionists. A major survey in 1990 confirmed that, for Protestants, the Anglo-Irish Agreement is still perceived to be the biggest single obstacle to peace. The Brooke Initiative was halted for lack of progress in July 1991.
- **1993:** In November 1993, however, the prime ministers of Ireland and the United Kingdom announced the Downing Street Agreement, offering for the first time the possibility of addressing the constitutional and security problems together as part of a peace package.

The agreement appeared to copper-fasten, in quite unprecedented terms, Northern Ireland's right to determine its own constitutional status, and its right to remain in the United Kingdom until a majority in Northern Ireland wishes to change it. Second, the government of the Irish Republic has undertaken to "forward and support proposals for change in the Irish Constitution" as part of an agreed settlement. Third, Sinn Fein might become involved in political talks when they have demonstrated a willingness to abandon violence. Some of these possibilities had been floated before. Now they are accepted in a formal agreement between two governments.

The possible involvement of Sinn Fein in political talks was a particularly significant development. All previous attempts to reach a political settlement in Northern Ireland were confined to constitutional parties, leaving the ending of violence for later discussion. The Downing Street Declaration introduced for the first time the possibility of combining the political and security strands of Northern Ireland's problems. Almost a year later the IRA announced a complete cease-fire, and was soon followed by the main loyalist paramilitary organizations. In February 1995 the two governments released an agreed Framework Document, and talks about a political settlement are planned for later in the year. Whether or not they will take place in a spirit of political compromise remains to be seen.

A tractable conflict?

Twenty-five years of failed initiatives, until the 1994 IRA cease-fires, seem to provide a strong argument that the Northern Ireland conflict is intractable. There is, however, an alternative analysis. It argues that the conflict is neither unchanging and sterile, as Churchill claimed, nor incapable of solution, as Rose implies. This analysis is based on a closer scrutiny of the same evidence, first on violence and then on political intransigence.

1   The controls on violence

Insufficient distinction is made between the terms "conflict" and "violence." The tendency to confuse them is not new. It arose around the turn of the last century from the willingness of the new discipline of sociology to regard society rather as a machine that occasionally breaks down, and sociologists as mechanics, whose role was to identify the fault and point out how it might be fixed. This is a view of society that regards conflict as dysfunctional, as evidence that something has gone wrong in the social body. This view of conflict still dominates some departments of sociology.

But there has been an alternative strain of conflict analysis, weaker but never quite defeated, represented by George Simmel in Germany almost a century ago (see Lawrence, 1976) and more recently by Lewis Coser (Coser, 1956). In this view it is as pointless to attack conflict as to attack the ageing process. Conflict is neither good nor bad, but intrinsic in every social relationship from marriage to international diplomacy. Whenever two or more people are gathered, there is conflict or potential conflict. The real issue is not the existence of conflict, but how it is handled.

Reference has already been made to the tendency for ethnic violence, unless rapidly addressed, to spiral out of control. During the early 1970s many observers believed that the upsurge of violence in Northern Ireland could lead to only two outcomes: the belligerents would either be shocked into an internal accommodation, or propelled into genocidal massacre. Neither has occurred. Two decades later there is still no settlement and the level of violence, though remarkably persistent, has not intensified. On the contrary, there is evidence that violence has diminished rather than risen in intensity. It reached a peak in 1972, when 468 people died. Since then it has gradually declined to below 100 in each year since 1981 until its rise in 1991 to over 100. The ratio of civilian to military deaths has diminished, and the number who have died from direct violence between the communities has almost disappeared; in 1992 it is difficult to find any examples of the direct sectarian confrontations which had been the main form of violence in 1969 and 1970 (McGarry and O'Leary, 1990: 318–41). This is not to diminish the awful tragedy of those who have suffered. Nor is it to suggest that paramilitary violence is dwindling away and will peter out; its pattern over the last twenty years has been spasmodic and subject to sudden increases. The point is that there are mechanisms operating in Northern Ireland – social, military, and paramilitary – which conspire to keep the level of violence under control but are not strong enough to eliminate it.

Ninety years ago Simmel used a domestic analogy to illustrate the danger of assessing the seriousness of a conflict by its outward expression. He described two married couples, one a model of harmony, considerate towards each other, always in agreement; the other given to spectacular public arguments. The real picture, he pointed out, may be completely different The agreement of the first couple may be based on a realization that their marriage is fragile and threatened; they cannot afford the risk of the one final quarrel that may topple them into divorce. The second couple, on the other hand, confident in the strength of their relationship, can afford to make every disagreement exuberantly public.

The same principle of refusing to take the visible expression of conflict at face value can be applied to ethnic conflicts. Developments during the early 1990s in Eastern Europe are reminders that countries which appeared to be insulated against ethnic conflict were in fact not. Ethnic identity, like the seeds discovered in the Egyptian pyramids, can lie dormant for centuries and, given the right conditions, spring into life. The only solution that history has shown to be completely effective in removing it is genocide. If that is not socially acceptable, we must look for better ways of handling it.

There is an analogy here with the treatment of cancer. Until recently cancer was seen as a terminal condition. Now each year sees a statistically measurable improvement in the survival possibilities for cancer victims. There has been a corresponding switch in treatment. Patients are no longer prepared for death but encouraged to enjoy a normal life. Ethnic conflict should be regarded in the same way, as a permanent but not a terminal condition – one to be tackled and improved.

2   Politics in context

"The Northern Irish problem" is a term widely used both in Northern Ireland and outside it as if there were an agreed and universal understanding of what it means. Richard Rose's conclusion that "there is no solution" to the problem is correct, within his own terms. The problem lies with his terms. These regard the problem as a constitutional one, with the implication that improvement is inconceivable without political accord. It is more accurate, and more productive, to consider the issue, not as a "problem" with the implication that a solution lies around the corner for anyone ingenious enough to find it, but as a tangle of inter-related problems:

• There is a central constitutional problem: what should be the polit-

ical context for the people of Northern Ireland? Integration with Britain? A united Ireland; independence?
- There is a continuing problem of social and economic inequalities, especially in the field of employment.
- There is a problem of cultural identity, relating to education, to the Irish language, to the whole spread of cultural differences.
- There is a problem of security; people are being killed and maimed because of it. Some even think there is a problem of religious difference.
- There is certainly a problem of the day-to-day relationships between the people who live here.

All of these are elements of the problem, but none can claim dominance. Each affects the others. Any approach to change needs to take into account all elements of the problem. Educational reforms will be frustrated if they are not accompanied by the removal of fundamental inequalities in the distribution of jobs. It is foolish to seek a political settlement that does not acknowledge that each tradition has cultural expressions which are non-negotiable to them but anathema to many of their opponents. It is ridiculous to devise security policies – peace lines; undercover operations – without trying to anticipate their effect on community relationships. To gauge progress along the single track of political negotiation – no matter how important that is – is rather like gauging a person's health by the condition of their kidneys. Important, yes, but any more important than bowels, liver, or heart?

A multilateral analysis suggests the need for a multilateral prescription. At certain times there is a chance of movement on some of these issues, while on others progress is impossible. In such circumstances it makes sense to adopt a pragmatic approach, with initiatives determined by opportunity and circumstances. Push where there is give. If one element of the problem seems intractable, accept it as such, at least in the short or medium term. Then get on with progress on the other elements. During the last three years there have been changes in the educational and fair employment fields which would have been unthinkable just five years ago.

The issue of cultural pluralism is firmly on the agenda: the law now requires every primary-school child in Northern Ireland to be introduced to the concepts of cultural diversity and mutual understanding. Despite the political stalemate at macro level, there has been some movement in the political undergrowth at local government level.

Eleven of Northern Ireland's 26 councils are currently operating a power-sharing regime, often involving rotation of the chair, and 18 have agreed to implement a community relations programme with specific and binding requirements.

These are undramatic but significant changes, but they should not be presented as the first glimmerings of a bright future. Progress towards a more general political solution has been more disappointing. It is not easy for politicians to abandon overnight the rhetoric and suspicion nurtured over centuries and appear, phoenix-like, at peace talks, ready to draw up new plans on a clean slate. Politicians have the same prejudices and weaknesses as the rest of us. In Northern Ireland, as in the Middle East, there has been too much eagerness to regard the first meeting of the protagonists as an end rather than a start. When the first meeting takes place, it will be necessary to leave space for the exposition of old sores and the repayment of old scores. Only later can the poultices be applied.

The Downing Street Agreement between the British and Irish governments, signed in November 1993, offers for the first time the possibility of addressing the constitutional and security problems together as part of a peace package. Peacemaking, especially between conflicting ethnic groups, is a long process. Let us hope for the best. But let no one believe that, even if political talks are successful, the other elements of the problem will meekly solve themselves. I am an optimist, but I believe that an optimist is one who plans for the worst rather than expects it.

Acknowledgements

This chapter is based on a paper entitled "Intransigent Ethnic Conflicts: Prospects for Peacemaking," presented at Haverford College on 12 November 1991. I would like to record my thanks to the Rockefeller Foundation, at whose centre at Bellagio part of the work for this paper was carried out, and to the Woodrow Wilson Center for Scholars in Washington DC.

References

Boyd, A. 1969. *Holy War in Belfast*. Tralee: Anvil Press.
Churchill, W. 1934. *History of the First World War*. London: Cassell.
Coleman, J. 1971. "The dynamics of conflict." In Marx, 1971.
Coser, L.A. 1956. *The Functions of Social Conflict*. Glencoe, IL: Free Press.
Darby, J. 1976. *Conflict in Northern Ireland*. Dublin: Gill and MacMillan.
Marx, G. (ed.). 1971. *Racial Conflict*. Boston: Little, Brown.

McGarry, J., and B. O'Leary (eds). 1990. *The Future of Northern Ireland*. Oxford: Clarendon Press.

Rose, R. 1976. *Northern Ireland: A Time for Change*. London: Macmillan.

Shibutani, T., and K. Kwan, "Changes in life conditions conducive to interracial conflict." In Marx, 1971.

Stewart, A.T.Q. 1977. *The Narrow Ground*. London: Faber and Faber.

Townshend, P. 1983. *Political Violence in Ireland*. Oxford: Oxford University Press.

12

Political autonomy and conflict resolution: The Basque case

José Manuel Castells and Gurutz Jauregui

1 Introduction

"The Basque Country," *Euskal Herria,* and *Vasconia* are all names referring to a territory divided between Spain and France. It encompasses the Spanish provinces of Navarre, Alava, Guipúzcoa, and Biscay and the ancient countries of Lapurdi, Zuberoa, and Lower Navarre in the Atlantic Pyrenees Department of France. This division has left the continental Basque Country in the north traditionally dependent on France, while the peninsular Basque Country, in turn, is dependent on the Spanish State.

Situated between an oceanic basin and the Ebro River, the territory spreads over 20,644 sq km. The peninsular zone is highly industrialized, although it is undergoing a structural crisis, particularly in Guipúzcoa and Biscay, and to a lesser degree in Navarre and Alava. The economy of the continental area is sustained by its primary sector, but other economic activities, such as tourism, are expanding.

While there have been constant claims for autonomy in the Basque territory controlled by France, the French government has never conceded any degree of political control. This article, therefore, deals exclusively with the peninsular, or Spanish, area. The Spanish Basque territory is itself politically divided into two autonomous communities: the Statutory Community of Navarre and the Autonomous Community of the Basque Country.

The Autonomous Community is governed by a basic law called the Statute of Autonomy. From a political and institutional point of view, this statute offers solutions to problems that persist in the Basque Country as a whole.

The Basque Country has always maintained a very notable singularity. It has its own language, *Euskera* (or Basque), which is of pre-Indo-European origin and is spoken by over one-fourth of the population. There is also a peculiar political-institutional framework, consisting of self-government through provincial parliaments, which has been historically respected by the Castilian monarchy (as well as that of France up to the 1789 revolution).

The nineteenth century was particularly hard on the peninsular Basque Country, because the majority of the population supported the losing faction in this period's two great dynastic wars (the Carlist Wars). The four provinces opted for defence of monarchic autocracy, the right to their own Church of the Old Regime, and, with unquestionable intensity, the continuation of the Basque Country's political uniqueness. During the second civil war, the Basque territory was the stage for war operations and a defeat which, for the first time in its history, resulted in the disappearance of its autonomous government. The only exception was an agreement to share taxes collected with the Spanish State.

It was precisely this formula, known as the "economic contract," which enabled Basque provincial institutions to undergo vigorous industrialization. This started with tremendous force at the end of the last century in Biscay, thanks to the sale of iron to England. This led to the accumulation of large sums of capital which were soon distributed to the adjacent territories. The Basque Country led Spain in industrialization and, subsequently, in development and standard of living.

Throughout this century, because of the appearance of the nationalist phenomenon, the Basque Country has made continuous demands for recognition of its political reality. The reign of Alfonso XIII brought no response to this growing demand. The monarch limited himself to conserving the economic contracts regime. It was during the Second Republic (1931–39) that the Basque Country (as well as Catalonia) articulated its strong will to obtain an autonomous political regime.

Its concept was based on the Statute of Autonomy and followed the decentralized model of the Weimar Republic. The Statute was obtained at the late date of 1936, in the midst of the Civil War, at a time when the Spanish Republican government needed to attract Basque support in the struggle against fascism and the insurgent military forces. Franco's regime suppressed all signs of Basque identity. Perhaps as a consequence of this overt oppression, when the political transition to democracy occurred after Franco's death, claims for autonomy, particularly in the Basque case, became an essential issue to be resolved. This was due both to the intensity of the claims as well as to political violence with clearly separatist objectives. For this reason, the Spanish Parliament approved a new Statute of Autonomy covering the provinces of Alava, Guipúzcoa, and Biscay. It was proclaimed on 18 December 1979. The Spanish legislators believed that an autonomy generous to the wishes of the Basque representatives would end terrorism and serve to integrate a territory that had traditionally been reluctant to take part in the Spanish political sphere.

2 Basque singularity

2.1 Basque nationalism and violence

Basque nationalism was founded by Sabino Arana in 1893. Historically, three main traits have characterized its ideology. These are: centripetism, regenerationism, and ethnocentrism. They have in turn spawned a series of strategic-political aspects. But the three traits have stood out, as they have directly conditioned the origins of ETA, as well as its subsequent development.

Centripetism
Basque nationalism is rooted in the radical contrast between the Spanish and the Basque, viewing the two as naturally antagonistic. Along these lines, the concept of the Basque Country as antithetical to the concept of Spain emerges. This antithesis is the the main factor, the cause and reason for the very existence of Basque nationalism. The nationalist claim is thus supported by the idea of the Basque Country's "occupation" by the foreign state of Spain. Ideologically

speaking, Basque nationalism is therefore not only configured as an "anti-system" political movement, but also as anti-Spain.

Regenerationism

Historically, Basque nationalism has always tended to be projected as a community movement endeavouring to respond to the Basques as a whole, aiming to establish itself as the only legitimate representative of the Basque community. This regenerationist trait continues today within the complex world revolving around ETA and its subsidiary political and cultural bodies, social, youth, and student movements.

Ethnocentrism

This third trait is a direct consequence of the two previous ones. It characterizes the "community" served by the movement as the Basque ethnic community exclusively, and both confuses and identifies this with the nationalist community, so that any non-nationalist is considered non-Basque.

This has given rise to a deep sense of community rooted in the autochthonous or indigenous community, as significant to Basque identity as the nationalist claim itself. The intrinsic tension between the various social classes was substituted for a double Basque Country/Spain and autochthonous/immigrant tension, so that the nationalist community always appeared as a monolithic bloc without a crack, facing the "external enemy."

The initial strategy of Basque nationalism, based on the rejection of the Spanish, and the subsequent refusal to intervene in Spain's political affairs, was significantly tempered in later years. Such a compromising and possibilist policy, however, always met with firm opposition among certain intransigent sectors claiming to possess ideological legitimacy. Therefore, from the beginning, Basque nationalism has been embroiled in an internal debate between the need for a possibilist strategy to overcome the Basque/Spanish antagonism and the ideological bases of radical and uncompromising nationalism. This same dialectic between the possibilist and radical strategies prevailed during the Francoist period and the democratic transition that followed.

ETA (meaning "Basque Country and Freedom") was founded in 1959, in the middle of the Francoist period. At its start, ETA had to choose between two alternative, nationalist models: that of the European ethnic minorities, or that of the emerging third world nationalism. The former defines its strategy from the perspective of restructuring and reforming European national states in order to attain a federal Europe made up of different peoples. The latter bases its entire strategy on a radical and absolute antagonism between the dominant country and the colony, such that resolution of the conflict must inevitably lead to the violent expulsion of the colonizer and the substitution of the old colonial power for a new, autochthonous power.

While a certain initial ambiguity was to be seen, all data tip the scale towards ETA's ultimate adherence to the third world model. ETA proposed strict activism and a radical break with the "oppressor country," which led to the organization of a military branch as early as 1960, and the first act of violence in the summer of 1961. Why? Several factors must be considered:

(*a*) One must take the post-war social and political situation of the Basque Country into account. For Basques, the post-war era was marked by disappointment and setbacks. These had begun even earlier, with the relative failure of the policy of compromise adopted by the moderate Basque Nationalist Party (Partido Nacionalista Vasco, PNV) during the Second Republic and the mutual distrust between the nationalists and the Spanish Republican regime. They continued with the abandonment of the Basques by the Western powers during the post-war period, and the sense of annihilation of Basque identity, marked by the progressive and alarming disappearance of the Basque language. Enormous numbers of immigrants, and rapid and profound social and economic transformations, with the resulting environmental degradation, contributed further. Behind all this, of course, loomed the omnipresent Francoist repression, which nipped in the bud the slightest signs of opposition. These factors not only inclined ETA's stance towards uncompromising nationalism, but also led its members to act on their theories.

The situation fostered the latent feeling that the autochthonous Basque community was dying out. This feeling represents a fundamental element in ETA's development. It is logical if one considers the marked ethnocentric character of historical Basque nationalism, which linked the nation's existence indivisibly to the survival of its language. It was, and still is, believed that if the Basque language were to die, the Basque Country would cease to exist.

(*b*) Conditions tended to encourage the view of the Basque Country as a country occupied by Spain. In the context of a highly industrialized society and a powerful working-class movement, evidence emerged of brutal repression capable of smothering even the most insignificant manifestations of the Basque identity. Consequently, the anti-colonialist movement's methods of fighting back were adopted. It was held that the Basque Country constitutes a Spanish colony.

(*c*) Activism, an expression which may be understood as the sublimation of praxis to the detriment of theory, has become the mark of identity best defining ETA. This activism conditions in an absolute manner the organization's theoretical activity and, especially, its political strategy.

As a radical and intransigent nationalist movement, ETA believes that the Basque people must stand up, not only to Francoism, but to Spain, in order to recover their national identity. For this reason, it is defined as a national liberation movement rather than just another political party. ETA's attitude is not exclusively political, but fundamentally regenerationist.

This is how the great drama of ETA was produced, a drama which is played out on an ideological stage. It raises the questions of how to apply a third world guerrilla strategy to an industrialized society and, in the area of praxis, how to make a third world guerrilla strategy with mass action compatible with current institutional political activity within the democratic system. In practice, this twofold drama is currently reflected in the contradiction between ETA's armed struggle and the political struggle of *Herri Batasuna* (HB), or People's Unity.

2.2   The specificity of the Basque party system

The Basque party system is clearly a multi-party system, with seven political forces having parliamentary representation, resulting in a very marked fragmentation. It could be said to be a very accentuated "polarized-pluralist" system, in that an absolute compatibility exists between the two ends of the continuum, represented by Alava Unity (Unidad Alavesa, UA; see p. 230) and HB.

The multi-party nature and the polarization of the system are derived from the fact that, interwoven into Basque political life, are four important cleavages which, in order of importance, are the following: violence versus non-violence; nationalism versus non-nationalism; provincialism versus non-provincialism; the left wing versus the right wing.

Violence versus non-violence

Throughout the Francoist period and during the first few years of democracy, ETA was generally supported and accepted within Basque society. In the last 15 years, however, ETA has begun to squander irretrievably the respect and acceptance it enjoyed during Franco's dictatorship. One by one, the various political groups, including the nationalists or left-wing parties, have opted not only to turn their backs on ETA, but to reject it actively. Only one sector of the nationalist left wing, represented by HB, maintains a supportive position of political collaboration with it.

The result, in political terms, is that the entire set of political parties with parliamentary representation, with the exception of HB – which has 13 of the 75 members of parliament – now overtly rejects violence in general and ETA in particular. Despite the fact that only a minority in Basque society supports violence, this violence, nevertheless, represents the principal problem, that is to say, the problem whose resolution is a precondition for that of all the others.

The qualitative incidence of violence in Basque society is much higher than HB's true electoral support; and there are several reasons for this. First, the violence emerged historically as a means of solving important political problems, which led to ETA's justification or, at least, prevented any radical opposition to it up until recent years. Second, ETA and HB believe that these problems have not been solved by the Statute of Autonomy. Third, ETA's armament capacity is very significant, provoking numerous acts of violence.

Nationalism versus non-nationalism

Basque society is politically as well as culturally split into two broad sectors; the nationalist sector, which represents 65 per cent of the votes, and the non-nationalist sector, with 35 per cent. From a sociological point of view, nationalism is dominant. It also dominates from a political viewpoint, although it is conditioned by the presence of PSOE (Partido Socialista Obrero Español), Spain's majority party. Nationalism has been fragmented into four political parties (currently five) which vie for a similar political market. Many recent events in Basque politics can be explained by this fact.

In the nationalist sector, PNV, the major party, holds 22 out of the 75 seats. The four remaining nationalist political forces combined hold 28 seats in parliament. This has led to internal movement in each of the parties aiming to consolidate their respective electoral spaces, and it has led to a rearrangement of the nationalist space occupied by political parties.

Significantly, one of the nationalist parties, HB, defends ETA's violence and its members actually serve as the organization's political spokespersons. This position makes it difficult, if not impossible, for HB to be integrated into or form a coalition with any other nationalist force or to adopt common agreements with other democratic nationalist political forces.

The non-nationalist sphere coincides almost exactly with the Spanish party system as far as its presence is concerned, but not in its electoral weight. PSOE, the party governing in Madrid, is supported by 20 per cent of the voters in the Basque Country in contrast to approximately 40 per cent in the rest of Spain. Similarly, PP (Partido Popular, the main Spanish opposition party, has an electoral support of 8 per cent in contrast to 26 per cent in the rest of Spain. These political parties lack the autonomy to carry out policies independent of guidelines issued by their directive bodies in Madrid. There are two basic reasons for this lack of autonomy; their limited electoral weight with respect to the rest of Spain, and their scant influence, given their peripheral nature, in their own internal party decisions.

Provincialism versus non-provincialism
Since 1986, a "territorialization" of the party system has been taking place, leading to the development of provincial sub-systems of the political parties. Potentially, this could lead to a dismantling of the core system. Signs of this trend include the appearance of UA, which enjoys an electoral support of 18.5 per cent in the province of Alava, and the concentration of one part of the nationalist vote, the PNV, in Biscay and the other part, consisting of HB, Basque Solidarity (Eusko Alkartasuna, EA), and the Basque Left (Euskadiko Ezkerra, EE), in Guipúzcoa.

Left wing versus right wing
This split is currently weakened and blurred. Of course, this reflects a generalized symptom in the developed world springing from a series of complex causes which we shall not go into here. However, in the Basque case this vagueness arose long ago and results from several causes, which have simply been accentuated by generalized

factors that have appeared elsewhere. The result is that since 1986, a coalition government has existed made up of two majority parties, PNV (centre/right-wing nationalist) and PSOE (centre/left-wing non-nationalist).

3   The significant political problems

Setting aside the issue of violence, it would be appropriate to review briefly the main political problems which the Statute of Autonomy has attempted to address.

3.1   The right to self-determination

This represents the principal problem in that, to a great extent, it encompasses the remaining political problems. As Basque national-ism has historically held the attainment of independence as its final objective, this entails exercising the right to self-determination in one concrete sense of the term: the achievement of an independent Basque State.

In article 2 of the Constitution, the Autonomous Communities are granted ample autonomy, but the unity of Spain is considered to be indivisible. This implies the impossibility of territorial segregation. This is arguably the main obstacle to the disappearance of political violence and to the permanent normalization of the country.

3.2   Territoriality

This problem is closely linked to the previous one. It is manifested in two ways. Firstly, because the Basque Country includes territory in both Spain and France, Basque nationalism has aspired toward uniting the entire territory under one political power. The contro-versy, therefore, reaches beyond the concrete scope of the Spanish Constitution and into France.

The second territorial problem has to do with Navarre, one of the four provinces within the Basque territory in Spain. In Navarre, nationalism is very weak. At the time the Basque Statute of Auton-omy was approved, the majority political forces in Navarre decided not to be included, choosing instead to constitute their own Autono-mous Community. This situation is complicated further because the Navarrese decision was the fruit of a fully democratic agreement.

3.3   Language and culture

As has been previously pointed out, the defence of language and culture constitute one of the most significant aspects of the nationalist claim. The Statute establishes a very broad system of language and cultural development in education, public administration, and society in general. Nevertheless, important problems exist in carrying out and developing this system.

3.4   Financial autonomy

One of nationalism's demands has been for the maintenance of the traditional system of economic contract, consisting of the right of Basque institutions to exact taxes and agree with the state on the necessary contributions.

3.5   Police forces

This represents an historical problem which, under Franco, became extremely serious. Traditionally, Basque institutions had their own police forces, but during the dictatorship those forces were replaced by a repressive police organization which earned the hatred of practically the entire Basque society. The Statute of Autonomy sets down the guidelines for an autonomous Basque police force run by the Basque Administration.

4   The Statute of Autonomy

Having reviewed the main problems faced by the Spanish democratic system in resolving the Basque dispute, let us examine the response applied to them.

4.1   General characteristics

The Basque Country attained its Statute of Autonomy in 1979, after Spain's approval of its democratic Constitution a year earlier. The Statute represents a proposed political solution to the serious historical controversy which has significantly affected relations between the Basque Country and Spain, and has conditioned the development of the Spanish political system itself over the last two centuries.

From a legal standpoint, the Spanish constitutional text is quite open-ended, in that it refrains from defining the terms and scope of autonomy too rigidly. Such content was to be specified in each of the Statutes of Autonomy, with an overall constitutional framework defining the limits for the different provinces. This flexibility represents an obvious advantage from a political point of view, in so far as it has facilitated negotiations concerning the content of each Statute of Autonomy, particularly the Basque Statute, and has allowed negotiators greater leeway. At the same time, however, the flexibility leads to some imprecision when legally interpreting the statutory precepts.

The Basque Statute of Autonomy's text appears to be conditioned by these two factors. It reflects both a highly complex political controversy and the flexible nature of the constitutional norms regulating the autonomous State. This leads to several consequences.

The Basque Statute clearly pushes to the limit all possibilities provided by the Constitution. This tendency can be seen in the wording's emphasis on the nature of the Statute as a "pact" (e.g. in the Preliminary Title and Additional Resolution, the latter also sustained in the First Additional Resolution of the Constitution), and especially in delineating spheres of responsibility.

A second consequence, derived directly from the first, is the vagueness in some key precepts of the statutory text – a deliberate and conscious vagueness reflecting the conflicting and unclear Constitution–Statute relationship. The Statute's core objective is to provide a way out of a problematic and controversial situation, and for this reason it is highly indecisive and deliberately nebulous concerning the most problematic aspects. Certain issues were simply not dealt with, in the hope that they could be tackled later on, once the autonomous framework was under way. The very ambiguity of the constitutional text favours this lack of clarity and ultimately allows for the avoidance of discussion of these controversial issues. This vagueness affects not only the Constitution–Statute relationship but also the internal makeup of the Basque Autonomous Community itself and, to an even greater degree, the Autonomous Community/ Historical Territory relationship.

A third consequence is the legal imprecision of the statutory text. From a formal viewpoint, the Statute is a legally faulty document, and it repeatedly suffers from a lack of technical quality. Its imprecision reflects the Statute's own indefiniteness, which makes sense given the circumstances of its creation and discussion. It must be taken into account that the statutory text is the synthesis of a long and arduous negotiation process first among the Basque political forces and then between these and the central government.

Some additional causes ought to be added to this. It must not be forgotten that the Basque Statute was the first to be approved after the Constitution, which meant it lacked a frame of reference or models for comparision. One must also take into account the haste with which the statutory text was created and made official. This was principally due to the need to resolve speedily Basque political demands for autonomy.

Another point worth bearing in mind is that the Statute has a dynamic nature, with a clear potential for extension, for example to the historical territories.

4.2 The Statute's fundamental aspects

4.2.1 Nationality
In accordance with the power invested by article 2 of the Spanish Constitution, the Statute of Autonomy of the Basque Country defines, in its article, the Basque People or Euskal-Herria as a nationality. Contrary to appearances, the affirmation of nationality does not have legal effect. There are several reasons for this.

First, concerning the "plurinationality" of the Spanish State, the constitutional text limits itself to recognizing the existence of nationalities and regions, without ever legally defining the distinction between these two concepts. Furthermore, from a practical perspective, the distinction between nationalities and regions lacks real effect. It does not necessarily determine the institutional-legal structure of the Statutes of Autonomy, nor does it establish respective responsibilities. The adoption of one term over the other is up to the statute-writing legislators. In fact, there have been cases where Autonomous Communities invested with full powers have not denominated themselves "nationalities" (for example, the Canary Islands).

From this legal-constitutional perspective, the expressions "nationality" or "region" are replaced by the term "Autonomous Community," applicable to each and every territory acceding to the economy. It represents a sociological definition lacking legal effects, although it does have important political connotations, especially in the Basque case. Indeed, the expression "nationality" is linked to the uniqueness, in terms of intensity as well as diffusion, of the Basque demand for a nation, which is reflected in the Additional Resolution of the Statute (discussed immediately below).

4.2.2 Historical rights

The Additional Resolution of the Statute of Autonomy of the Basque Country establishes that:

the acceptance of the autonomy regime established in the present Statute does not entail a renunciation by the Basque People of the rights which, as such, could have corresponded to them by virtue of their history, rights which can be updated in accordance with what is established by legal ordinance.

This resolution is a programmatic Declaration with implicit reference to the First Additional Resolution of the Constitution. Similar to Navarre's autonomic norm, it has important legal consequences regarding the Basque Country–State relationship, as well as the internal organization of the Basque Autonomous Community itself.

As far as the Basque Country–State relationship is concerned, the resolution implies statutory acknowledgment of the connection between historical statutory rights and the current autonomy regime. Such an admission is not simply declarative, but rather has important material effects. Indeed, the Statute of Autonomy of the Basque Country boasts a qualitative uniqueness, as shown by its granting of significant and distinct powers, whose approval is directly based on the admission of historical rights.

This is clear in the case of the subjects which provoked the most arduous debates before agreements in the statutory project were reached; education (art. 16) and the autonomous police (art. 17). Both areas are explicitly sustained based on the Additional Resolution of the Spanish Constitution and historical statutory rights. The same thing occurs with respect to the Economic Contract (Art. 14).

The second group of consequences refers to the internal, institutional structure of the Basque Autonomous Community itself and, more concretely, to the organization of historical territories. The statutory recognition of such territories, as well as their legal-political institutionalization and the granting to these of substantial powers, are based on the cited recognition of historical rights.

4.2.3 Language and culture

Article 6.1 establishes that "Euskera, the Basque People's own language, is to share with Spanish the status of official language in the Basque Country. And all its inhabitants have the right to know and use both languages." In accordance with this precept, the Basque language, besides being official along with Spanish, is recognized as the Basque People's own language. The qualification of "own" implies the uniqueness of Euskera as the official language of the Basque Country, but its legal status as one of two official languages is of more importance. This entails, independently of its reality and weight as a social phenomenon, the admission of Euskera by the public powers as a normal means of communication, amongst themselves as well as among private subjects, with full legal validity and effects.

According to article 6.2, it falls to the Basque institutions to regulate the linguistic officiality, to arbitrate and regulate the measures and means necessary to assure the knowledge of the languages, while taking into account that, in accordance with article 6.3, no one can be discriminated against on the grounds of language.

Finally, article 6.5 foresees that, with Euskera being the heritage of other Basque territories and communities, the Basque Country may ask the Spanish Government to draw up treaties or conventions establishing cultural relationships with these other countries where these territories or communities are located, in order to safeguard and foment Euskera. This allows for two alternatives: either Spain can sign treaties with other countries at the request of the Basque Autonomous Community, or the Basque Autonomous Community can itself engage in "transnational" activities. In the latter case, the community is empowered to reach beyond the strict State limits to cooperate with other regional bodies in the defence and development of Basque language and culture, but such activities do not constitute a strict manifestation of international law.

The Statute limits itself to establishing the basic design of linguistic policy. Its practical application and development are regulated by the Basic Law of Normalization of the Use of Euskera, passed by the Basque Parliament on 24 November 1982.

4.2.4 Territoriality

THE HISTORICAL TERRITORIES. Article 2 configures the Autonomous Community of the Basque Country as an aggregate of the provinces of Alava, Guipúzcoa, and Biscay, as well as Navarre, in case the latter should decide to be incorporated in accordance with the procedure established by the Constitution. Several aspects of article 2 are worth noting.

Firstly, the voluntary nature of the historical territories' participation in the configuration of the Autonomous Community of the Basque Country is significant. Such participation is not formulated as a factual reality, but rather as a right to take part, its voluntary character reflecting the precepts laid down by the constitutional act.

Secondly, the internal boundaries are defined by the provinces which historically constituted the Basque Country: this accords with traditional statutory agreements. In historical Basque agreements, as well as the current statutory text, the terms "province" or "historical territory" have a double meaning: as administrative entities serving to organize the State's administrative services (as such, they are comparable to the rest of the provinces); and as quasi-sovereign institutional autonomies, markedly political in nature (traits specific only to the Basque Community provinces).

Given the traditional self-governing capacity of historical territories, an internal organization of a federalist state has been designed. Within it, regional and provincial institutions and authorities exist side by side, giving rise to some important consequences.

Finally, there is a notable absence of even implicit reference to the townships (with the exception of the almost marginal one in article 8), in contrast to the great, historical importance given them in the previous statutory agreement period, as well as subsequently in the diverse waves of claims for autonomy.

THE SPECIFICITY OF NAVARRE. According to the volunteer principle, Navarre holds a generic right to inclusion in the Autonomous Community of the Basque Country. Certain specifications are given as to how its integration must come about. Its right is explicitly acknowledged in the Constitution (Transitory Resolution 4a), Statute of Autonomy of the Basque Country (article 2), and the Law of Improvement of the Statute-laws (Additional Resolution 2a).

When the Constitution was being written, Navarre decided not to be integrated into the Autonomous Community of the Basque Country, opting instead to constitute an individual Statutory Community. If, in the future, Navarre were to decide to incorporate itself into the Autonomous Community of the Basque Country, such an integration would have to take place in accordance with constitutional and statutory guidelines regulated in Transitory Resolution 4a of the Constitution, article 47-2a of the Statute of Autonomy of the Basque Country and Additional Resolution 2a of the Organic Law of Reintegration and Improvement of the Navarre Statutory Regime, respectively.

4.2.5 Material competencies

Certain subjects are covered under the First Additional Resolution of the Constitution, denoting the statute writers' efforts to force the constitutional guidelines to the limit in such matters. In the remaining issues concerning competencies, an ample attribution of competencies to the Basque Country is similarly envisaged. This is shown by the 39 subjects considered to fall exclusively under the authority of the Autonomous Community, thus expressing the capacity for real self-governance.

This same extensiveness led to a substantial part of the subject matter reserved for the State being qualified in the Constitution with phrases such as "not to the detriment of ...," "in the framework ...," "in accordance with ...," etc. This solution has been a constant source of conflict because of its obstinate attribution to the State of essential, ruling authority.

Apart from those already mentioned (police, education), a series of additional, specific competencies exist in the Statute. They correspond to matters of undeniable significance, in which a certain degree of overlap with the State is articulated – for example, health care and communications. The quantitative and qualitative level of competence is certainly extensive, even comparable to that of a state within a federal system. But the vagueness in the attribution of some applications has led to constant recourse to the Constitutional Court in order to resolve the conflicts arising.

4.2.6 Citizenship

Citizenship is regulated by article 7 of the Statute of Autonomy of the Basque Country, which in turn is closely linked to article 139 of the Spanish Constitution. According to the cited constitutional precept, all Spaniards have the same rights and obligations in any part of the State territory. This implies the exclusion of the possibility of a specific Basque citizenship, as differentiated from the rest of the Spaniards, which could affect the social, economic, administrative, or civil order (excepting, in this latter case, those indicated in articles 149.01.18 of the Spanish Constitution and 10.5 of the Statute of Autonomy of the Basque Country).

Therefore, the political condition of being Basque alluded to in article 7 refers exclusively to exercising political rights, and solely within the Statute's framework. Three cases are included: citizens with administrative residence in the territory of the Autonomous Community; residents abroad, if their last administrative residence was in the Basque Country and if they retain their Spanish nationality; and descendants of residents abroad, if they make an explicit request and keep their Spanish nationality.

4.2.7   Economic Contracts

The Economic Contracts provisions constitute a fundamental aspect of the Statute of Autonomy of the Basque Country. They are an institution without equivalent in any other autonomous community except Navarre. They constitute the most obvious expression of the acknowledgement and application of Basque historical rights.

The Economic Contracts involve a unique system of regulation of tax relations between the State and the Basque Country. Their statutory basis is found in article 40 of the Statute of Autonomy, which establishes that the Basque Country will have its own Autonomous Tax Department to exercise and finance its competencies adequately. Its development is regulated by Law 12/81, by which the Economic Contract with the Autonomous Community is approved (modified by the Law of 2 August 1985, by which the Economic Contract is adapted to the establishment of IVA (value added tax), which will remain in force until 31 December 2001.

The contract system implies that the Provincial Governments of the Historical Territories can carry out the collection, management, liquidation and inspection of all taxes, except those related to customs and those collected by fiscal monopolies.

Distribution of the money paid in is established in the following way. First, the Provincial Governments add the amounts determined by a Basque parliamentary law to the money paid in to the general Basque Tax Department. A global quota is established, with the Basque Country's share paid to the State as a "contribution towards all State charges not assumed by the Basque Autonomous Community."

Every five years, the methodology for designating the quota is determined, and rules for the following five years are established. This is done through a law voted on by the General Legislative Assembly of Spain after previous agreement by the Combined Commission of the Quota. For its part, the Commission must annually update the quota. The Combined Commission of the Quota is made up of one representative from each of the Provincial Governments, representatives from the Basque Government, and an equal number of representatives from the State Administration.

5 Autonomic praxis

Having pointed out the principal political problems of the Basque Country, and the responses provided to them by the Statute of Autonomy, it is appropriate to weigh the practical results achieved in these twelve years of autonomy.

5.1 Violence

ETA's activity has had serious consequences for the whole of Basque society. Its activity has left hundreds of families torn apart by death, injuries, imprisonment, and exile. It has caused deep splits and internal conflict in Basque society and the nationalist movement, it is contributing to an economic crisis, and it is threatening the stability of the democratic system.

In recent years all Basque political forces except for HB have actively opposed violence. In January 1988, the forces opposing violence subscribed to the Ajuria Enea Pact, an agreement to normalize and seek peace for the Basque Country. Since the signing of this agreement, ETA has found itself in a progressively more delicate and difficult political situation. Socially, Basque society's rejection of ETA is becoming more and more generalized and intense. Politically, ETA and HB are weaker and ETA has suffered numerous arrests, thus debilitating its operative capacity. Nevertheless, it still maintains a significant ability to carry out terrorist activity.

In any case, violence is being more and more clearly dissociated from the Basque national construction process, particularly from statutory development. While recognizing that the violence has a clear political component and that certain characteristic claims, such as the right to self-determination, have not been acknowledged, virtually all Basque political forces now agree that political violence has no justification whatsoever.

5.2 Self-determination

Traditionally, the right to self-determination has been expressed as a demand for an independent, national State. But important changes are now occurring due to the state–nation crisis, which, as is becoming clearer, suggests that self-determination no longer constitutes a synonym for independence. This is increasingly apparent in Europe, where two alternatives to the national problem are now proposed. One is the creation of new national states; the other, the transformation, surpassing, even disappearance of existing ones.

In Europe today, political change is taking place on three levels. Nation states, though remaining the typical, dominant form, are affected by a serious crisis. Certain supra-state bodies of integration have come into play; they are still weak but have a clear mandate to become stronger quickly. There is also the resurgence or, in some cases, consolidation of certain social formations proclaiming their own political power.

According to the classical conception of sovereignty, nation states have historically tended to be self-sufficient. Perhaps the most explicit expression of such self-sufficiency is the traditional conception of the border as a rigid line denoting the separation between specific territories under the sovereignty of each state. However, the intensification of trade, the mobility of people as a consequence of economic well-being and the ease of travel, and the progressive similarity of culture resulting from the exchange of goods, culture, and communications media are rapidly putting an end to this old concept of the border, substituting it with international cooperation and pulverizing the classical concept of sovereignty.

Intra-European relations, based until recent times on antagonism among the various nation states, are moving toward an enriching and positive cooperative relationship extending beyond state levels and structures. The prerogative of international relations is no longer exclusively that of the states. Regional entities and institutions have an ever-intensifying international presence and many of them are growing in importance: for example, trans-border cooperation conventions and private mercantile, professional, and cultural bodies.

These new realities are causing a profound change in the theoretical conceptions on which nation states have traditionally been founded. We are on the threshold of a new world. The nation-state/Industrial-Revolution symbiosis is tending to be superseded by new forms of political organization and structuring, which may reduce the nation state to a mere historical category comparable to the feudal state or the absolutist state. In seeking new kinds of legal-political structure, it is indispensable to avoid repeating the mistake committed by the liberal revolutionaries at the time of the nation states' formation. The new design of political power, manifested in Europe in the form of the European Union, must take into account the diversity of the collective peoples of which it is composed. Otherwise, it risks wiping out the existing formations.

To date, regions have lacked an official existence in the seat of the European Union. The presence of certain regions in the EU sphere has not been determined or favoured by the EU's institutions but rather by the internal, federal, or regional structure of the states to which they belong. Such is the case of the Länder Germans and, to a lesser degree, of some Italian regions. The solution to the nationalist problem in Europe seems intimately linked to the way in which the EU's institutional development proceeds. In such development, it would appear necessary to grant important protagonist status to the regions. While realizing that this would not be exhaustive, and while centring exclusively on the political, institutional sphere, we consider that such development could be based on five core concepts:

(i) Institutionalization of a two-level, federal structure in which not only states are represented, but also regions (Länder, Autonomous Communities, etc.). Perhaps this could be achieved by means of a Regional Council or Senate, with its own legislative authority its own political decision-making powers.

(ii) Direct participation of regions in matters of their particular interest or competence, by two means: (*a*) through an office or delegation near the headquarters of the Community institutions, without power of decision, but with a substantial informational and administrative capacity; and (*b*) through the state's central bodies in the negotiation and establishment of EU norms, as long as the matters affect their material competencies.

(iii) Execution, on the part of the regions, of EU decisions in all areas affecting their competence.

(iv) The regions' exercising of an intense and ample leading role in so-called "transnational relations," that is, all foreign activities meant to favour economic, social, and cultural development. These would entail, for example: visits abroad made by regional delegations; the invitation of representatives from foreign countries; participation in commercial or tourist activities; the organization of meetings, studies, and even the making of informal agreements with other European regions or foreign countries.

(v) Finally, in those regions which, like the Basque Country, are situated in a border area, it would seem indispensable to strengthen trans-border cooperation for the common good of the diverse regions. An open interpretation of article 8-A of the Single European Act, which defends the setting in motion of the internal market in an area without internal borders, could enormously facilitate the development of border regions, thus making the creation of supra-state regional centres possible and resolving historical conflicts.

In significant sectors of Basque nationalism, and with reference to the right to self-determination, an important change of orientation can be perceived in recent years. There is an implicit renunciation of the attainment of an independent sovereign state, substituting this claim for a demand for protagonist status within the European Union.

5.3 Territorial integration

As has already been indicated, the Statute establishes an arrangement based on the territories' will. Navarre did not consent to becoming part of the inter-Basque institutional group, choosing instead to remain outside. The three remaining provinces did consent without raising any problems, at least in the beginning. Nevertheless, the composition of internal representation, which was of a clearly federal type and was created with equal numerical representation for the three provinces, was soon the subject of significant complaint in Biscay, the province with the largest population, because its genuine weight appeared to be reduced. As a consequence of the predominance of nationalism in this province, this dissatisfaction was not demonstrated explicitly in the years that followed.

Another, more important fissure is that produced in Alava. This province has the smallest population; yet the political capital of the Autonomous Community lies here, and most of the latter's administration takes place in it. Based on a supposed "victimization" – which has no basis in fact, since Alava has undoubtedly been the province profiting most from the autonomy – "Alava Unity," a political force whose economic origins are very unclear, has emerged. This party opposes nationalism, considering it contrary to Alava's specific interests. It involves a strictly provincial, political force, although a relatively important one, which puts into question the territorial integrity of the Basque Country, though its discourse is basically centred on the rejection of nationalism. In summary, in a

Basque Country undergoing an upheaval due to problems of a very diverse nature, even the problem of its own territory has yet to be resolved.

5.4 Public security

In accordance with the Statute text, and by agreement with the State Administration, in 1980 the Basque Autonomous Police emerged. Since then their numbers have been increasing steadily. Currently, approximately 5,000 officers have been deployed throughout the territory, with the deployment in the capital cities not set to be finalized until 1995.

Since its appearance, this police force under the authority of the Basque Government has been involved in a tough confrontation with the State police force, with the latter jealously hanging onto its authority over public order, an authority which was justified by the battle against ETA terrorism. The central Administration has been clearly reluctant to favour the deployment of a police force dependent on a nationalist government which, moreover, showed initial misgivings about joining in the anti-terrorist struggle. This led to the central powers' disputing the Statute text concerning the fundamental role reserved for the autonomous police.

At the end of the 1980s, the central and Basque governments reached an agreement in which the autonomous police were acknowledged as a police force with full powers, and, as such, their leading, even exclusive, function in the ordinary sphere of citizen security was granted. The agreement coincided with an undeniable involvement of the autonomous police in the fight against terrorism. Because their officers are originally from the Basque Country, and thus are highly familiarized with the population and area, they have been quite successful in the anti-terrorist struggle – a fact that has turned them into a target, currently only in threat, of the terrorist organization, ETA.

One issue remains to be resolved. The autonomous police force still lacks a clear legal framework, since no legal resolution has been passed allowing for the development of a Statute and governing the organization's function, composition, and regulations. Thus, we find ourselves with an important police force, devoid of sufficient legal regulations.

Problems have also arisen between the autonomous police and the local police. The latter depend on the town halls and play important roles in the provincial capitals. Vagueness concerning these police forces' jurisdiction has been an additional source of conflicts when different groups take action in the same matters. Therefore, what is needed is a law ordaining the different areas of authority and clearly designating the distribution of activity among the different police forces operating in the same territory.

Finally, the State Administration's aim of monopolizing the judicial police, specializing in investigating crimes and tracking the perpetrators, has not been achieved in the Basque Country. This is a result of the "full capacity" nature of the autonomous police. One last precaution taken by the central Administration has to do with the relative prohibition of the autonomous police's use of powerful weapons, thus avoiding their intervention in activities beyond their responsibilities as police officers. Despite these problems, the current deployment of the autonomous police is taking place normally.

5.5   The regime of linguistic co-officiality

In addition to granting the native language, Basque, a status equal to that of Spanish, an important policy promoting Basque is also being implemented in the form of economic subsidies for publishing and education. Several years ago, a television channel (ETB), dependent on the Autonomous Community and broadcasting only in Basque, was also inaugurated.

The implantation of bilingualism in public administration has been questioned, particularly with respect to autonomous and municipal areas. The State Supreme Court has ruled, since 1984, that the valuing of Basque language abilities on tests for selecting civil servants discriminates against citizens who do not know Basque. The basis of such examinations is thereby nullified. The injustice of such declarations and their contradiction of what is established in the Constitution and the Statute have led the Constitutional Court to break with said doctrine, establishing a practice of implanting bilingualism in public offices.

The pragmatism and undeniable gradualism of co-officiality applied to administration ought to avoid conflict in such delicate matters. Nevertheless, the privileges supposedly conceded to Basque have been used by State political parties as missiles in the electoral battle, thus sparking yet another conflict. The Socialist Party's access to the government (they are the prime advocates of revising the co-official policy) has relieved the tension, while at the same time entailing a slowing down of measures of public support for Basque.

An open debate is currently taking place on the legal nature of education centres teaching exclusively in Basque (*Ikastolas*), and the support they receive from the Basque Government. The Socialist Party, which is in charge of educational policy, is attempting to equate them with all other public centres, depriving them of the additional economic support they have enjoyed to date. The issue has yet to be closed.

5.6   The possibility of historical rights

The importance of the Additional Resolution of the Spanish Constitution has already been pointed out. In it, the Basque People's non-renunciation of their historical rights is admitted, as is the need to bring them up to date. It is worth noting that, in practice, the uniqueness of Basque autonomy lies in this recognition. Current demands do not entail a return to legendary rights, but a recognition of certain, exceptional areas of power reserved exclusively for the Basque political institutions. The conferring of such matters has previously been reviewed in a pact with the State, and has signified special recognition of the Basque Country, reaching beyond the highest levels of autonomy held by the other Autonomous Communities. In addition, and through the pact system itself, certain matters not contained in the statutory text, such as transportation, roads, and local civil servants, have been permitted to be taken on by the Basque Autonomous Community. Related to this, it turns out that a constitutional clause which originally appeared to be purely declarative has become the main basis for Basque autonomous singularity.

6   Conclusion

It is true that the Statute of Autonomy has not proven capable of resolving some of the Basque Country's traditional demands. Nevertheless, it is providing satisfactory results. The Statute of Autonomy is demonstrating its validity as an effective instrument for recovering Basque identity. The progress made in the last twelve years is substantial and the necessary foundations have been laid for a recovery of the Basque language and culture. It also serves important functions in educational material. A Basque Parliament and Government exist with ample authority to develop their own institutional policies, always within a global framework designed by the Spanish Constitution, and their own public administration with an extensive decision-making capacity. The Basque Autonomous Community has a relatively strong spending power, allowing it to plan the Basque economy, albeit within the limits of the Spanish economy and international conditions.

The issues still pending are extremely varied, and their solution depends on very diverse conditions. Some of the problems are indigenous to the Basque Country. This is the case of the social division between the nationalist and non-nationalist worlds. As a result of this split, Basque society has yet to achieve an acceptable degree of homogeneity and social integration. It is a destructured society and therefore suffers internal conflict and strife. Something similar occurs with respect to violence. It involves a problem with clearly political origins, but which at the current time has no justification whatsoever. It is a basically indigenous problem whose solution mainly, although not exclusively, lies within the Basque society itself. In order to resolve the problem of violence, as well as that of homogenization of Basque society, an institutional leadership by the Basque Government is desperately needed. This type of leadership occurred during the Second Republic and the Civil War.

Among the various indigenous problems, the current delicate economic situation in the Basque Country stands out. Basque industrial activity has traditionally revolved around the iron and steel industry. The crisis in this sector is producing a genuine dismantling of the Basque industrial fabric, which, for the moment, has not adapted itself to current technological changes. Terrorism causes additional difficulties for economic recovery, since foreign investors are clearly reluctant to intervene in the Basque economic recovery, even though this is a developed country with a large industrial culture.

Another large set of problems arises from the non-recognition of the right to self-determination on the part of the Spanish Constitution. This is a fundamental and delicate issue for which the Spanish State has not yet managed to find an adequate solution. The problem has lost much of its potency in the expectation of possible solutions provided by the final design of the construction of Europe. Therefore, an adequate response from the Spanish State, as well as from the European Union, will be crucial in order to resolve this and other similar matters existing in Western Europe. An inadequate policy could ignite and destroy Spanish democracy and subsequently European unity. As an example of this statement, the fact that HB (the majority party in Guipúzcoa, with great influence in the entire Basque territory) does not acknowledge the legitimacy of the Spanish Constitution and Basque Statute and refuses to participate in parliamentary political life is highly upsetting to Basque democratic stability.

The third set of problems is that related to territorial integrity. Basque nationalism has always set its sights on the unification of these seven historical Basque territories. In this aspiration, the Basque Country, which sociologically and historically represents a single unit, is nevertheless, politically divided into three different entities: the Basque Autonomous Community; Navarre; and the continental Basque country. In the case of Navarre, there is no legal problem whatsoever in carrying out its integration. The problem is political, in so far as the Navarrese majority parties have preferred not to join the rest of the Basque Community to date. The final solution to this problem will depend, in the end, on the Navarrese themselves. Therefore, the Navarrese issue cannot by any means be considered a structural problem of the Basque Country, but is rather a specific problem of nationalism. As far as the French Basque territories are concerned, it is true that it would currently be legally impossible to integrate them into the Basque Autonomous Community. However, it is also true that even if such a union were viable, citizens would almost certainly reject it, at least as things stand today.

One final set of problems remains: those derived from the application of the Statute of Autonomy. Despite the Statute's approval, the relationship between the State and the Autonomous Community still involves conflict, as can be seen by the numerous occasions on which the Constitutional Court has had to intervene to resolve conflicts over competencies. There is mutual distrust between the two administrations, expressed by the State in its continued attempt to reduce Basque authority and by the Basques in their permanent stance of demand-making. Although time has passed, some significant competencies which, according to the Constitution and the Statute, correspond to the Autonomous Community, have yet to be transferred. A process of mutual and loyal collaboration between both administrations is, therefore, indispensable in order to resolve, once and for all, this age-old controversy.

13

Ethnic and racial groups in the USA: Conflict and cooperation

Mary C. Waters

Introduction

This paper argues that the historical experiences of groups in the
United States significantly shape the various cultural lenses through
which people understand inter-ethnic conflict. Specifically, the mode
of incorporation of a people into the social and cultural structure of
the United States, along with their subsequent treatment, influences
three aspects of that understanding at both the individual and group
levels:

1. The meanings attached to racial and ethnic identities: are these
   oppositional identities, immigrant identities, or symbolic identities?
2. The relationship of the group and its component individuals to
   the state: do they trust the institutions of the state to be fair and
   honest? Do they see systematic oppression, and the power of the
   state exercised against them, or do they see the state as an instrument of power to be used by their own group or as a neutral
   arbiter among groups?
3. The meanings attached to incidents of hate crimes, violence, and

intergroup encounters: are they perceived as temporary, accidental and individualized, or as permanent, systematic, and institutionalized?

The empirical material used to amplify this argument is a study of four major bias incidents in New York City in the period 1987–1992. Subsequent to these incidents, the well-publicized rioting in Los Angeles occurred, a racially-tinged event that caused considerable death and destruction of property. While Los Angeles is not discussed here, the four New York incidents examined remain particularly worthy of analysis.

This paper focuses on understanding the roles, reactions, and perceptions of three groups of people: West Indian immigrants, African-Americans, and white ethnic Americans. It explores the little-known fact that most such incidents in New York City during the past five years have involved West Indians as victims. Nevertheless, these incidents have generally been reported and understood in terms of the long-term racial problems involving whites and blacks in the United States. However, I differentiate the experiences of West Indians and American blacks, and trace how those differences contribute to different understandings of causes and consequences of hate crimes in New York City.

The paper proceeds as follows: First, I trace the historical distinction in the United States between groups defined in terms of ethnicity and in terms of race. I explore the differences in the ways these groups have been incorporated into the American society and polity and the differences in how they have experienced violence.

Second, I examine the ways in which some of these distinctions have broken down in the last 30 years or so, with the large-scale immigration of non-Europeans following upon changes in American immigration laws in 1965.

Third, I introduce a typology of three groups – involuntary minorities, voluntary minorities, and the dominant white group (who are themselves descendants of voluntary minorities). In New York City these three groups are represented by African-Americans, West Indians, and white ethnics, such as Italian-Americans, Polish-Americans, and Irish-Americans.

Part 4 of the paper describes the four major bias incidents, and traces the popular understandings of what happened in each of these groups in the Howard Beach case, to illustrate the general differences in their perceptions. I conclude with general principles of intergroup relations which can be abstracted from analysis of these incidents.

237

Race and ethnicity in the United States

Americans generally distinguish between *race* relations and *ethnic* relations. The term "race' commonly refers to distinctions drawn from physical appearance while the term "ethnicity" commonly refers to distinctions based on national origin, language, religion, food, and other cultural markers (Stone, 1985). The history of the groups defined as ethnic has been one of increasing inclusion in society, economic and social assimilation, and a decline in the salience and determinacy, though not the existence, of ethnic identities (Takaki, 1987; Lieberson and Waters, 1988; Waters and Lieberson, 1992; Neidert and Farley, 1985). Ethnic groups have generally been identified in cultural and social spheres but have not been given explicit legal status as a group (Glazer, 1987, Thernstrom, 1987).

In contrast, the history of racial groups has been marked by a greater degree of conflict and continued exclusion (Takaki, 1987; Blauner, 1972). Racial groups continue to be very separate from other groups in American life in terms of socio-economic status, residential segregation, and intermarriage (Lieberson and Waters, 1988). Moreover, since 1965, groups defined as racial or language minorities have been given explicit legal status and recognition by the government. The four federally designated minority groups are blacks, Native Americans, Hispanics, and Asian-Americans (Thernstrom, 1987).

The different experiences of groups defined racially and ethnically have in part been explained by the different modes of incorporation of the groups into American society (Lieberson, 1961; Blauner, 1972). European ethnic groups are generally composed of voluntary migrants and their descendants who chose to come to the United States. Those defined racially, such as blacks, Native Americans, Mexicans in the South-West, and Puerto Ricans, have generally been incorporated into the United States historically through conquest or the forced migration of slaves.

As Lieberson (1961) argues, the mode of incorporation of a group into the society has long-range effects on the probabilities of conflict and the extent to which that conflict becomes violent. He describes two different situations of initial contact: (1) subordination of an indigenous population by a migrant group; and (2) subordination of a migrant group by an indigenous racial or ethnic group. The first case has much more potential for conflict than the second.

In United States history, the initial violent confrontations between white settlers and the indigenous Indian, and later the Spanish, populations conformed to the first model by generally resulting in the formation of "racial" groups. The later successive assimilation of white European immigrants conformed to the second model and led to the formation of "ethnic groups." Lieberson identifies the United States after the subordination of the indigenous Indian population as belonging to the second type of society, as the core American group subordinated the incoming immigrant groups. The forced migration of black Africans as slaves does not fit Lieberson's model.

Post-1965 immigration and the breakdown of the racial/ethnic dichotomy

The growth in the size of the non-white voluntary immigrant population since 1965 challenges the dichotomy which once explained different patterns of American inclusion and assimilation: the ethnic pattern of assimilation of immigrants from Europe and their children and the racial pattern of exclusion of America's non-white peoples.[1] The new wave of immigrants includes people who, though still defined "racially," have migrated voluntarily, and often under an immigrant legal preference system which selects for people with job skills and education that puts them well above their "co-ethnics" in the United States economy. Though generally defined as members of minority racial groups in the United States, these new immigrants do not necessarily share the racial and minority identities imposed on them when they arrive. Black immigrants to New York City from the Caribbean nation states – the subject of my current research – provide an example of a group that challenges these theoretical distinctions. They are voluntary migrants from societies in which blacks are the majority to a society in which blacks are a stigmatized minority (Waters and Mittelberg, 1992).

These immigrants have a degree of ethnic identity along with their racial identity as black. Thus individual immigrants can identify themselves as Jamaican or Haitian as well as black. While some aspects of racial oppression are no doubt the same throughout the world,[2] the fact remains that these immigrants are entering a society in which they are assigned immediately to membership in a group which has its own history of oppression and minority status. For instance, these immigrants are defined as black for purposes of affirmative action accounting for employment and for voting rights enforcement statistics.

239

These Caribbean immigrants have a complicated relationship with their new identities. Most of them try to distance themselves from American blacks. They emphasize their own cultural and ethnic identity which distinguishes them from American blacks. They declare that Jamaicans and American blacks are different groups with different values, customs, traditional foods, dialects, and so on (Bryce-Laporte, 1972; Buchanan, 1979; Dominguez, 1975; Foner, 1985, 1987; Justus, 1976; Sutton, 1973; Sutton and Makiesky, 1973; Bonnett, 1990; Waters, 1991b; Apollon and Waters, 1990). They also point to the different reactions and relations with whites foreign-born blacks and American blacks have.

West Indians generally do not expect racism and racist reactions from whites to the same extent as American blacks. West Indians tend to be more open to whites and more oblivious to racial slights. They have grown up in societies where the majority of people are blacks: as a result they have had less personal experience with racism of the kind that American blacks have encountered all their lives. Thus they expect less racism and interpret most interactions with whites as owing to their own individual characteristics rather than to their racial characteristics. They describe the American blacks as hypersensitive to issues of race, while the American blacks describe the foreign-born blacks as naïve in their acceptance of whites.

American society in general and whites in particular have tended not to recognize these distinctions. They have generally defined American blacks and foreign-born blacks as similar in their identities as blacks, thus equating racial and ethnic identities under the umbrella of a single racial identity (Waters, 1991; Woldemikael, 1989; Bryce-Laporte, 1972; Kasinitz, 1992). This lack of recognition by outsiders of ethnic differences within the racially identified group tends to promote a common racial identity. The factors uniting African-Americans and Caribbean-Americans are a common racial identity based on skin colour, their historical roots in Africa, and the shared aspects of their histories as victims of racism in European colonialism and slavery.

Thus, the distinction between groups defined by race and those defined by ethnicity which has characterized American society throughout its history is challenged by the increase in non-European immigrants since 1965. These include large numbers of people who, though members of a racial group, blacks, are being incorporated into American society as voluntary immigrants trying to maintain an ethnic identity which recognizes their non-American roots. The distinctions developed by the anthropologist John Ogbu to explain education performance in different societies is a starting point for understanding the positions of these immigrants in the United States.

Voluntary and involuntary minorities

Ogbu (1978, 1990) has developed a theory about the cultural differences between voluntary migrants and involuntary minorities, a difference which corresponded in the past with the historical distinction in the United States between racial and ethnic groups, but which, as we have seen, is now more complicated.

Ogbu has examined the question of why minorities stemming from involuntary migrants in a variety of countries around the world do not perform well academically, especially when compared to the academic achievement of voluntary immigrants. He argues that the persistent underperformance of minorities in these societies cannot be completely explained by "conflicts in cognitive, communication, social interaction, teaching and learning styles" (Ogbu, 1990: 144). He maintains instead that the history of the mode of incorporation of the group into the society, the history of how the minority group was treated by the dominant group, and the history of how the minorities responded to that treatment must be taken into account because these histories give rise to different cultures and identities.

The important distinction Ogbu makes is between immigrant "voluntary minorities" who have chosen to move to a society in order to improve their well-being, and castelike "involuntary minorities" who were initially brought in to the society through slavery, conquest, and colonization. He argues that voluntary and involuntary minorities have very different understandings of what it means to be a minority, which are a result of the historical experience of how they were incorporated into society and the cultural adaptations they made to the treatment they were subjected to by the dominant group. Voluntary migrants who are subject to discrimination and exclusion because they use their home country and culture as a frame of reference

do not measure their success or failure primarily by the standards of other white Americans, but by the standards of their homelands. Such minorities, at least during the first generation, do not internalise the effects of such discrimination, of cultural and intellectual denigration. (Ogbu, 1990: 8)

They develop "immigrant identities" which *differ* from the dominant group in society's identities, but are not necessarily *opposed* to those identities.

The situation differs greatly for involuntary minorities who do develop oppositional identities:

For involuntary minorities there were no expectations of economic, political and social benefits. Resenting their initial incorporation by force, regarding their past as a golden age and seeing their future as grim in the absence of collective struggle, they understood that the American system was based on social class and minority conditions. (Ogbu, 1990: 150)

The coping responses that different groups develop for dealing with problems with the dominant group thus reflect the different histories and social psychologies of the groups. Ogbu argues that voluntary migrants have a

greater degree of trust for white Americans, for the societal institutions controlled by whites, than do involuntary minorities. Such immigrants acquiesce and rationalise the prejudice and discrimination against them by saying in effect, that they are strangers in a foreign land [and] have no choice but to tolerate prejudice and discrimination. (Ogbu, 1990: 152)

The involuntary minorities do not have a homeland with which to compare their current treatment, or in which to root their identities. Thus, Ogbu argues, they do not see discrimination against them as a temporary barrier to be overcome. Instead, "recognizing that they belong to a subordinate, indeed a disparaged minority, they compare their situation with that of their white American peers. The prejudice against them seems permanent, indeed institutionalised" (Ogbu, 1990: 153). This also leads to distrust of the institutions controlled by the dominant group. This understanding of their situation leads the involuntary minorities to conclude that solidarity and challenges to the rules of the dominant society are the only way to improve their situation. Ogbu describes the psychological orientation that develops among involuntary minorities as being "oppositional" in nature: "They do not see their social identity as different from that of their white oppressors, but as opposed to the social identity of white Americans" (Ogbu, 1990: 155). These "oppositional identities" mean that the involuntary minorities come largely to define themselves in their core identities in terms of their opposition to the dominant group.

For blacks in America, Ogbu argues, the very meaning of being black involves *not* being white. The strong value put on solidarity and opposition to rules perceived as being against them means that when a member of the group is seen as cooperating with the dominant society's institutions, his or her very identity is called into question. In

Ogbu's work, the young black student who tries to achieve in school is accused of "acting white."

The identities of the dominant groups

The last group under review are the descendants of voluntary minorities from European countries, who are now in the later stages of assimilation. My earlier studies have examined different social psychological ways of experiencing an ethnic or racial identity in the United States depending on whether one is a member of an ethnic group that is assimilating or a racial group that is still experiencing exclusion and discrimination (Waters, 1990). The groups which have achieved a degree of individual and group social mobility adopt ethnicity as a symbolic, voluntary identity which is intermittent in its effects on the individual and freely chosen as a valued personal asset (Waters, 1990; Gans, 1979). These ethnic identities have few costs but many benefits for the individual, such as psychological feelings of closeness to other group members and of originality and special-ness which come to an individual by virtue of being included in the group.

People who assert a symbolic ethnicity do not give much attention to the ease with which they are able to slip in and out of their ethnic roles. It is quite natural to them that in the greater part of their lives, their ethnicity does not matter, it is largely a matter of personal choice and a source of pleasure. This approach to their own ethnicity leads to a situation where whites with a symbolic ethnicity are unable to understand the everyday influence and importance of skin color and racial minority status for members of minority groups in the United States. The way in which they think about their own ethnicity – the voluntary, enjoyable aspects of it – makes it difficult to under-stand the contemporary position of non-whites. Since their own ethnicity is a voluntaristic, personal matter, it is difficult for white ethnics to understand that race or ethnicity for others is influenced by societal and political components.

For these white ethnics, invoking an ethnic background has increasingly become a voluntary, individual decision. Invoking their ethnic background is done for the enjoyment of the personality traits or for the rituals associated with their ethnicity. For them ethnicity itself takes on certain individual and positive connotations. The process and content of a symbolic ethnicity then make it increas-ingly difficult for white ethnics to sympathize with, or understand,

243

the experience of a non-symbolic ethnicity, the experience of racial minorities in the United States.

Identities and bias incidents

While Ogbu's distinction between voluntary and involuntary minorities was developed through analysis of ethnographic work among minority groups in state schools, I will extend the theory in order to analyse the ways in which minority groups respond to violent incidents and the criminal justice system. Voluntary and involuntary minorities have different responses to incidents of racial violence and in turn these will differ from the responses of the white dominant group. The three different types of response will be partly determined by the historical experiences of the groups and the resulting meaning that membership in the groups has for the individuals. Involuntary migrants experience discrimination and violence as systemic; the criminal justice system is viewed with distrust and with the suspicion that it is part of the systematic institutional racism which caused the violence in the first place.

Voluntary minorities view the violence as directed at them because of their membership in the group and also see the group perpetrating the violence as part of the dominant society. However, they have more trust in the state as an arbiter of justice; the criminal justice system is not automatically implicated in the incidents and there is a desire to deal with the incidents according to "the rules."

The dominant group has yet another reaction. Its members generally do not consciously experience themselves as members of any group but instead understand themselves to be individuals first and foremost. Members of both voluntary and involuntary groups are accustomed to seeing their identities and group membership as an integral part of how society and other individuals respond to them – calling forth discrimination or accommodation or some sort of conscious reaction to their identities. But members of the dominant group invoke their identities in a voluntary manner, only for their own purposes and generally believing that their identities as white or as some other ethnicity (Italian, Irish, etc.) do not matter very much. As a result, they experience and understand bias incidents in an individualistic manner.

Examined in this context, then, the four racial incidents in New York described here prove to be more complicated than a simple black–white distinction would allow. The violence has not occurred between American whites and American blacks who share a long history of racial hatred, violence, and conflict. Instead, much of it has occurred between native whites and foreign-born blacks. As soon as these incidents became publicly known, however, American black and American white political leaderships and the media started to define the situation in terms of black–white conflict. Thus the people involved in the incidents have been caught up in a rhetoric and an intergroup dynamic that has been going on between white and black Americans. These immigrant individuals are thus identified as being members of a group – black Americans – to which they may or may not see themselves as belonging. The next section of the paper analyses the specific incidents of bias in light of these further distinctions.

Incidents of bias in New York City

New York is a city of some 7.3 million people. In 1990 whites comprised 43 per cent of the population, blacks 25 per cent, Hispanics 24 per cent, and Asians 7 percent. One-third of the city's population is foreign-born, with approximately 100,000 newcomers arriving each year. (It is estimated that between 25 and 40 per cent of the black population are foreign-born.) The 1980s were generally a time of economic prosperity for the city, which gained new jobs in the service industry while a long-term decline in manufacturing jobs continued. But the situation changed at the end of the decade. Since 1989, the city has been in an economic recession and job losses have been recorded in all sectors of the economy.

In the late 1980s and early 1990s New York City became a symbol of racial tension and violence for the nation. Beginning with the murder of Michael Griffith in Howard Beach in December 1986, a series of incidents occurred in the boroughs of Brooklyn and Queens which have suddenly made neighbourhood names stand as code words for racial hatred, modern-day lynchings, and the failures of blacks and whites to live together in peace. The Howard Beach incident, where Griffith was killed, was followed in 1989 by the killing of another African-American, Yusuf Hawkins, in Bensonhurst, fire bombings in Canarsie, a long boycott of a Korean grocer in Flatbush by African-Americans, as well as riots and the deaths of Gavin Cato and Yankel Rosenbaum in Crown Heights in 1991. While the generally all-black neighbourhoods of Bedford Stuyvesant, Brownsville, Harlem, and the South Bronx were the symbols of the failures of American race relations in the 1960s, these areas have been replaced

245

with neighbourhoods which are white or interracial as the sites of our failures in race relations in the 1990s.

In the parlance of the city police department, interracial violence or threats of violence are defined as "bias incidents." The police have a bias-investigation team which decides whether or not to classify a particular incident or crime as a bias incident. The Bias Crime Unit has been collecting statistics of bias incidents in New York since 1981, using the definition of a bias crime developed by the California Racial Ethnic and Religious Crimes Project: "Any act to cause physical injury, emotional suffering or property damage, which appears to be motivated, all or in part, by race, ethnicity, religion or sexual orientation" (DeSantis, 1991: 86).

From 1981 to 1986 the total annual number of confirmed bias cases was never more than 300. But after the well-publicized Howard Beach and Tawana Brawley[3] cases, the numbers increased to 463 in 1987 from 265 in 1986. In the last four years the number of cases has remained at this same high level. There were 550 cases in 1988, 527 in 1990, and 540 in 1991. The strict definition of a bias crime means that many incidents of cross-racial violence are not classified as bias crimes. There must be an explicit mention of race, ethnicity, or sexual orientation surrounding the crime for it to be so classified. This has implications because the different parties to these incidents will differ on whether or not the crime had anything to do with race.

The crimes reported as bias crimes (also called hate crimes) varied in severity. In 1991, of the total 540 incidents, 140 were relatively minor incidents of phone calls or letters laced with slurs. The total number also included 11 swastikas painted on synagogues and homes. Most of the incidents did not involve physical injury, the three murders and 146 assaults constituted 28 per cent of the total bias crimes reported. However, the largest category of crimes were those related to race. In 1991, 121 incidents were aimed at blacks, 70 at whites, 38 at Hispanic people, 10 at East Indians, 6 at Chinese, and 2 at Koreans. In general, they involved groups of attackers against one or two victims. They have also generally involved young people: 60 per cent of victims and perpetrators were under age 18. While these official statistics probably include all of the homicides and extremely serious racial incidents, advocacy groups caution that most bias incidents go unreported. It is estimated that as many as 80 per cent of incidents are not reported to authorities, because victims either do not know about how to go about reporting the incidents, do not believe anything will be done about them, or are intimidated through fear of further violence if they report what happened to them.

As I have noted, this paper focuses on the four bias incidents in New York City which resulted in sustained attention in the media and an appreciable rise in bias incidents reported to the police. After each racial incident reported here, the number of cases recorded in the following month surged to peak levels.

Although these bias incidents have been widely reported, it has not been widely noticed that three of these racial incidents have involved Caribbean-American immigrants as the victims. Only the killing of Yusef Hawkins in Bensonhurst involved an African-American.[4] The four incidents referred to here include the 1986 Howard Beach incident, in which a Trinidadian immigrant, Michael Griffith, was attacked by a gang of whites and chased onto a busy highway, where he was struck by a car and killed. The second incident, known as Bensonhurst after the name of the neighbourhood in which it occurred, happened in August 1989, when an African-American youth, Yusef Hawkins, was killed by a gang of whites, apparently because they thought he and his friends were coming to visit a neigh-bourhood girl. The third case, the Korean grocery boycott in January 1990, involved a dispute between a Haitian-American shopper and a Korean-American shop owner. This dispute escalated into a major political incident in which a boycott by blacks against Korean gro-ceries and firebombings and fights resulted.

The final incident, in August 1991, was the one which occurred in the Brooklyn neighborhood of Crown Heights. An Orthodox Jewish driver lost control of his car and hit and killed a seven-year-old black immigrant boy from Guyana named Gavin Cato. A dispute over whether a Jewish ambulance refused to treat the dying boy inflamed tensions in the mixed Jewish–Caribbean black neighbourhood and a few nights of rioting resulted. In the first night of rioting a Jewish student from Australia, Yankel Rosenbaum, was stabbed and killed. Before it was over, 163 people were arrested and 66 civilians and 173 police were hurt.

An analysis of the reactions of the participants in all of these inci-dents shows that in general their understandings reflect the differences outlined here among the African-Americans as involuntary minorities, the West Indian immigrants as voluntary minorities, and the white ethnics as dominant symbolic ethnics. Because of space limitations only the Howard Beach incident will be described in detail here.

Howard Beach

Howard Beach was the first incident to bring nationwide attention to race relations in New York. On 19 December, 1986, four men were travelling on a main thoroughfare in the section of the borough of Queens known as Howard Beach when their car broke down. The four were Michael Griffith, aged 23, whose family had come from Trinidad 18 years ago when he was 5 years old; the boyfriend of Michael's mother, Cedric Sandiford, 36, who had immigrated from Guyana when he was a teenager; Timothy Grimes, 18, the boyfriend of Cedric's niece, and Curtis Sylvester, 19, a cousin of Michael's whose family also came from Trinidad. Sylvester stayed with the car while the three other men walked into the main part of Howard Beach to get help.

The men were spotted by a group of young white men who were leaving a party in the neighbourhood. That group included Jon Lester, 18, originally a South African, who had immigrated from England with his family four years earlier; Scott Kern, 18; and Jason Ladone, 17. The white men spotted the black men, who had stopped in a pizza parlour to get something to eat. Lester, who was the leader of the white group, had apparently gathered its members together, shouting, "There's niggers at the pizza parlour. Let's get them" (Breindel, 1987: 22).

As the black men walked up the street the whites pounced on them. They first taunted the blacks and then began beating them. Grimes was hit once before he managed to escape. Griffith and Sandiford tried to get away but the white teenagers caught up with them along a fence that bordered the Shore Parkway and continued their assault. Sandiford feigned unconsciousness. Griffith, severely beaten, dove through a three-foot hole in the fence and staggered onto the parkway. He was struck and killed by an automobile driven by Dominick Blum, 24, of Brooklyn, a court officer and the son of a policeman.

Meanwhile, various witnesses of the beatings and the incident of whites chasing the blacks had called the police. When the police eventually responded, they found a dazed Sandiford walking along the parkway and the body of Michael Griffith by the side of the parkway. However, instead of immediately believing Sandiford and treating him as the victim of the beating he had endured, they treated him as if he were a suspect of a crime. "When police found the beaten

Sandiford, they had him spread against the car and searched him, [in Sandiford's words:] 'he searched me, ripped off my coat. Then he started asking me about some crimes committed down the road. He started treating me like a criminal.' " The police then allowed Sandiford to call Michael's mother, Jean Griffith, to inform her that her son had been killed. While Sandiford was talking to Mrs Griffith and trying to calm her, the detectives made him hang up the phone (Hynes and Drury, 1991: 139).

The bare facts of the case – that these men were attacked by a mob of whites only because they were black and walking on a public street in an all-white neighbourhood – brought about immediate widespread attention. The crime was generally condemned, leading to demands for quick action by the police, the mayor, and black leaders.

Almost immediately, radical leaders of the African-American community became involved in the case. The insensitive treatment of Sandiford by the police added fuel to the charges of black leaders that the crime was not limited to the white mob who had chased the men, but instead was part of the systematic, institutionalized conspiracy of whites to keep blacks down and occasionally to kill them. Sandiford at first cooperated with the police and the district attorney investigating the case, but the African-American activist lawyers, C. Vernon Mason and Alton Maddox, advised him to withdraw his support and to refuse further cooperation. They argued that the police were involved in a conspiracy to protect the driver of the car that had hit Griffith. As I have stated, Dominick Blum, the driver of the car, worked for the criminal justice system as a court reporter and his father was a policeman. It was this tie to the criminal justice system which suggested to the black leaders that a cover-up of Blum's complicity in the crime was quite possible. Investigating detectives quickly concluded that Blum could not logically have been part of the mob (since his car was proceeding on the highway and since he had been elsewhere). But the activist lawyers, along with the Reverend Al Sharpton, a well-known African-American community figure, accused the district attorney and criminal justice system of taking part in a cover-up.

Mason and Maddox, originally from Georgia, and Sharpton, from Brooklyn, had represented victims of white violence in the past. They were explicit about using the Howard Beach murder as a metaphor for black–white relations throughout the country:

On the day Sandiford vowed not to co-operate with Santucci [the Queens district attorney], Maddox met with a small group of black reporters in a tiny room of the Abyssinian Baptist Church and told them that black activists throughout the city were "developing an agenda that is bigger than Michael Griffith", an agenda that included sharpening the lines between friends and enemies of the black community. "Never again will we lose our children," Maddox told them. "It would be better that we would all be eliminated today than for us to continue living like we're living in this city and this state." (Hynes and Drury, 1990: 99)

Mason and Maddox were explicit about not trusting the criminal justice system to investigate the crime fairly and counselled the victim's family not to cooperate. In further writing about the Howard Beach incident, the political analyst Jim Sleeper (1990) pointed to this insistence on the guilt of Blum by the black leaders in spite of convincing evidence that it was not possible, as evidence that the anger and perceptions of the black leaders were leading to situations in which they cut themselves off from other groups which might otherwise naturally be their allies in city politics.

In addition to Maddox, Mason, and Sharpton, the major figures in the Howard Beach group were the Reverend Herbert Daughtry of the Black United Front and Sonny Carson of Black Men against Crack. These African-American leaders called for boycotts against pizza parlours citywide, and white-owned businesses in Howard Beach became the initial targets.

These reactions of the African-American leaders reflect the particular lens through which blacks as involuntary minorities see black–white race relations. These leaders see the oppression and discrimination directed against blacks as something permanent, best confronted by challenging the rules of the system through racial solidarity. The tactic of not cooperating with the criminal justice system is a sensible one once the white-controlled state is perceived as systematically biased against your group. From this perspective, the actual guilt or innocence of Dominick Blum no longer mattered, since all whites are symbolically guilty for creating the violent and racist society which protected the white mob attacking the four black men in Howard Beach.

Details indicate how the family and co-ethnics of Michael Griffith at first interpreted what happened to him differently from the radicalized political leaders. Jean Griffith, the 42-year-old nurse's aide who was the mother of the slain boy, stated: "It still doesn't sit in my mind what whites did to my son ... But I don't feel that whites are all the same. I've worked with children and most of the kids are white. I worked with one white child that I loved so much that when I got home at night I called his house to see how he was doing" (Hynes and Drury, 1990: 47).

When the special prosecutor Charles Hynes and his staff were waiting with Jean Griffith and Sandiford for the verdict at the trial of the white attackers, he reported that the mother of the slain boy was quite calm. Rather than issuing demands about the verdict or ultimatums she said to him: "Relax ... whatever the jury does is one thing, but the Lord will provide, and do what He has to do in His own good time" (Hynes and Drury, 1990: 297). Sandiford also did not go on the record with blanket accusations against all whites or with remarks which would heighten polarization of the races. After the verdict of guilty for two of the whites accused in the killing, a reporter "asked Sandiford if the convictions said something about the value of black life in America. 'No sir,' he replied, 'It says something about the value of human life in America'" (Hynes and Drury, 1990: 300).

This interpretation squares with the reports of researchers who have argued that West Indians and American blacks have different expectations about race relations. Coming from societies in which blacks are in the majority, West Indians report that they are not sensitized to racial conflict as American blacks are. In a sense, then, when racism does strike, as in the case of Howard Beach, the West Indians are deeply shocked and report being surprised. Michael Griffith's mother told the *Trinidad Express* newspaper: "My son's death opened the eyes of the public ... racism was something we read about in the Deep South. Maybe it was there all along in New York but I never really experienced it" (*New York Carib News*, 1987: 4).

Philip Kasinitz (1992: 247) stated that the West Indian people he interviewed for his book on West Indian politics in Brooklyn also reported that Howard Beach educated them to see things in a different light than they had before. He reports that a young Trinidadian woman about Michael Griffith's age told him: "We from the Caribbean don't think about racial matters as much. I think we have been very naive."

The reactions of the family of Michael Griffith and the words of the victim Cedric Sandiford provide a quite different interpretation of the situation. It may be that this different response resulted from different perspectives: the black political leaders were trying to make a political statement while the family were reacting to the tragedy that had befallen them. Still, the systematic difference between the

Caribbean approach to understanding and coming to terms with these tragedies seems to differ from the African-American pattern of responses. That different reaction seems to correspond more closely to the model of voluntary minority as opposed to involuntary minority cultural identities which we have outlined.

Evidently the reactions of the West Indian participants and the black-American leadership diverged on the issue of whether the racism that had killed Griffith was so pervasive that all whites and the institutions of the criminal justice system should also be held responsible and should not be trusted to bring justice to the situation. In contrast, the reactions of the accused white boys and their families diverged on a more fundamental issue – whether race was involved at all in the killing. The parents of the Howard Beach defendants denied that it was racial. "I wish they would get off this racial angle," said Joanne Ladone. "It was a confrontation between two groups of people – not black and white but human beings" (Hynes and Drury, 1990: 235).

Whites generally use two approaches to make the point that race was not involved in the attacks. One is to deny that their identities as whites have anything to do with their actions – in a sense, to adopt a "raceless" interpretation in which the altercations are not bias crimes at all because the racial and ethnic identities of the participants had nothing to do with the encounters. The defence tried to bring into evidence the past criminal records of Griffith and Sandiford in an effort to prove that they had not been chased and attacked because of their race, but because they were suspected of being in Howard Beach to commit crimes and the whites were defending their community. (This, of course, is a ridiculous argument since the white attackers had no way of knowing the criminal records of the men. Black skin was being taken as a marker of dangerous intruders, itself a racist assumption which brings us full circle to the conclusion that the blacks were attacked only because of their race.)

The second way in which whites tended to deny that racism had anything to do with the incident involved arguing that the defendants could not be racist since they had friendly personal relations with black people. Jon Lester's mother stated: "Jon is not a racial person," noting that her son had been dating a black girl for some time (Hynes and Drury, 1990: 236). Sleeper (1990) reports that in his job as a waiter Lester had become friendly with a number of African-Americans, one of them a lawyer who defended him without charge when he had been arrested earlier for possessing a gun. This fact convinced

Sleeper that Lester could not be a complete racist. Not only did he like some black people, but some black people liked him.

As we see, then, the three groups involved in Howard Beach had distinctly different interpretations of the situation which can best be understood by the types of identities they had developed over time.

Competing perspectives, multiple realities

The major conclusion stemming from Howard Beach and the other incidents in New York is the fact that these racial incidents can be viewed from different perspectives, each of which is equally legitimate and real to the particular groups of participants. These perspectives include an either/or perspective on the history of American race relations in which the divide that matters is whether or not the participants are white or black, a mosaic, multi-cultural pluralist perspective that looks at each of the groups involved and the ethnic and racial backgrounds and histories they bring to understanding the others' actions, or a non-ethnic, non-racial approach which sees these interactions as involving atomized individuals. The perspective evoked is related directly to the historically determined nature of the groups to which the individuals belong.

Three general themes emerge from these particular cases:
(1) the role of the media and the importance of looking at the differences between what élites and ordinary people believe;
(2) the role of violent events in highlighting and shaping group boundaries;
(3) the complexities of the position adopted by the state in dealing with bias incidents.

1   The media and the role of élites

The role of the media in defining the situation is often pivotal, differing at times from the perspective of the participants involved. Analysts and policy makers should beware of what Heisler (1990: 26) has described as "ethnic nominalism": defining groups by an objective characteristic and then assuming that people defined so subjectively identify themselves with this group. Applied to this case, the circumstance that whites tend not to see the differences between West Indian and American blacks does not mean that West Indian and American blacks identify with each other or that they see the world in the same way.

Accounts of the violence in the media tend to give some details of these multifaceted events but also they tend to force those details back into a black/white cultural lens, thus losing a grip on the different perceptions. That is partly because the people themselves are seeing these events in the black–white focus, and partly because as Americans, reporters and authorities see the incidents in a black–white focus.

Élites who speak for a group may or may not share the same agenda as its rank-and-file membership. In the cases of Howard Beach, the Korean grocery boycott, and Crown Heights, the leadership of the protest movements was drawn primarily from American blacks although the victims were Caribbean-Americans. It is at least an open question whether it is a case of ethnic nominalism to gloss over the differences between Caribbeans and Americans in reporting the incidents as involving "blacks" and in assuming that the leadership of the American black community interpreted and responded to the situation in the same way as the Caribbeans directly involved in the incidents. In the case of American society, where ethnic and racial groups have social status but not official political status as a group, there is no elected representative of the "black point of view." Leaders of protests in most of these situations were in fact protesting against a local government with a black American mayor and a black American police commissioner.

The media can define the groups involved and can also elevate spokespersons into the functional equivalent of an elected leader of a group or community. This has a circular effect, since the way people come to understand the "truth" of a situation they did not witness is in part through the accounts and interpretations of leaders who speak for them. This reinforces the leadership of certain spokespeople for the group and affirms their membership in the group for the individuals who have their identities and interpretations spoken for in the press.

But even when the incidents are open-and-shut cases of white violence against black American victims, as in Bensonhurst, an analysis of the ways in which the participants understand the components of their own identity is crucial in gauging how interventions by the criminal justice system, public demonstrations, and media coverage will be interpreted.

Not all black Americans have as much at stake in an oppositional identity as the radical black American leaders I have described here. The middle-class blacks who have found opportunities within the economic and political system are indeed moving towards a social identity and place in society which is less influenced by their colour than those blacks still outside the economic mainstream (Wilson, 1978). Thus they will develop a social identity which is more similar to that of a voluntary minority or a symbolic ethnicity – an identity which may differ from that of other groups but will not differ in terms of experienced oppression. Thus, Mayor Dinkins and the moderate black political leadership do not share the distrust and systemic interpretations of the black underclass and their radical leaders. (At least they do not share these interpretations to the same degree.)

However, in the city's politics it is the radical leadership and their disaffected poor constituents who generally speak for the people affected by these bias incidents. These radical black leaders "cater to the cluster of left-out working class and poor blacks (some in the middle class too) best described as the disenchanted" (Kilson and Cottingham, 1991: 525). As West (1991: 225) argues, these national non-elected black leaders "highlight the traditional problems of racial discrimination, racial violence and slow racial progress." It is this group's interpretation of the causes and consequences of the racial violence that influences the rhetoric of race relations played out in the media around these bias incidents, not necessarily the rhetoric that would be adopted by middle-class or immigrant blacks.

Élite leaders and spokespeople for a group involved in racial or ethnic violence may have their own agenda in reacting to the experience of violence. The existence of a threatening outside enemy who has harmed a member of the group is a powerful force to unite the members of the group to each other and to a strong leadership, disregarding the many interests other than racial or ethnic ones, such as growing class divisions and growing divisions based on nativity, which might disunite them.

2   Defining and shaping boundaries of the group

These incidents point up the role that such public political events play in defining the boundaries of groups and the internal and external definitions of belonging to particular groups. The nature of belonging to groups partly involves the group's history *vis-à-vis* the state and other groups. This relationship is shaped during such pivotal moments as these incidents of racial violence. So, for instance, while average immigrants from Trinidad to New York might have thought of themselves primarily as Trinidadian or West Indian before the murder of Michael Griffith, they may come closer to identifying themselves as black Americans afterwards. It was obvious that Griffith was killed for the colour of his skin and not for his identity as an immigrant.

Griffith was defined in the press and in the criminal justice process as a black American. This outside definition might tend to reinforce the black-American identity of the average Trinidadian immigrant reading and listening to accounts of the murder in the media.

Finally, while this immigrant might understand the event as an incident of racial violence and hatred but not necessarily as systematic oppression, the interpretations offered by African-American leaders in the press and the behaviour of the police in the incident itself might serve to reinforce the perceived veracity of the definition of the situation by the African-American involuntary minority. Thus, Caribbeans in New York at the time could come away from this event with the perception that their earlier, more trusting approach to American institutions had been naïve. This could signal the assimilation of these voluntary black immigrants into the historical experiences and resulting psychological identities of the involuntary black-American minorities.

These case studies dramatically indicate the continued vast importance of race as a master status in the United States. Especially in these street encounters of racial violence in New York, the colour of a person's skin takes precedence over all other aspects of the person's identity or roles. These incidents demonstrate the involuntary character of race identity for minorities in this society and the enormous importance attached to race.

The aftermath of some of these incidents brings home to black immigrants in New York that, regardless of the differences and separation they see between themselves and black Americans, they are likely to be seen by the wider society only as "blacks." This serves to heighten political and social solidarity between black Americans and black immigrants and increase the degree of identity shift for these individual immigrants. These incidents lead to voluntary immigrants becoming socialized to think of themselves as involuntary minorities, with all the anger and sense of helplessness that entails.

3   The role of the state

Finally, these case studies elucidate principles and guidelines for the state in dealing with incidents of bias. The understanding of hate crimes differs depending on whether one sees them through the lens of race and the history of racial oppression in the United States, or through the lens of ethnic antagonism and intergroup rivalry. The state's position and directives *vis-à-vis* the participants should recognize these different interpretations. In the one view, the State (in its white, official form) is seen as part of the institutionalized racism and oppression of one group (blacks) in favour of another (whites). In another view, that of a pluralist society with a variety of groups, the state can be seen as neutrally adjudicating in the course of group conflicts, fights, and misunderstandings. In a third view, the primary players are seen to be individuals who happen to belong to groups, a circumstance that has little to do with the course of events. This perception is expressed in the argument by the whites accused in these cases.

These findings about the different reactions of different groups to these incidents imply different roles and responses for the state *vis-à-vis* the various groups. The apparatus and procedures in place in New York for dealing with bias incidents will only lead to a peaceful resolution if the responses of the criminal justice system, politicians and the police are appropriate to the understandings and reactions of the various groups and individuals involved.

The reactions of whites with a symbolic ethnic identity who are part of the dominant group in society will most likely fail to involve awareness of racial and ethnic factors perceived by members of the minority groups. In dealing with these white ethnics, the state must insist on the racial and ethnic nature of such crimes. For far too long in the United States certain whites have perpetrated violence on subordinate groups, counting on a blind eye from the state. To change that dynamic requires official recognition of the existence of racial and ethnic crimes, and the establishment of institutional mechanisms for distinguishing such crimes from individual crimes having nothing to do with group membership. The establishment of bias crime units and investigation teams such as those in New York is a step in this direction. It is important to understand that members of a dominant group tend not to recognize the ways in which one's membership in that group influences behaviour and attitudes.

In dealing with the identities and attitudes of voluntary migrants, the state has a different set of problems and objectives. One lesson drawn from the New York experience is that the state should not ratify existing categories for classifying ethnic and racial groups. If West Indians are treated and defined as part of the American black

group, without recognition of their different cultures and understandings they might bring to conflict situations, they will eventually
start to identify themselves as such. It is still an open question
whether voluntary immigrants from the Caribbean will assimilate to
being black Americans or to being a distinctive type of black ethnic.
If our analysis is correct, the type of social identity they ultimately
develop might influence their reactions to the various institutions in
society; whether they see themselves as an ethnic group in a fluid and
open society or whether they see themselves as a caste-like minority
in a permanently disadvantaged position.

The authorities need to listen carefully to the nuanced interpretations of the groups involved in bias incidents. Not least, care
must be taken to ascertain whether the leaders of particular protests
actually represent the constituency they claim to represent. If West
Indians are indeed less inclined than black Americans to experience
such attacks in the light of historical racial attacks and enmity, they
are more likely to see discrimination and racism as aberrations to be
dealt with and overcome. The failure of the media and official government agencies to recognize or publicly discuss such differences
between West Indians and American blacks could have long-term
implications.

In the specific case of West Indians and the bias incidents in New
York, the authorities need to recognize that, as voluntary immigrants,
West Indians generally have a greater degree of trust of the system
than they are given credit for. The government can build on the
trust already there, *not* by denying that discrimination has taken
place and *not* by reacting as if the West Indians have an oppositional
identity simply because they are black, but by emphasizing the neutrality and fairness of the institutions and people in place to deal with
the incidents.

The final case of involuntary minorities is the most difficult for state
officials. It is essential to understand the logic of their history and the
nature of their identities. Involuntary minorities with oppositional
identities require greater reassurance by the state, since they see
systematic oppression where dominant group members only see
accidents or individual rather than group events. These oppositional
identities tend to lead to the expression of grievances and hostility
outside of established procedures if only because of a lack of trust in
criminal justice institutions. Special care must be taken to demonstrate the state's neutrality and commitment to equal justice.

This is an especially difficult goal, since one way in which the state generally guarantees neutrality is to have minority representation. Such representation may work better for voluntary immigrants than for involuntary minorities such as black Americans. For them, the presence of members of their group in government may not be enough. An oppositional identity presupposes that members of the group who work within the power structure instead of outside it or against it are betraying their group. In accord with the analysis developed by John Ogbu in the field of education, and developed further here, an African-American official of the government or the police risks being accused of "acting white" simply because of his or her ties to a power structure which is perceived as being anti-black in its very nature. Black representatives in the government need to be prepared for the possibility that their very identity as a member of the black group will be challenged. To demonstrate how they can be both members of the black group and part of the power structure requires proof that the power structure is not opposed to the group identities. Considering the way in which past history has shaped the development of oppositional identities, this is bound to be a very difficult undertaking.

Notes

1. Asians are an exception to this dichotomy. Those who stress the castelike experience of Asians point to the severe restrictions on their immigration as examples of the ways in which their racial status gave them a very different experience.
2. Migrants from Caribbean countries are all coming from societies where racism exists. There is much literature describing the racial stratification in the Caribbean (Hoetink, 1967). But there is also growing evidence that immigrants to the United States from these countries tend to "forget" or consciously downplay the racism which existed in their home society. There is also a very big difference between the racism which exists in countries where blacks are the overwhelming majority and those, like the United States, in which they are the minority.
3. Tawana Brawley was a young woman in upstate New York who was found beaten and cut and who claimed that she was raped and attacked by a white policeman. Although the incident did not occur in New York City proper, it became a cause for some of New York's most outspoken black political leaders and aroused a great deal of concern and anger in New York's black community. It was later discovered that the entire claim was a hoax. Tawana was apparently a very troubled young woman who inflicted the wounds on herself and concocted the story. While the fact that the incident was a hoax appears to be accepted by the majority of law enforcement and moderate black leaders in the area, and while Tawana has confessed that it was a hoax, a very considerable minority of blacks in New York – some might argue a majority of inner-city poor blacks – still believe that Tawana was telling the truth and that there has been a cover-up. I do not deal with the Tawana Brawley case in this paper because it was a hoax and not a real incident, and because it did not occur inside New York City. At the same time, many of the statements made about the case by African-American leaders will fit the analysis I am making here.
4. In this case, yet another West Indian might just as easily have been a victim, because one of

259

the boys along with Yusef on the night he was killed and who was also attacked by the mob was a West Indian, Luther Sylvester.

References

Apollon, Katia M., and Mary C. Waters. 1990. "Haitian Americans and Black Americans: An Analysis of Race and Ethnic Identities." Paper presented at the Meetings of the Society for the Study of Social Problems, Washington, DC.

Blauner, Robert. 1972. *Racial Oppression in America*. New York: Harper and Row.

Bogen, Elizabeth. 1987. *Immigration in New York*. New York: Praeger.

Bonnett, Aubrey W. 1990. "West Indians in the United States of America: Some Theoretical and Practical Considerations." In A.W. Bonnett and G. Llewellyn Watson (eds), *Emerging Perspectives on the Black Diaspora*. Lanham, MD: University Press of America.

Breindel, Eric. 1987. "The Legal Circus." *The New Republic* 196: 20–3.

Bryce-Laporte, Roy. 1972. "Black immigrants: The Experience of Invisibility and Inequality." *Journal of Black Studies* 3: 29–56.

Buchanan, Susan H. 1979. "Language and Identity: Haitians in New York City." *International Migration Review* 13: 298–313.

———. 1983. "The Cultural Meaning of Social Class for Haitians in New York City." *Ethnic Groups* 5: 7–30.

Cheng, Lucie, and Yen Espiritu. 1989. "Korean Businesses in Black and Hispanic Neighborhoods: A Study of Intergroup Relations." *Sociological Perspectives* 32, no. 4: 521–34.

DeSantis, John. 1991. *For the Color of His Skin: The Murder of Yusef Hawkins and the Trial of Bensonhurst*. New York: Pharos Books.

Dominguez, Virginia R. 1975. *From Neighbor to Stranger: The Dilemma of Caribbean Peoples in the United States*. Occasional Papers no. 5. New Haven: Antilles Research Program, Yale University.

Evanier, David. 1991. "Invisible Man." *The New Republic* (14 October): 21–6.

Foner, Nancy. 1985. "Race and Color: Jamaican Migrants in London and New York City." *International Migration Review* 19: 708–27.

———. 1987. "The Jamaicans: Race and Ethnicity Among Migrants in New York City." in Nancy Foner (ed.), *New Immigrants in New York* (New York: Columbia University Press), pp. 131–58.

Gans, Herbert. 1979. "Symbolic Ethnicity: The Future of Ethnic Groups and Cultures in America." *Ethnic and Racial Studies* 2 (January): 1–20.

Glazer, Nathan. 1987. Introduction, in Takaki, 1987.

Goldman, Ari L. 1990. "Other Korean grocers give to those in Brooklyn boycott." *New York Times*, (14 May): B5.

Heisler, Martin O. 1990. "Ethnicity and Ethnic Relations in the Modern West." In Joseph V. Montville (ed.), *Conflict and Peacemaking in Multiethnic Societies* (New York: Basic Books), pp. 21–52.

Hoetink, H. 1967. *The Two Variants in Caribbean Race Relations*. London: Oxford University Press.

Hornung, Rick. 1990. "Fear and loathing in City Hall: How Dinkins Misplayed the Flatbush Boycott." *Village Voice* (29 May): 31–4.

Hynes, Charles J., and Bob Drury. 1990. *Incident at Howard Beach: The Case for Murder*. New York: G. P. Putnam's Sons.

Justus, Joyce B. 1976. "West Indians in L.A.: Community and Identity." R. S. Bryce-Laporte and D.M. Mortimer, *Caribbean Immigration to the United States*. RIIES Occasional Papers no. 1. Washington, DC: Smithsonian Institution, Research Institute on Immigration and Ethnic Studies.

Kasinitz, Philip. 1992. *Caribbean New York: Black Immigrants and the Politics of Race*. Ithaca, NY: Cornell University Press.

Kilson, Martin, and Clement Cottingham. 1991. "Thinking about race relations." *Dissent* (Fall): 520–30.

Klein, Joe. 1991. "Deadly Metaphors." *New York Magazine* (9 September): 27–9.

Lee, G. Fiyun. 1991. "Racism Comes in All Colors: The Anti-Korean Boycott in Flatbush." *Reconstruction* 1, no. 3: 72–6.

Lieberson, Stanley. 1961. "A societal theory of race and ethnic relations." *American Sociological Review* 26 (December): 92–110.

Lieberson, Stanley, and Mary C. Waters. 1988. *From Many Strands: Ethnic and Racial Groups in Contemporary America*. New York: Russell Sage Foundation.

Logan, Andy. 1991. "Around City Hall." *The New Yorker* (4 November): 106–12.

Navarro, Mirey A. 1990. "For a Store Owner, Boycott Raises Fears of Misunder-standings." *New York Times*, 17 May.

Neidert, Lisa, and Reynolds. Farley. 1985. "Assimilation in the United States: An Analysis of Ethnic and Generation Differences in Status and Achievement." *American Sociological Review* 50, no. 6 (December): 840–50.

Ogbu, John. 1978. *Minority Education and Caste: The American System in Cross-Cultural Perspective*. New York: Academic Press.

———. 1990. "Minority Status and Literacy in Comparative Perspective." *Daedalus* 119, no. 2 (Spring): 141–68.

Rieder, Jonathan. 1990. "Trouble in Store." *The New Republic* (2 July): 16–22.

———. 1991. "Gown of Thorns." *The New Republic* (14 October): 26–31.

Sims, Calvin. 1990. "Black Customers, Korean Grocers: Need and Mistrust." *New York Times* (17 May): B1, B4.

Sleeper, Jim. 1990. *The Closest of Strangers: Liberalism and the Politics of Race in New York*. New York: W.W. Norton.

Stafford, Susan B. 1987. "The Haitians: The Cultural Meaning of Race and Eth-nicity." In Nancy Foner (ed.), *New Immigrants in New York* (New York: Columbia University Press), pp. 131–58.

Stone, John. 1985. *Racial Conflict in Contemporary Society*. Cambridge, MA: Harvard University Press.

Sutton, Constance R. 1973. "Caribbean Migrants and Group Identity. Suggestions for Comparative Analysis." In *Migration: Report of the Research Conference on Migration and Ethnic Minority Status and Social Adaption* (Publication no. 5). Rome: United Nations Social Defense Research Institute, pp. 133–48.

Sutton, Constance R., and Susan R. Makiesky. 1975. "Migration and West Indian racial and ethnic consciousness", in H.I. Safa and B.M. Du Toit (eds), *Migration and Development: Implications for Ethnic Identity and Political Conflict* (Paris: Mouton & Cie.).

Takaki, Ronald (ed.). 1987. *From Many Shores: Perspectives on Race and Ethnicity in America*. New York: Oxford University Press.

Thernstrom, Abigail. 1987. *Whose Votes Count? Affirmative Action and Minority Voting Rights: A 20th Century Fund Study*. Cambridge, MA: Harvard University Press.

Wallace, Michael. 1971. "The Uses of Violence in American History." *American Scholar* 40, no. 1: 81–102.

Waters, Mary C. 1990. *Ethnic Options: Choosing Identities in America*. Berkeley: University of California Press.

———. 1991a. "The Role of Lineage in Identity Formation Among Black Americans." *Qualitative Sociology* 14, no. 1 (Spring): 57–76.

———. 1991b. "The intersection between race and ethnicity: generational changes among Caribbean immigrants to the United States." Paper presented at the American Sociological Association Annual Meeting, Cincinnati, Ohio, August.

Waters, Mary C., and Stanley Lieberson. 1992. "Ethnic Differences in Education: Current Patterns and Historical Roots." *International Perspectives on Education and Society* 2: 171–87.

Waters, Mary C., and David Mittelberg. 1992. "The Process of Ethnogenesis among Haitian and Israeli Immigrants to the United States." *Ethnic and Racial Studies* 15, no. 3 (July): 412–35.

West, Cornel. 1991. "Nihilism in Black America." *Dissent* (Spring): 221–6.

Wilson, William Julius. 1978. *The Declining Significance of Race: Blacks and Changing American Institutions*. Chicago: University of Chicago Press.

Woldemikael, T.M. 1989. *Becoming Black American: Haitians and American Institutions in Evanston, Illinois*. New York: AMS Press.

14

Ethnic conflicts and minority protection: Roles for the international community

Asbjørn Eide

The increased salience of ethnic conflict and violence poses new challenges for the international community. Traditional peace-keeping efforts are not necessarily applicable any more; new tools are needed, together with a fresh understanding of the nature of emerging conflicts. This chapter examines the need for common standards for defining and analysing ethnic and minority disputes, and examines roles and practices that may prove useful in defusing conflicts.

1 Why should the international community be concerned with ethnic conflicts?

Two different factors come into play. One is what I shall call the humanist impulsion towards a morally based civilization, the other is the concern with a stable international order.

The humanist impulsion: This is the primary drive behind the concern with protection of human rights worldwide. It is based on the premise that every human being is born and should remain equal in dignity and rights, irrespective of race, colour, ethnic or national origin, sex, and so forth. This motivation to identify with all fellow human beings has emerged as a gradual process over centuries, in revulsion against past wars of religion or nationalist adventures, against discrimination and hatred. The humanist impulsion also affects, to an increasing extent, governments in their external relations.

The humanist quest gathered momentum in this century in reaction to massive violations, such as those of the extreme nationalism engulfing Europe from 1930 to 1945; the Holocaust, the mass extermination of Gypsies, and other manifestations of intolerant ethnonationalism. The cosmopolitan, humanist drive for a global civilization has manifested itself in the adoption of the Universal Declaration of Human Rights, undoubtedly the most important document ever adopted by any international organization.

The importance of a stable international order: International security is increasingly understood not as nationalist, competitive security, but as an inclusive, cooperative security for a peaceful world. This, in turn, is required to trim the enormous military expenses caused by past confrontation. Other underlying concerns include the common interest in facilitating global economic interaction, including communication and tourism; the common concern with avoiding environmental deterioration; and other international matters, including the avoidance of terrorism. These, among other factors, generate a concern – partly altruistic in its humanist motivation, and partly self-interested – in having a prosperous international environment.

Is there an "international community"?

The concept of an international community presumes the existence of a broad range of common values and coordinated interests among states. A broad set of common values has indeed been formulated in the Charter of the United Nations. While the Cold War made it impossible to implement those values through concerted action, the prospects seem immensely better now. Nevertheless, it would be wrong to hide the fact that states have very ambiguous interests, both in relation to specific ethnic conflict and in regard to human rights issues in specific countries. States have special interests which may deviate considerably from their general interest in the preservation of a peaceful international order.

Special interests related to particular conflicts may be derived from hegemonic or geopolitical concerns of influence and dominance, or from ethnic identification with one of the parties to the local conflict. Countries having large numbers of their own kith and kin living in other countries (sometimes referred to as "national minorities") are tempted to respond to demands for support in cases where those minorities get into trouble. Examples abound in the recent past, including: the Turkish concern with the Turkish-speaking minority in Cyprus, which led to a military intervention; the Indian concern with the Tamils of Sri Lanka, which led to a traumatic peace-keeping effort; the Armenian concern with the majority population in the Azerbaijani enclave of Nagorno-Karabakh, which is verging on a war between Armenia and Azerbaijan; the Russian concern with the fate of the people in South Ossetia, which might lead to direct Russian intervention; and – possibly even more dangerous – the risks associated with the growing problems faced by Russian-speaking populations in Latvia and Estonia.

The combination of hegemonic interests, ethnic identification, and geopolitical concerns thus causes many states to have ambivalent attitudes in response to specific conflicts. Many other states want to avoid becoming involved, because of unforeseeable consequences. It is possible to observe, however, an increasing preference for handling such issues through inclusive international organizations. Nevertheless, these organizations are affected by the ambiguities of their member states. As repeatedly stated, most recently by the Secretary-General of the United Nations in his *An Agenda for Peace* (A/47/277, S/24111), "The United Nations is a gathering of sovereign states and what it can do depends on the common ground that they create between them."

He added, however, that while the adversarial decades of the Cold War made the original promise of the United Nations impossible to fulfil, the January 1992 summit represented an unprecedented recommitment, at the highest political level, to the purposes and principles of the United Nations Charter, and *An Agenda for Peace* constituted an effort to indicate the way in which the emerging post-Cold-War common ground could be used to advance more effective roles in peace-making by the international community through the United Nations. Let the present article be a contribution to the reflection on how this can be done in regard to ethnic conflicts involving minorities.

2 International roles in conflict prevention and resolution

Two basically different, but complementary, approaches will be examined here. One is based on evolving law, and has three main components: standard-setting; supervision of implementation; and settlement of disputes over the application of the standards. The other is based on diplomacy, and has three other main components: preventive diplomacy; peace-making; and peace-keeping. Between them there is an evolving relationship, and they are increasingly combined to achieve a joint fourth major task: peace-building. I shall first explore briefly the two approaches, and then examine the possibility of closer harmonization between them.

The legal approach to minority issues

The concern here is with international efforts to establish standards on how governments should deal with their inhabitants, and the implementation of such standards. This is intimately linked with the evolution of international organizations, through the League of Nations and later the United Nations, and through regional organizations.

For simplicity's sake, three major stages of relevance to minority and ethnic group rights will be examined here. The first concerns the arrangements connected with the peace settlements after the First World War. The League of Nations, while appearing to be a global organization, was mainly a European–Latin American organization with Japan as one of the few Asian members. The end of World War I was, in many ways, the victory of nationalism over empires in and around Europe, but most colonial empires remained intact.

For Europe, nationalism was seen as a progressive step, strongly endorsed by Woodrow Wilson, the president of the United States who played a major role in the Versailles negotiations. It was made a significant guideline for the organization of the new international order. The nationalist ideology, requiring states to be congruent with nations in the ethnic sense, had a strong appeal. It was, of course, impossible to implement it fully. Whichever way state borders were drawn, groups of different nationalities were bound to be found inside many of the new or the restructured states. Therefore, provisions for protection of national minorities became the major preoccupation.

It is often believed that the Versailles settlements constituted a

266

major advance for minority protection.[1] This is hardly tenable. Minorities became much more exposed than before, owing to the endorsement of the nationalist ideology as a cornerstone in the international legal order. The system of minority protection was established mainly in order to sweeten the pill. Unfortunately, the nationalist pill turned out to be deadly dangerous. It facilitated the emergence of numerous authoritarian regimes across Europe and ended with the devastation of World War II, initiated by the high priest of nationalism, Adolf Hitler.

The second stage set in at the end of World War II. The lessons of malignant nationalism had been learned; the new international order was to be based on pluralism and tolerance. The foundation was the International Bill of Human Rights, whose basic principle was the equality of every human being irrespective of national or ethnic origin – and also irrespective of race, religion, and sex. States were expected to create equality for everyone before the law and to give everyone equal protection by law.[2]

Another core element in the new international order was the principle of territorial integrity. The existence of different nationalities within a state should not be a reason for dividing it up, provided pluralism and equal respect were provided for members of all groups. While the right to self-determination was recognized, it was understood as self-determination of peoples, not of nations, and was essentially related to the dismantling of colonialism and the prevention of occupation. The essential point is that the right to self-determination should belong to the collectivity of persons living within the territory concerned – the colony, or the occupied territory. Self-determination was no longer intended to have an ethnic basis. The group living in an inherited territory should have the right to govern itself.

In this new world, the problem of minorities was not expected to be of great significance. If states behaved according to the principle of pluralism, the different groups would have no particular difficulty. The freedom of religion (UDHR art. 18, ICCPR art. 18), to which every individual was entitled, would make it possible for members of religious groups to assert their religious identity; freedom of expression and information (UDHR art. 19, CCPR art. 19) made it possible for groups to use their own language as a basis for expression and communication; freedom of association (UDHR art. 20, ICCPR art. 22) would make it possible to organize cultural and political associations along ethnic lines if they so wished.

Nationalism was not dead, however, neither in the collective mind of the majority nor among the ethnic minorities. Many of the former sought to use the state as a vehicle for their particular nationalist self-assertion, for instance by elevating their language to be the only official language; the latter, in resistance, increasingly sought to have a reserved domain for themselves, to opt out altogether, or to have borders redrawn in order to join other states where their own ethnic group dominated.

From the very beginning of the post-war period, some half-hearted efforts were made to develop mechanisms for the protection of minorities.[3] There was little enthusiasm, however, and not much happened apart from the reassertion of the freedom of all individuals to preserve their religious, cultural, and linguistic identity, alone or in co-operation with others (ICCPR article 27).[4]

Nationalist and ethnic tensions increased in the 1970s and 1980s. By 1989/90 it was becoming clear that nationalism was reasserting itself with a vengeance, and the minority problem had to be addressed more seriously. Some progress has been made in recent years, in that a Working Group under the Human Rights Commission has been able, after 14 years of debate, to adopt a Draft Declaration on the Rights of Minorities. Efforts have also been made within the Council of Europe. A Draft European Language Charter and a Draft European Minority Convention have been prepared but the prospects for their adoption remain uncertain.

Standard-setting is also proceeding in relation to the rights of indigenous peoples.[5] These are, in most cases, small and very vulnerable groups who inhabited regions subsequently settled or occupied by more assertive and modernizing groups. The indigenous peoples have generally been marginalized, pushed into the hinterlands. Many of them, however, have shown great resilience, and have been able to develop their own culture further, influenced, but not absorbed, by the more technology-intensive culture around them. In recent years, their representatives have become active at the international level, developing their own international network of organizations and participating with great energy in a working group within the United Nations on the drafting of rights of indigenous peoples.

The Conference on Security and Co-operation in Europe has also, to an increasing extent, sought to elaborate standards relating to minorities. Within the CSCE, however, this does not take the form of precise legal standards but rather as broad political principles. The Helsinki Final Act of the CSCE refers both to the rights of minorities and to territorial integrity. The relation between these two has become a major issue in recent years. The dominant position, however, is that minority rights have to be solved in preservation of the territorial integrity of the inherited state.[6]

The significance of standard-setting for the resolution of conflicts

Collective standard-setting is, basically, a dialogue (or multi-party discussion) in search of common solutions to common problems. It can work in so far as the problems are fairly common and if underlying values are broadly shared. Its primary function is preventive.

Through the application of standards adopted at the international level, governments can defend their policies against militants both inside majority groups and among minorities. The existence of standards reduces the range of legitimate options, consequently reducing the degree of uncertainty about outcomes. This can be reinforced by the desire to try to be seen from the outside as conforming to civilized standards.

Secondly, the adoption of international standards for the treatment by governments of their own subjects, including minorities, affects the policies of external actors. They have, through reference to the internationally adopted standards, a framework by which to assess the performance of states and governments in their internal affairs, and can take this into account in the formation of their bilateral relationship with that state, in development policies and other matters.

In some circumstances, the process of standard-setting can in itself contribute to conflict resolution. The most interesting case is that of the UN Working Group On Indigenous Peoples' Rights. Via this group, indigenous peoples' representatives have joined in a dialogue with governments from countries in which indigenous peoples live to discuss the best ways of handling situations involving minorities. Their debate about standards to be applied to indigenous peoples has already led to significant legal changes in several countries.

However, the dialogue becomes effective standard-setting only when there is a basis of real, not only token, agreement. In the real world there is often considerable ambiguity: governments might wish to be able to apply generally accepted standards but may find themselves in situations where this would be politically impossible or too costly for them. The standards could remain empty rhetoric unless international mechanisms existed to promote or ensure their application, also in times of stress.

Duty to cooperate and duty to prevent

All states belonging to the United Nations have, in accordance with article 56 of the Charter, undertaken an obligation to cooperate with the organization in promoting universal respect for and observance of human rights and fundamental freedoms for all without distinction as to race, sex, language, or religion (UN Charter, art. 55c). This obligation to cooperate in the prevention of human rights violation extends to all standards adopted by the United Nations in the field of human rights.[7]

International supervision of national implementation

Human rights bodies of the United Nations have developed several procedures for cooperative efforts to ensure respect for human rights.[8] One is supervision of the national implementation of adopted standards. Under the International Covenant on Civil and Political Rights (art. 2), all states party to the Covenant undertake to respect and ensure the provision to all individuals within their respective territories of all the rights contained in the Covenant, without distinction of any kind. Under article 40 of the same Covenant, the states are obliged to submit reports on the steps they have taken to implement those obligations, and those reports are to be examined by an elected international committee which carries out a dialogue with representatives of the state concerned on the degree to which the latter has complied with its obligations.

This formalized dialogue between governments and United Nations expert bodies is applied also to a wide range of other conventions. These reports are then examined by an expert body of the United Nations, which, in regard to each report, convenes representatives of the government concerned for a discussion of the progress made and the obstacles encountered. Admittedly, the dialogue is not always very satisfactory. Nevertheless, it is evolving and plays an increasingly important role.

Complaint procedures for, or on behalf of, individuals

A second, essentially preventive function is the availability of individual complaint procedures. Individuals who claim that they have been subjected to discrimination or other violations of human rights have the possibility, under strictly regulated rules, to address the committees of the international human rights bodies, in order to obtain a finding whether or not the alleged violation has taken place. This procedure is open only in regard to states which have accepted such procedures, and many states still fall outside this arrangement.

Such procedures are functioning reasonably well in regard to governments which are committed to the implementation of human rights and which do not face severe internal opposition to it. In many societies of the world, however, relations are not so harmonious. Religious conflicts, fundamentalism, ethno-nationalism, and profound social cleavages generate situations where governments are not willing or able to ensure compliance of human rights. The United Nations human rights bodies have tried to address these kinds of situations too, by developing mechanisms for responding to gross and systematic violations. A description of these procedures is found in *United Nations Action in the Field of Human Rights* (United Nations Centre for Human Rights, 1988: chap. XIV C).

The precarious assumption: Is only the government side at fault?

The predominant attitude held by human rights activists has been that it is the government which is at fault. The government is of course obliged to abstain from violations and has a duty to prevent them. Nevertheless, when violations occur, the government is held to be at fault.

The precariousness of this argument becomes obvious in cases of serious group conflicts. The duty to prevent violations also includes an obligation to protect from group violence – but what can the government do when the group violence is out of control?

One side of the coin is that the human rights normative system allows for suspension of some human rights under a state of emergency. What about the other side – restraining the violent opposing group? It may be alleged that this is the responsibility of the government, and that the government should take all means compatible with human rights to control such groups.

There should be no international encouragement of groups which engage in violence, and yet it occurs – as verbal endorsement of their self-determination claims, or even as direct intervention. Governments should not be excused for carrying out violations beyond what is permissible under a state of emergency, but more efforts should be made to find ways to restrain the opposing group. There are groups, such as the Khmer Rouge or Sendero Luminoso, which have no moral standing at all. But there are also armed secessionist groups which evoke strong sympathy in some circles, for instance the Sikhs, the Tamil Tigers, the Armenian community in the Azerbaijani enclave of Nagorno-Karabakh, or the South Ossetians in Georgia. Their drive for self-determination and external endorsement of it constitute major problems for international peace in our time.

Applicability to group conflict resolution?

Is the legal approach, based on human rights and minority standards, functional in regard to serious group conflicts? A major problem is that the parties in such conflicts have two basically different approaches to such situations. Governments consider it their absolute duty to maintain law, order, and territorial integrity whilst secessionist groups are convinced of their moral and legal right to self-determination.

Once the conflict has coalesced, the groups have formed, and polarization has occurred, one is no longer dealing with individuals or associations but with hardened and militant groups, either in confrontation with each other and/or the government. Outside governments may also be drawn in, providing support to the minorities, to the extent of being accused of illegal intervention.

Inter-state dispute settlement

Human rights issues are mostly dealt with in intergovernmental organizations through procedures very different from the traditional inter-state dispute mechanisms which are typical for normal international law issues. While international law has been traditionally understood as law regulating the relationship between states, human rights regulate the relationship between authorities and their subjects. Most outside states prefer multilateral channels or institutions to deal with such issues.

The International Court of Justice, established for the handling of disputes between states, has not been used much for these purposes. For instance, it is revealing that no state was prepared even to make use of the right under the Genocide Convention to bring Democratic Kampuchea to court for the massive human rights violations perpetrated by the Pol Pot regime (Kooijmans, 1991). Nevertheless, as also pointed out by Kooijmans (1991), inter-state dispute settlements are provided for in a number of instruments (CCPR, ICERD, the European Convention for the Protection of Human Rights and Fundamental Freedoms, etc.) and this option has been applied, particularly under the European Convention, in a number of cases. In issues involving minorities, however, the Court has not been much used either by the United Nations or by the Council of Europe or the CSCE.[9]

The procedures under the so-called "human dimension" of the CSCE contain considerable prospects for further development. These emerged out of the Vienna follow-up meeting, which started on 4 November, 1986 and ended on 15 January 1989, thus spanning the crucial years of the introduction of *glasnost* and the end of the Cold War. They have since been further developed through several subsequent meetings and consist of four stages:

(i)   exchange: states are obliged to respond to requests for exchange of information on issues under the human dimension of the CSCE;

(ii) bilateral consultations, to be held at the request of one state to clarify the information and the facts;

(iii) notification: other members can be notified, by any CSCE member, on questions emerging from these contacts which the notifying state finds important;

(iv) discussions at the annual meeting on the human dimension, which can be initiated by any state.

Procedures for fact-finding have since been further developed under the CSCE. They are intended partly to help in confidence-building and partly to help assess whether new members conform to CSCE principles. Such fact-finding can be of help at early stages in the conflict. Later, when the conflicts have hardened, it seems that much more comprehensive processes are required, involving a wide range of activities.

At the United Nations, the debate about new approaches is now being pursued with great vigour. A survey of possible and desirable activities has been outlined in the recent report by the United Nations Secretary-General, *An Agenda for Peace*, which was presented to the Security Council on 17 June 1992.

Preventive diplomacy
Preventive diplomacy is defined, in the Secretary-General's report, as "action to prevent disputes from arising between parties, to prevent

existing disputes from escalating into conflicts and to limit the spread of the latter when they occur." Such diplomacy is primarily addressed to inter-state disputes. The United Nations does not see it as its task to prevent disputes from arising between different parties inside a country – indeed, the main political activity inside a state is to bring up disputes. It is crucial, however, to ensure that the disputes do not escalate into violent conflicts. This is essentially what human rights, including the political rights underlying the required democratic governance, are about.

If international human rights bodies were sufficiently effective, they would guide the local parties to manage their disputes, in compliance with accepted human rights standards, through democratic channels. When this does not succeed, however, and conflicts do escalate into violence, other states can be affected in a multitude of ways – refugee flows, danger of intervention by the "mother country," crossborder terrorism, and disruption of trade, communications, and development activities. Preventive diplomacy is indeed required to limit the spread of such conflicts should they occur. Consequently, there should be a closer link between the activities of the human rights bodies and those of the political organs of the United Nations, including the Secretary-General.

Peace-making
This term is defined by the Secretary-General as "action to bring hostile parties to agreement, essentially through such peaceful means as those foreseen in chapter VI of the United Nations Charter. Chapter VI refers to negotiation, enquiry, mediation, conciliation, arbitration, judicial settlement, resort to regional agencies or arrangements, or other peaceful means as chosen by the parties themselves. The Charter had disputes between states in mind. Disputes arising between groups inside a state have been subject to international concern only in so far as they bring up human rights problems.

Unfortunately, only some aspects of the problems can be addressed by the international human rights bodies. They can ascertain whether the government, in its response to the conflict, has respected human rights norms. International human rights bodies have not, so far, seriously investigated the underlying causes in order to help the parties solve their conflict. There are, however, certain developments in that direction, such as advisory services, including the special rapporteurs and their recommendations.

At the political level of the United Nations, it has increasingly been recognized that hostile disputes inside countries can have serious international implications; consequently, there has been a growing tendency to deal with such disputes. Recent examples include the actions in El Salvador and Cambodia.

Peace-keeping
This is defined by the Secretary-General as the deployment of a United Nations presence in the field, hitherto with the consent of all the parties concerned, and normally involving United Nations military and/or police personnel and frequently civilians as well. The "consent" to which he refers is the consent of the states involved in a dispute. In several cases, however, disputes have arisen which are primarily domestic but have great international implications (the Congo, Cyprus, Lebanon), in which case consent strictly speaking is necessary only from the government. However, for a number of reasons, peace-keeping forces have not been intended for substantial military action; consequently, de facto consent is required also from organized groups which otherwise might start armed action against the United Nations peace-keeping forces.

In ethnic conflicts, as seen often in the recent past, local groups may not be willing to stop allied action when United Nations peace-keeping forces are deployed. This is why the Secretary-General now proposes the possibility of making use of **peace enforcement** units. This is a new and important, but difficult, departure. It is not a question of deploying large-scale UN forces to resist aggression by states, but to enforce agreements which are intended as steps in the solution of conflicts.

Peace enforcement appears particularly applicable in cases of cease-fires which are agreed to but very quickly violated, often by militants who want to upset the peace process and who succeed because of the response by the other side to the provocation. If the United Nations has the necessary presence to enforce the agreement, such provocations could be prevented, and, should they happen, the United Nations could take the necessary steps against the provocateur, thus avoiding the escalation which otherwise almost always results from provocation. As the Secretary-General points out, however, the task of peace enforcement can on occasion exceed the mission of peace-keeping forces and the expectations of peace-keeping force contributors. Peace enforcement units may have to be more heavily armed than normal peace-keeping forces, and prepared and trained for armed action. In ethnic conflicts such a presence may be essential, but it can still operate only where the parties are prepared to take steps towards peace and can agree on some interim measures towards that end.

In the case of Bosnia and Herzegovina, there has been a large degree of consensus in the United Nations on who is to blame and on the basic standards that should be implemented. The Serbs have had practically no external supporters and yet they have managed, by the relentless use of arms, to prevent the United Nations from making peace in the region to date. What has become very clear is that the UN has to play a more forceful role – still not interventionist, but operating at the consent of the host government and able to use force against recalcitrant groups.

Peace-building
The Secretary-General depicts the concept of peace-building as comprehensive post-conflict measures to identify and support structures which will tend to consolidate peace and advance a sense of confidence and well-being amongst people. Among the measures mentioned he refers to advisory and training support for security personnel, monitoring elections, advancing efforts to protect human rights, reforming and strengthening governmental institutions, and promoting formal and informal processes of political participation. The major thrust is towards good governance, which in turn is intimately dependent on a proper safeguard for human rights for all, including the different ethnic and religious groups.

However, peace-building can also be carried out preventively. When the international community consistently seeks to encourage the development and strengthening of the institutions for good governance, including such arrangements for pluralism as will satisfy reasonable demands by minorities, conflicts might not erupt in the first place. Consequently, there is common ground between human rights endeavours and those of peace settlement.

3 Reconciling the humanist impulsion and the quest for a stable international order: Requirements by the international community on how to manage minority conflicts

The humanist approach emphasizes freedom and equality, whereas the need for a stable international order emphasizes respect for authority and continuity. Sometimes these two considerations may appear to be in conflict; it is desirable to find ways to harmonize them.

Conflict resolution is not a single act but a complex process con-sisting of many steps. The international community is increasingly clarifying its requirements both as to the behaviour of the parties during conflicts and as to the final outcomes. An effort is now under way within the United Nations Sub-Commission on Prevention of Discrimination and Protection of Minorities to formulate guidelines for peaceful and constructive ways to handle situations involving minorities, regulating both processes and outcomes (Eide, 1990, 1991b). These are briefly outlined below.

(i) Paramount importance must be given in our time to equality, non-discrimination, and full participation of all individuals and groups. The current basis is the International Bill of Human Rights, founded on article 1 of the Universal Declaration:

All human beings are born free and equal in dignity and rights. They are endowed with reason and conscience and should act towards one another in a spirit of brotherhood.[10]

Equality in the enjoyment of human rights requires abstention from and prevention of discrimination; equality in dignity requires respect for the self-identification of the individual with her or his group, within a broader society of reciprocal tolerance between members of the different groups.

The intensity of religious, national, or ethnic conflicts can often be traced to a lack of respect for ordinary individual human rights on an impartial basis. Such conflicts could often have been prevented had there been full impartiality in the administration of justice, with special emphasis on equal and effective protection of all ethnic groups by law enforcement officials and security forces. The right to freedom of association, if applied without discrimination on ethnic grounds, would make possible the peaceful and open expression of policy preferences by such groups. Freedom of expression and information on an equal basis for all ethnic groups would make it possible for them all to express themselves and seek information in the language they prefer, including their mother tongue, orally and in writing. Freedom to participate in cultural life of the community, in accordance with UDHR article 26, means that individuals can preserve and develop the culture of the community constituted by each minority group.

Full and equal participation is provided for in several respects in the human rights system; see, for instance, article 21 of the Universal

Declaration, article 25 of the Convention on Civil and Political Rights, and article 1 of the Declaration on the Right to Development. Issues of a complex nature arise where constitutional and administrative arrangements, which depend on the nature of the different situations, are involved. When the political will is there, a wide range of options exists; some of these are examined in section (iii) below.

(ii) The rights and development of minorities must be promoted in a manner that is consistent with the unity and stability of states, in the light of the Declaration on Principles of International Law Concerning Friendly Relations and Co-operation among States (UN General Assembly Resolution 2625/25). This declaration spells out in greater detail the principles of the United Nations Charter. In the post-Cold-War period it may be possible to implement them more consistently than before.

Every government considers it a paramount task to maintain the political independence and territorial integrity of its state, and all other states are expected to respect its sovereignty and integrity. One qualification exists, however, namely, the right of peoples to self-determination. A major problem arises, in dealing with minority conflicts, when the ethnic group concerned lives compactly together in a region of the state, and claims that it is a "people" and therefore entitled, in accordance with the United Nations Charter, to self-determination. The most serious human rights problems occur during ethnic conflicts where the political status of the territory is made uncertain through such claims. When neighbouring states and/or the international community react in ambiguous ways to such claims or even endorse them, the future status of that territory is thrown into uncertainty. Efforts to find peaceful solutions are then blocked, and armed conflict is often very difficult to avoid, sometimes attracting external intervention. Outside states and the international community should insist on the application of general principles of international law, thereby limiting the options as to what is lawful and thus reducing the uncertainty with all its accompanying violence.

While the right of peoples to self-determination is generally recognized, the scope of its application is, unfortunately, still highly controversial. Some comments are required.

The claim, in a specific case, that a group has a right to self-determination implies that the group concerned is entitled to determine freely its political status and to pursue that collectivity's economic, social, and cultural development. Furthermore, every state has the duty to respect this right in accordance with the provisions of the Charter. The crucial problem arising in such cases is to decide who can be the beneficiaries, or subjects, of the right to self-determination: Who is the "self"? Who is a "people" as regards this right?

Sometimes the application of the principle is clear in theory, but difficult in practice. The people living in a colonial territory are entitled to self-determination. This means the people living in a territory beyond Europe, administered as a colony or under similar control by European states, or by states subsequently populated by people of European stock. Normally it means the people as a whole, including the different ethnic groups which together form the population within the inherited colonial boundaries. Separate ethnic groups cannot each on their own demand a right to self-determination.

A second case is that of alien occupation. The people living in a territory that has been subjected since the adoption of the United Nations Charter in 1945 to alien occupation or annexation not endorsed by a free and fair popular referendum, are entitled to self-determination. Also, the people as a whole hold the right, not the separate ethnic groups on their own.

Incorporations resulting from occupations, apart from the colonial ones, which have taken place prior to 1945, do not normally give rise to a right of self-determination. Many territories, in Europe and elsewhere, have at some stage in history been incorporated through occupation and military conquest into the state in which they now find themselves. To rearrange all such historical outcomes now would cause havoc to the international order. Few of the existing sovereign states have obtained their present borders through free and friendly developments. Nevertheless, over successive generations, the ethnic groups now constituting the state have developed networks and ties, both on the personal level (intermarriages and associations of many kinds) and on the material level (infrastructures of transport and communication, etc.). It would be highly destabilizing at the present stage to accept claims by peoples of territories which at some time in history were incorporated through occupation that they now have a right to self-determination.

The third case is that of federations formed by voluntary accession by member republics, and where it has been explicitly stated in their respective constitutions that they have a right to withdraw from such federations. In such cases, the federation itself is a voluntary arrangement, lasting as long as the parties to the federation find it appropriate, and therefore the withdrawal is justified as a utilization of a right existing from the very time of the combination into a federation. The most prominent examples are the dissolutions of the USSR and the Yugoslav federation. The right of self-determination, based on the principle of voluntary accession, is in such situations applicable only to the union republics, not to the smaller entities which may have various kinds of autonomies under the pre-existing order.

Beyond these cases, the question of unilateral right to self-determination is in doubt, overridden by the basic principle of territorial integrity. There is one important proviso, however: that the state conducts itself in compliance with the principle of equal rights and self-determination of peoples and is possessed of a government representing the whole people of the territory without distinction as to race, creed, or colour. It must be kept in mind that the most basic principle of self-determination is that of the right of popular participation in the government of the state as an entity. When the government does not allow all segments and all peoples living in the state to participate, the claim of self-determination by the excluded group becomes stronger.

National or ethnic groups, living compactly together on a territory inside a sovereign state, will therefore bear the onus of proving, in all cases other than those mentioned above, that they have a right under international law to secede; the presumption will be against such a right. If the right cannot be convincingly proved, through some kind of recognition by the international community, outside states cannot be entitled to encourage or support such efforts at self-determination.

The difficulty is that the international community has not established appropriate institutions and procedures to settle competing and controversial claims of self-determination versus territorial integrity. Intergovernmental institutions tend to shy away or to be evasive when confronted with such issues, finding them too politically volatile. State practice, however, generally conforms to the criteria outlined above.

International law prohibits external help to secessionists. The Declaration on Friendly Relations makes it clear that the right of peoples to self-determination cannot authorize, and shall not be used to encourage, "any action which would dismember or impair, totally or in part, the territorial integrity or political unity of sovereign and independent states possessed of a government representing the whole people belonging to that territory without distinction as to race, creed and colour." According to the same declaration, every state is obliged to refrain from any action aimed at the partial or total disruption of the national unity and territorial integrity of any other state or country.

All states have the duty to refrain from organizing or encouraging the organization of irregular forces or armed bands for the purpose of incursion into the territory of another state. This also goes for the so-called "mother country." Every state, furthermore, has the duty to refrain from organizing, instigating, assisting or participating in acts of civil strife or terrorist acts in another state (paras 1 and 2, principle of non-intervention, Declaration on Friendly Relations). Except for the cases mentioned above, all kinds of support to armed struggle for secession constitute violations of international law.

The right to self-determination, understood as a unilateral right, is not generally available to groups even when they live compactly together on a territorially defined area within a larger state. This does not exclude the possibility of peaceful, bilateral arrangements negotiated between the different groups living inside a state, aiming to transform the political structure without the use of violence. Populations living in different territorial parts of a state are, of course, free to decide peacefully on an amicable divorce, as long as this is not brought about by violence or external pressure.

(iii) Minority rights and development should be promoted in ways which do not endanger regional peace and security. Regional security is negatively affected by ethnic and religious conflicts, which often lead to serious dislocations and internal displacement of populations, international refugee flows, and strong temptations for or pressure on outside states to intervene, justified as humanitarian intervention. Conflicts are often started by minor episodes. In the beginning there may be nothing more than some feeling of unease about alleged discrimination. Such allegations are gradually combined with protests and political demonstrations. Rumours emerge and are easily believed. If at that stage security forces overreact, their response constitute a self-fulfilling prophecy which is then exploited by the self-appointed militants among the minority; they may respond in kind to the action of the security forces and this, in turn, may lead to new and more violent responses by the latter.

It should not be excluded from consideration that the violence is deliberately provoked by militants on both sides, for the purpose of agitating public opinion and creating firm and confrontational alignments, leading eventually to massacres and reprisals by both sides.

Eventually this can degenerate into a guerrilla/counter-guerrilla process, bringing about full polarization, where extralegal executions, even liquidation, become part of the process, with internal repression on both the majority and the minority side.

This can ultimately develop into a cataclysm of infantile regression. For the self-appointed leaders of the minority the stakes have by this time become so high that they are no longer prepared to seek an accommodation with the government, which they might have warmly welcomed at an earlier stage in the evolution of the conflict; nor does public opinion permit the government to take conciliatory measures towards the minority. For the leaders of the minority, international support, either from the "mother country" or by other states, becomes crucial. Since the principle of non-intervention initially holds states back from providing such support, the strategy by minority leaders may be to provoke such strong repression from the majority side that potential outside helpers can justify their action as humanitarian intervention.

Had the parties applied humanitarian standards strictly in their encounters, when armed force is also used, escalation to such levels might not have happened. But while an international presence to constrain the parties might be helpful, recent experiences show that even this may not be enough, because of the irrational conflict dynamics.

The best way to prevent external intervention is to find constructive, domestic solutions based on consistent confidence-building efforts. It is also desirable to develop international mechanisms that make it possible for the parties to address the international community for purposes of conflict resolution.

(iv) For minorities to preserve their dignity as members of a particular community based on religion, language, or culture, they may need protection against other groups who might seek to block them from doing so. They may also need preservation and protection of the material basis of their culture and lifestyles, or material support sufficient to preserve that culture and lifestyle. This will undoubtedly require special measures. These can span a wide range of possibilities.

(v) Development processes can reduce or intensify national and ethnic conflicts. Development and modernization increase national and ethnic identification and inter-ethnic cleavages when economic disparities result, creating prosperity for some groups and relative or absolute deprivation for others. In addition, groups attach different values to different kinds of development. Some emphasize environmentally safe and sustainable developments which preserve traditional lifestyles and the established cultural basis of dignity, while others favour quick technological transformation even when environmental degradation results and lifestyles are disrupted.

Minorities have just cause for reacting when they live compactly together in a peripheral part of the country and are subjected, without having been properly consulted or having given their free and informed consent, to economic processes which profoundly affect their livelihood, and which result from policies and decisions adopted by central authorities influenced by the dominant majority. The problems become particularly severe when natural resources are exploited in such a way that the possibility of survival on the basis of the traditional way of life is destroyed.

On the other hand, ethnic relations can be improved when development projects are directed towards improving the conditions of minorities living in areas which have been lagging behind in economic development, provided they are properly involved in decision-making related to those projects.

(vi) Measures adopted to protect minorities must also respect human rights of majorities and of all individuals in the country. Two points need to be addressed here:
(*a*) While minorities shall be allowed to preserve their identity and traditions, this cannot be used to enforce rules and regulations violating internationally recognized human rights.
(*b*) The preservation of identity, including self-government, cannot be used to deprive members of other groups of their human rights. A group constituting a numerical minority at the national level is often the majority within a specific region; should that minority be allowed to form and exercise local authority in that region, its rules and regulations must fully respect the internationally recognized human rights of members of other groups living there.

4 Conclusions

Problems of ethnic conflicts and minority issues are central to the international agenda in our time. There is an increasing need for a combination of the insights gained by international standard-setting and implementation, on the one hand, and conflict resolution practices, on the other.

Conflicts cannot be solved ad hoc, without the application of basic standards; all actors have to adapt to a common framework demanded by the international community. This, however, can be done only at the early stages, when the parties are behaving rationally. When conflicts have gone beyond the rational stage and become cataclysmic, there is a need for a much more complex, patient, step-by-step process to make them return to rationality and adaptation to norms of civilization. Peace enforcement will often be required but is tremendously difficult; the tactics and strategy of peace enforcement as a prelude to peace-building have yet to be learned.

Notes

1. This article was completed in 1993 and has not been updated. The literature on ethnic conflict and minority protection has grown exponentially during the last few years. Updated bibliographies are found, e.g., in Alan Phillips and Allan Rosas, *Universal Minority Rights* (pp. 363–79), published by Åbo Akademi University Institute of Human Rights (Åbo, Finland) in cooperation with Minority Rights Group, London, 1995. A comprehensive bibliography is contained also in Asbjørn Eide, *Peaceful and Constructive Resolution of Situations Involving Minorities*, United Nations University Monograph Series on Governance and Conflict Resolution (forthcoming).

   On abbreviations: UDHR stands for the Universal Declaration of Human Rights, adopted by the United Nations General Assembly in 1948. ICERD stands for the International Convention on the Elimination of All Forms of Racial Discrimination, adopted by the General Assembly in 1965. ICCPR stands for the International Covenant on Civil and Political Rights, adopted by the General Assembly in 1966.

   References to the literature on the minority protection under the League of Nations can be found in Thornberry, 1991. Capotorti (1979) provides a useful analysis of the content of those arrangements.

2. The basis of the International Bill is the Universal Declaration. For a detailed examination of the articles of the Universal Declaration and its follow-up in subsequent standard-setting, see Eide et al., 1992.

3. For a recent and comprehensive review, see Bokatola, 1991.

4. Capotorti (1979) remains the most comprehensive analysis of the implications of article 27. For an examination of the interpretation of the article by the Human Rights Committee, see Tomuschat, 1983.

5. For a review of efforts to draft minority rights, see Alfredsson, 1982 and 1991; Barsh, 1986; Hannum, 1988.

6. See further below, and Ermacora, 1991.

7. See further Boven, 1992.

8. A useful survey of these procedures is found in United Nations Center for Human Rights, 1991.

9. See CSCE Supplementary Document to Paris Charter; CSCE Valetta Mechanism; CSCE

Moscow report (in list of instruments). The Conference on Security and Co-operation in Europe (CSCE) was in November 1994 renamed the Organization for Security and Co-operation in Europe (OSCE).
10. ICERD is a major tool in ensuring non-discrimination on racial or ethnic grounds.

References

Alfredsson, G. 1982. "International Law, International Organisations and Indigenous Peoples." *Journal of International Affairs* 36, no. 113.

———. 1991a. "Equality and Non-Discrimination: Minority Rights." Report to the Council of Europe in connection with the Seventh International Colloquy on the European Convention on Human Rights. Document H/Coll (90) 6. Strasbourg: Council of Europe.

———. 1991b. "Discussion Paper on Human Rights, Fundamental Freedoms and the Rights of Minorities." Submitted to the Third Strasbourg Conference on Parliamentary Democracy, SXB.COF (III) 8. Strasbourg.

Andrysek, Oldrich. 1989. *Report on the Definition of Minorities*. SIM Special no. 8. Utrecht: Netherlands Institute of Human Rights.

Barsh, R.L. 1986. "Indigenous Peoples: An Emerging Object of International Law." *AJIL* 80: 369.

Bokatola, Isse Omanga. 1992. *L'Organisation des Nations Unies et la Protection des Minorités*. Brussels: Bruylant.

Boven, Theodore C. van. 1992. "The Security Council: The New Frontier." *Review of the International Commission of Jurists* 48 (June): 12.

Capotorti, Francesco. 1979. *Study on the Rights of Persons belonging to Ethnic, Religious and Linguistic Minorities*. UN Doc. E/CN.4/Sub.2/384/Rev.1.

Eide, Asbjørn. 1990. *Possible Ways and Means of Facilitating the Peaceful and Constructive Solutions of Problems Involving Minorities*. Preliminary report to the United Nations Sub-Commission on Prevention of Discrimination and Protection of Minorities. UN Doc. E/CN.4/Sub.2/1990/46.

———. 1991a. "Minority Situations: In Search of Peaceful and Constructive Solutions." *Notre Dame Law Review* 66, no. 5: 1311–53.

———. 1991b. *Possible Ways and Means of Facilitating the Peaceful and Constructive Solutions of Problems Involving Minorities*. Progress report to the United Nations Sub-Commission on Prevention of Discrimination and Protection of Minorities. UN Doc. E/CN.4/Sub.2/1991/43.

Eide, Asbjørn, and Jan Helgesen (eds). 1991. *The Future of Human Rights Protection in a Changing World*. Oslo: Norwegian University Press.

Eide, Asbjørn, Gudmundur Alfredsson, Göran Melander, Lars Adam Rehof, and Allan Rosas, with the collaboration of Theresa Swinehart. 1992. *The Universal Declaration of Human Rights. A Commentary*. Oslo: Scandinavian University Press.

Ermacora, F. 1991. "Rights of Minorities and Self-Determination in the Framework of the CSCE." In Marcel Brus, Sam Muller, and Serv Wiemers (eds), *The United Nations Decade of International Law: Reflections on International Dispute Settlement* (Dordrecht/Boston/London: Martinus Nijhoff).

Kooijmans, P.H. 1991. "Inter-State Dispute Settlement In the Field of Human

Rights." In Marcel Brus, Sam Muller, and Serv Wiemers (eds), *The United Nations Decade of International Law: Reflections on International Dispute Settlement* (Dordrecht/Boston/London: Martinus Nijhoff).

Tomuschat, C. 1983. "Protection of Minorities under Article 27 of the International Covenant on Civil and Political Rights." *Völkerrecht als Rechtsordnung Internationale Gerichtsbarkeit Menschenrechte. Festschrift für Hermann Mosler* (Berlin: Springer-Verlag), pp. 949–79.

United Nations Centre for Human Rights. 1988. *United Nations Action in the Field of Human Rights*. New York: United Nations.

United Nations Centre for Human Rights, and United Nations Institute for Training and Research. 1991. *Manual on Human Rights Reporting*. New York: United Nations.

15

The right to autonomy: Chimera or solution?

Hurst Hannum

One of the most frequently voiced solutions to ethnic conflict, at least where there is some degree of territorial separation among competing groups, is to grant "autonomy" to the minority group. As will be seen, autonomy can include a wide range of political, economic, and other powers. However, in order to assess what degree of power should be devolved in a particular situation, one must focus on the underlying goal that creating autonomous structures is designed to serve.

On a continuum of political power, many analysts would place autonomy higher than the ability to protect minority rights but lower than the independent statehood which may result from the exercise of a people's right to self-determination. This is probably accurate, although it should be remembered that autonomy is not a term of art in international law, and that the term has been used to describe a plethora of different arrangements.[1]

Most ethnic conflicts grow out of the dissatisfaction of a group which is a numerical minority within an existing political unit (normally a state) with its share of political and economic power *vis-à-vis* the larger society. This relative powerlessness may be combined with a desire to strengthen or renew shared cultural characteristics, such as language or religion. In many situations, the minority views itself as having been subject to varying degrees of repression under the existing system.

The development of autonomous arrangements to serve the interests of a territorially based group (which is often, although not necessarily, ethnically and culturally distinct from the dominant society) may respond to three primary needs. In its broadest sense, autonomy may be an expression of the self-determination of a people or society, where that people's choice falls short of independent statehood. Autonomy may also be a means of ensuring that a state is truly democratic, so that all significant segments of society are able to participate effectively in the political and economic decisions which affect their lives. Finally, autonomy may be viewed primarily as a means of ensuring that fundamental human rights are protected, by ensuring that the larger polity can only intervene within the autonomous community within certain specified limits.

Democracy and democratization seem to be on everyone's lips today, and it may be appropriate to begin with an analysis of autonomy as a component of **democratic governance**. In this context, autonomy can exist within a wide variety of structures, from classic federalism to arrangements of confederation, consociation, devolution, or decentralization. Our concern today, however, is not to define these terms more specifically,[2] and the particular form of autonomy adopted may depend on historical and other factors as well as upon the relative substantive powers of the central and autonomous governments.

Autonomy as a response to the need for more democratic forms of government may be based on either regional or ethnic concerns, although there may evidently be an overlap in these categories when an ethnic group is regionally concentrated. When the primary concern is to ensure that the legitimate interests of peripheral regions are adequately addressed by the central government, devolution of power to sub-state entities is clearly consistent with democratic theories and the ultimate sovereignty of the state as represented by the central government.

There is no democratic requirement that a state be organized as a "unitary" system or led exclusively by a strong central government. The commitment to a unitary state expressed publicly by many central governments is unpersuasive as a theoretical paradigm, unless it is supported by arguments based on functional efficiency or political necessity. It is often said that "the government is best which governs least," and ensuring that issues are considered by the lowest appropriate level of government has long been thought to be politically desirable.[3]

The idea of creating separate institutions to respond to *ethnic* concerns, on the other hand, is *not* necessarily compatible with traditional notions of democracy. Indeed, there is no political role for ethnic minorities as such in either capitalist or socialist doctrine, which are based respectively on the individual or the masses, not on discrete non-economic units such as linguistic or cultural groups. The traditional Westminster model of democracy is based strictly on "one person, one vote"; its individualistic orientation does not encourage the representation of groups or segments of society *per se*.[4]

Of course, one may wish to redefine democracy in order to avoid situations in which identifiable segments of society seem to be permanently excluded from power, and protection of individual rights, as well as majority rule, is essential to democracy. The Westminster model works only when political parties can compete meaningfully for power and actually achieve it on a regular basis. It is the likelihood that today's majority will become tomorrow's minority that is the ultimate brake on the abuse of power by the government of the day; where this alternation of power does not exist – as was the case in Northern Ireland, where the nationalist Catholic minority had no chance of sharing power with the unionist Protestant majority, despite a formally fair electoral system – merely free and fair elections may not be sufficient.

Ultimately, of course, demands for democracy based on ethnicity may threaten the state itself. Appeals to nationalism, and even racism, are often couched in terms of expressing the democratic will of the majority, although one cannot maintain that democracy requires ethnic, religious, or linguistic purity. The conclusion must be that ethnically based autonomy arrangements are probably not required to achieve democracy, at least in its narrow definition as rule by the majority. This is important, for many contemporary demands for autonomy respond as much to decades of non-democratic government as they do to legitimate concerns over ethnic identity or minority rights. In such situations, one should look carefully at what purpose autonomy is designed to serve and distinguish between demands for greater political power for its own sake and demands for democratic government.

Self-determination is the right of peoples to "freely determine their political status and freely pursue their economic, social and cultural development."[5] Although it is beyond the scope of this paper to analyse the precise meaning of self-determination today, even a preliminary understanding of this principle requires a certain historical perspective. While its philosophical origins may be traced back farther, self-determination became a political force in the nineteenth century. It was a principle of political organization openly based on ethnicity, most often expressed in linguistic and religious terms. The "nation-state" – an independent entity which corresponded to an ethnic, cultural, linguistic, and historically identifiable nation – became the paradigm.

However, even strong advocates of the principle of self-determination, such as US President Woodrow Wilson, subordinated self-determination to larger geopolitical concerns, and the victors at Versailles recognized claims to statehood based on their own views as to what arrangements might be more likely to keep the peace, or serve other political concerns, rather than on any inherent "right" of peoples to statehood. Those groups or nations which did not achieve statehood had to be content, in some cases, with specific rights guaranteed to them as minorities. And, of course, claims for self-determination were recognized at Versailles only in so far as they pertained to new, altered, or defeated states; they were not considered to be universally applicable.

The United Nations Charter refers to the "principle" of self-determination only twice, although this vague principle soon became a widely recognized right. This right, however, had a different philosophical and political basis than the ethnically based principle of self-determination developed during the preceding century.

The right to self-determination recognized by the United Nations is best described as an absolute right to decolonization, based on territory rather than ethnicity.[6] While there were exceptions to this territorial principle (e.g., the division of British India and the former Belgian colony of Rwanda-Urundi), ethnicity was consciously deemed to be irrelevant to the overriding goal of freeing African, Asian, and other non-self-governing territories from European control. The principle of the inviolability of territorial integrity – irrespective of the ethnic composition of the population – is invariably found in conjunction with UN references to self-determination, and this principle was forcefully reiterated in 1964 in one of the earliest and most important resolutions adopted by the Organization of African Unity.

Despite the practical limitation of international recognition of the right to self-determination in the colonial context, the legal and political documents which proclaim the right are expansive in their scope. The two international covenants on human rights (which remain the only legally binding treaties to proclaim a right of self-determination) state, "All peoples have the right of self-determination." Self-determination thus remains a force in the post-colonial era, although those who would now claim its benefits seek to return to the pre-1945 ethnic basis of self-determination, rejecting the UN's insistence on the territorial integrity of existing entities during the colonial era.

In the present context, it is perhaps sufficient to mention some of the unresolved issues that confront anyone who seeks to invoke the right of self-determination today. First, of course, is the definition of the "self." Must the self be ethnically homogeneous, or is the majority in an existing multi-ethnic state the appropriate self to decide that state's political future? Is there not a right to remain together as well as a right to separate? If the self is determined ethnically or culturally, then why should existing administrative borders which surround ethnic minorities be considered sacrosanct, as most commentators seem to assume? If one supports the right to self-determination of Croats in Yugoslavia, should not this right also extend to Serbs in Croatia? Or to Albanians in Serbia?

Once the appropriate self is identified, there remains the question of what the self has the right to determine. In the examples just cited, there is an assumption that self-determination may lead to secession, but this assumption should not be accepted automatically. As already noted, the principle of national unity and territorial integrity has been reaffirmed by the United Nations and other international bodies at least as frequently (and as fervently) as has the right to self-determination.

Self-determination is a relative, not an absolute, right, and different levels of self-determination may be appropriate for different selves. Should the right of self-determination as defined by international law always permit secession? Or should secession be seen solely as a matter to be determined within the political discretion of the states and communities involved?

It is noteworthy that statements of the European Community with respect to the recognition of new states which formerly constituted parts of the Soviet Union or Yugoslavia are carefully framed in the context of the *dissolution* of an existing state, not the secession of one part of a state from the rest. Whether or not this position accurately reflects the factual situation, it does reflect the continuing fear on the part of the international community that any recognition of a right to secession would invite widespread chaos.

If secession is excluded as a legal right encompassed within the right to self-determination, this does not necessarily imply that self-determination has lost its relevance. Rather, it suggests that we may be in the process of developing yet a third definition to the right of self-determination, distinct from both the ethnically based approach of the nineteenth century and the territorially based anti-colonialism of the post-1945 period.[7]

Although it is too early to conclude that such a newly defined right has crystallized in international law, the implications of such a development for the resolution of ethnic conflicts on the basis of devolution of power is obvious. Under this new definition, autonomy and self-government may be the primary expressions of a people's right to self-determination, although the definition remains too vague at present to offer us much guidance as to the degree of autonomy which it may require.

The third reason for asserting a right to autonomy is to **protect human rights**. Here, too, developments since 1945 have tended to ignore ethnicity and the collective or community aspects of rights in favour of a more individualistic orientation. It is significant that the only widely accepted formulation of minority rights, found in article 27 of the Covenant on Civil and Political Rights, refers to "persons belonging to" minority groups, not to rights of the groups themselves.[8] This, of course, is in stark contrast to the post-Versailles concern with minority rights, as embodied in the so-called Minorities Treaties imposed on defeated or new states after World War I and whose implementation was a concern of the Council of the League of Nations.

In the past few years, the international community has recognized that the issue of minority rights needs to be addressed more directly, and several instruments do set forth norms related to the rights of national and/or ethnic, religious, and linguistic minorities.[9] These include the document adopted in 1990 at the Copenhagen Meeting of the Conference on the Human Dimension of the Conference on Security and Co-operation in Europe, and the proposal for a European Convention for the Protection of Minorities submitted by a group of experts to the Council of Europe in 1991. A draft European Charter for Regional or Minority Languages is also being prepared under the auspices of a Council of Europe committee of experts, and a Declaration on the Rights of Persons Belonging to National or Ethnic, Religious and Linguistic Minorities was formally adopted by the UN General Assembly on 18 December 1992.

Pending adoption of these and other instruments and the creation of mechanisms for their effective enforcement, there remain many "individual" rights of particular importance to ethnic communities. More than 100 countries have ratified the two international covenants on human rights, which guarantee, *inter alia*, rights to culture, privacy, language, association, religion, and education.

The fears of many ethnic groups are based on violations of such fundamental rights as the right to due process, freedom from discrimination, and personal liberty and security. Governments which discriminate against certain groups or which repress linguistic or cultural expression obviously contribute to ethnic conflict and violate "minority rights," although redress for such violations does not depend on the existence of special categories of group rights.[10]

An increasingly important human right is the right to "effective participation" in the economic and political life of a country. Originally developed in the context of consulting rural populations with respect to economic development plans, this right also is rooted in article 25 of the Covenant on Civil and Political Rights, which deals with participation in public affairs.[11]

What should be underscored is that this is a right to *effective* participation, not just the ability to cast a vote freely. Participation is not control, but it also is more than the purely numerical democracy suggested by the Westminster model. Like the emerging right to autonomy, the right to participation is not yet well defined, but it has great potential as a tool for ensuring that people – whether individuals or group – have a voice in the formulation of policies which directly affect them.

Demands for autonomy generally contain elements of all three categories of needs identified above: the protection of human rights; guarantees of real democracy; and responsiveness to the principle of self-determination. However, "autonomy" should not be viewed as an end in and of itself. Too often, it is used merely as a catchword, an ill-defined example of what Professor Jauregui has called "the pulverization of the classic concept of sovereignty." To be meaningful, demands for autonomy should respond to the specific needs of minority groups and individuals. These needs must include, at a minimum, respect for what might be termed the "traditional" human rights: the right to life and liberty and to freedom from discrimination. Added to these are other basic rights of freedom of association and religion.

However, autonomy can and should include more, although precise arrangements will vary with the particular circumstances. Greater group or regional control over language, education, and local decision-making power is often essential to provide ethnic groups with sufficient control over their own lives and cultures so that they need not feel threatened by the dominant society. At the same time, new forms of effective participation in the central government may need to be developed – which presupposes that a central government does retain legitimate authority to act in some spheres which will have an impact on ethnic or regional communities.

Greater devolution of powers to sub-state regions, or even separation, should remain a possibility, but one that can become reality only after a lengthy process in which the true wishes of all parties can be accurately ascertained. This may mean a long and cumbersome series of referenda or plebiscites, but it is the only way to ensure that fundamental decisions will accurately reflect the wishes of the people involved, as opposed to the often opportunistic demands of the political leaders of the moment.

Autonomy is not a panacea. It is, nevertheless, an appropriately flexible vehicle for constitutional and political change. In order to deal successfully with ethnic conflict, I would join Professor Darby's "plea for pragmatism," even while recognizing that extremism and rigidity might be more politically attractive positions to adopt and maintain. Autonomous arrangements will succeed in defusing conflict only where they are based on mutual respect and tolerance, and that should remain the ultimate goal of attempts at meaningful conflict resolution.

Notes

1. See, generally, H. Hannum and R. Lillich, "The Concept of Autonomy in International Law," *American Journal of International Law* 74 (1980): 858, reprinted in Y. Dinstein (ed.), *Models of Autonomy*, Transaction, 1981.
2. An excellent summary of these concepts may be found in C. Palley, *Constitutional Law and Minorities*, Report No. 36 (London: Minority Rights Group, 1978).
3. This "principle of subsidiarity" has been endorsed by the European Union to guide future development of its institutions and competence.
4. Of course, even very individualistic societies such as the United States may deviate from the one-person, one-vote principle when other factors are sufficiently important. The US Senate is geographically based on states, irrespective of population, and recent legislation designed to increase minority representation in Congress encourages the delimitation of electoral

boundaries to facilitate the election of minority candidates rather than to respect geographic coherence.

5. International Covenant on Economic, Social and Cultural Rights, art. 1; an identical article is found in the International Covenant on Civil and Political Rights.

6. One of the most important assertions by the United Nations of the right to self-determination is contained in General Assembly Resolution 1514 (XV) of 14 December 1960, which was entitled Declaration on the Granting of Independence to Colonial Countries and Peoples.

7. H. Hannum, *Autonomy, Sovereignty, and Self-Determination: The Accommodation of Conflicting Rights* (Philadelphia: University of Pennsylvania, 1990).

8. The only other group-oriented international instrument is the 1948 Convention on the Prevention and Punishment of the Crime of Genocide, which has been ratified by over 100 states but contains no effective implementation machinery.

9. See, generally, H. Hannum, "Contemporary Developments in the International Protection of the Rights of Minorities," *Notre Dame Law Review* 66 (1991): 1431.

10. Unfortunately, one of the least well-known international bodies concerned with the protection of minority rights is the Committee on the Elimination of All Forms of Racial Discrimination, whose mandate extends to non-discrimination towards ethnic as well as racial groups. While the Committee is able to do little more than make recommendations to states which are parties to the Convention on the Elimination of All Forms of Racial Discrimination, its examination of periodic state reports does present an opportunity for non-governmental organizations to challenge a government's view of minority relations in a particular state.

11. See, generally, H. Steiner, "Political Participation as a Human Right," in *Harvard Human Rights Yearbook* 1 (1988): 77.

Contributors

AIRAT R. AKLAEV is Research Fellow at the Department of Sociology of Inter-ethnic Relations, Institute of Ethnology and Anthropology, Russian Academy of Sciences. He received a Ph.D. in history in 1989. He is the author of over 20 articles and papers in Russian and English, and has conducted fieldwork in Georgia, Estonia, Uzbekistan, and Tuva. Resesarch interests include studies of ethnic minority identities and ethnic conflict, and language issues in ethno-political conflicts in emerging nations.

ABILABEK ASANKANOV is Chairman of the Ethnology Department of History at the Kyrgyz State University, Bishkek, Kyrgyzstan.

HIZKIAS ASSEFA is Director of the Nairobi Peace Initiative, Kenya.

JOSÉ MANUEL CASTELLS is Professor of Administrative Law at the University of the Basque Country. Dean of the Faculty of Law, he has published extensively in the fields of public administration, public policies, and regional policy. He is a member of the Gernika Gogoratuz Peace Research Centre, Donostia (San Sebastián).

JOHN DARBY is Director of the Ethnic Studies Network, University of Ulster at Coleraine, Northern Ireland.

SILVO DEVETAK is Director at the European Centre for Ethnic and Regional Studies of Maribor University, Maribor, Mladinska.

296

ASBJØRN EIDE, b. 1939, Dr. Jur. h.c., Lund University, 1991, is Director of the Norwegian Institute of Human Rights and a member of the United Nations Sub-Commission on Prevention of Discrimination and Protection of Minorities.

KLARA HALLIK Ph.D. is Senior Fellow in the Institute of International and Social Studies at the Estonian Academy of Sciences, Tallinn.

HURST HANNUM is Professor at the Fletcher School of Law and Diplomacy at Tufts University, Massachusetts, USA.

GURUTZ JAUREGUI is Professor of Constitutional Law and head of the Department of Constitutional and Administrative Law at the University of the Basque Country. He has published extensively on ethnic violence, ethnic nationalism, political decentral-ization, and theory of democracy. In English, he has published *Decline of the Nation-State* (Reno/Las Vegas/London: University of Nevada Press, 1994). He is a member of the Gernika Gogoratuz Peace Research Centre, Donostia (San Sebastián).

VICTOR KREMENYUK is Deputy Director of the USA and Canada Studies Institute in Moscow.

S.D. MUNI is Professor and Chairman of the Centre for South, Central and Southeast Asian Studies at the Jawaharlal Nehru University, New Delhi, India.

EMIL PAYIN is Director of the Centre for Ethno-Political Studies, Foreign Policy Association, Moscow.

KUMAR RUPESINGHE, b. 1943, Ph.D. in Sociology, City University, London; London School of Economics; Secretary-General, International Alert, London; Senior Researcher, International Peace Research Institute, Oslo (PRIO); Chair, Interna-tional Peace Research Association's Commission on International Conflicts and their Resolution (ICON); and Coordinator, United Nations University Programme on Governance and Conflict Resolution. Has published and edited many articles and books, including *Conflict Resolution in Uganda* (London: James Currey, 1989); *Ethnic Conflicts and Human Rights: A Comparative Perspective* (Tokyo: United Nations University Press, 1989); and a three-volume ICON book series (London: Macmillan, 1992).

VALERY TISHKOV, b. 1941, is director of the Institute of Ethnology and Anthropology at the Russian Academy of Sciences in Moscow from 1989. Formerly Minister of Nationalities of the Russian Federation; General Secretary of the Division of His-tory, Russian Academy of Sciences (1976–82) and head of American Ethnic Studies at the Institute of Ethnology and Anthropology (1982–1989). Has published numer-ous articles and books, including *The National Liberation Movement in Colonial Canada* (Moscow: Nauka, 1978); *History and Historians in the USA* (Moscow, 1985); co-author, *Native Peoples of the US and Canada in a Contemporary World* (Moscow, 1990).

MARY C. WATERS is Professor of Sociology at Harvard University. She received a B.A. in Philosophy from Johns Hopkins University, an M.A. in Demography, and an

M.A. and PhD in Sociology from the University of California at Berkeley. She has written two books on white ethnics in the United States: *From Many Strands: Ethnic and Racial Groups in Contemporary America* (with Stanley Lieberson) (New York: Russell Sage Foundation, 1988), and *Ethnic Options: Choosing Identities in America* (Berkeley: University of California Press, 1990), and she is the author of numerous articles on immigration and ethnicity in the United States, including, most recently, "Ethnic and Racial Identities of Second Generation Black Immigrants in New York City," *International Migration Review* 23, no. 4 (Winter 1994). She has been a Guggenheim Fellow, a Visiting Scholar at the Russell Sage Foundation, and she is a member of the International Immigration Committee of the Social Science Research Council.

424 SB BR 2041
12/05/96 40000 SELF